STATE OF TRANSLATION

International politics is often conducted in two or more languages. The resulting interlingual relations involve translation, either by interpreters who are inserted into conversations between statesmen, or by bilingual statesmen who negotiate internationally in one language and then legitimize domestically in another. Since no two languages are exactly the same, what is possible to argue in one language may be impossible in another. As a result, political concepts can be significantly reformulated in the translation process. *State of Translation* examines this phenomenon in the case of how nineteenth-century Ottoman and later Turkish statesmen struggled to reconcile their arguments in external languages (first mostly French, then English) with those in their internal language (Ottoman, later Turkish), and in the process further entangled them. Einar Wigen demonstrates how this process structured social relations between the Ottoman state and its interlocutors, both domestically and internationally, and shaped the dynamics of Turkish relations with Europe.

Einar Wigen is Associate Professor of Turkish Studies in the Department of Culture Studies and Oriental Languages at the University of Oslo.

CONFIGURATIONS: CRITICAL STUDIES OF WORLD POLITICS

Patrick Thaddeus Jackson, series editor

For a complete list of titles, please see www.press.umich.edu

STATE OF TRANSLATION

Turkey in Interlingual Relations

EINAR WIGEN

University of Michigan Press
Ann Arbor

Published in the United States of America by the
University of Michigan Press
Manufactured in the United States of America
Printed on acid-free paper
First published September 2018

A CIP catalog record for this book is available from the British Library.

Library of Congress Cataloging-in-Publication Data

Names: Wigen, Einar, 1981– author.
Title: State of translation : Turkey in interlingual relations / Einar Wigen.
Description: Ann Arbor : University of Michigan Press, 2018. | Series: Configurations :
    critical studies of world politics | Includes bibliographical references and index. |
Identifiers: LCCN 2018021212 (print) | LCCN 2018031569 (ebook) | ISBN 9780472124138
    (E-book) | ISBN 9780472130948 (hardback)
Subjects: LCSH: Language and international relations—Turkey—History. | Diplomacy—
    Language—History. | Turkey—Foreign relations. | Turkish language—Political
    aspects—History. | BISAC: POLITICAL SCIENCE / International Relations / General.
Classification: LCC JZ1253.5 (ebook) | LCC JZ1253.5 .W54 2018 (print)
LC record available at https://lccn.loc.gov/2018021212

Cover: Ambassador Stratford Canning dining with the Kaymakam of Istanbul.
Watercolor; anonymous, ca. 1809. © Victoria and Albert Museum, London.

Contents

Foreword

The book you hold in your hands is one of the most innovative and pathbreaking books that we have published in the *Configurations* series to date. Einar Wigen's book is a fascinating expansion of the territory of international studies into the realm of translation: not translation as a metaphor, but translation as the concrete act of rendering something written in one language into another language. While there has been work in conceptual history that looks at how particular notions evolve and change over time, Wigen's focus on what is conserved and what changes when politically important concepts traverse cultural and linguistic boundaries participates in a broader movement to reveal the global connections surrounding and penetrating supposedly "national" histories. Just as comparative political theory looks to identify parallels and exchanges between traditions not easy to see when looking at the world as though it were composed of a grid of hermetically sealed separate societies, Wigen's work invites us to explore the ways that acts of sense-making in the Turkish context responded to and modified the European sources on which Turkish intellectuals drew—and helped to shape the Turkish political context in ways that have lasting effects.

What is perhaps most striking about Wigen's book is that it foregrounds a topic that *ought* to have been more central to international studies all along. If we think of the field at its broadest as dealing with the encounter with difference across boundaries—whether those boundaries are the putatively hard-edged borders of sovereign territorial states, the more flexible and fluid "contact zones" between cultures and civilizations, the regulatory frameworks of global commerce, or something else entirely—then the movement of key conceptual and philosophical notions into alien environments ought to provoke a clear line of research. But the topic has been strikingly understudied. Most intellectual histories are either implicitly bounded by linguistic communities, or else they deal with the emergence of a roughly homogenous intellectual community across multiple languages. Genuinely *global* intellectual histories are rare, in part because of the sheer weight of the experience in multiple domains required in order to tell such a story in a compelling way. And reception histories, in which the account treats one intellectual community as the recipient of notions imported from another, often run the risk of downplaying or ignoring the agency of the "recipients" of a notion born elsewhere. Looking instead to those who live on the boundary, those who have the unenviable task of figuring out what something means in one context and then rendering some kind of equivalent for it in another context, are from this perspective engaged in "international relations"—the specific variant that Wigen calls "interlingual relations." His may be the first book to explore this terrain, but hopefully it will not be the last.

Wigen adopts a thoroughly relational approach to the topic at hand, refusing the easy temptation of defining *in advance* what notions like "democracy" and "civilization" mean, and then tracking which elements of that meaning do or do not survive the trip from one language to another. He also rejects the approach (common in some forms of conceptual history) that seeks to abstract an essence from a pattern of word use, and thus inductively arrive at a stable meaning for a concept based on the inferred substrate from which particular usages derive. Instead, for Wigen, a concept *just is* the way that it is used, nothing less and certainly nothing more. This means that translation cannot possibly be the conservation or transportation of meaning from one context to another, but has to instead involve producing what Wittgenstein might have called a "family resemblance" between how terms are used in different contexts. In so doing, the translator is affected by a variety of contingent factors and navigating, as it were, a constitutively ambiguous sea—particularly when the notion being translated is a complex one imbued with a rich history of its own, and one with important implications for political and social life. In this way, translating "democracy" or "civilization" from various European languages into Turkish is inextricably wrapped up with other aspects of the relations between the Ottoman Empire and the state of Turkey on one hand, and those European countries on the other: as the European countries urge "democracy" and speak of "civilization," it matters a great deal what sense is made of those notions in Turkish. The question here is not whether the translators "got it right," but more what sense the process of translation made and makes in the context of ongoing engagement.

As a result, Wigen does not and cannot provide anything like a comprehensive *theory* of interlingual relations. Instead, he provides a thoroughly configurational *explanation* of how particular outcomes came about. It is in the very character of this kind of approach not to be able to specify actors, sites, and controversies in advance; instead, they emerge from the careful effort to trace just how sense was made at particular junctures. We are thus presented with a detailed narrative that discloses the twists and turns that lead to the kinds of understandings of these key political terms operative today in Turkey. This might be thought of as a kind of inventory of resources that could be drawn on in contemporary political debates, but personally I prefer to think of it as a prelude to future structured discussions. Recognizing that "translation" is no automated technical process, but a highly contingent and contextual one, shows us both the similarities *and* the differences that persist in discussions about the key commonplaces that form our common political vocabulary.

Patrick Thaddeus Jackson
Series Editor, Configurations

Acknowledgments

I have been grappling with the subject matter of this book since I first spent a year at the Norwegian Institute of International Affairs (NUPI) in 2005. At NUPI I encountered Iver B. Neumann, whom I now count as my friend and mentor. Iver has guided my theoretical pursuits and helped me generously ever since. In the autumn of 2005, I started attending Bernt Brendemoen's Turkish classes at the University of Oslo with the vague idea of writing a work on Turkish conceptual history inspired by Neumann's books, *Russia and the Idea of Europe* (1996) and *Uses of the Other* (1999). Brendemoen's friendship, patience, and generosity in teaching Ottoman and Turkish language and helping me with sources have been invaluable. Of equal importance, his love for all things Turkish is contagious. Both Neumann and Brendemoen have my heartfelt gratitude. Helge Jordheim helped provide an academic home for me as a doctoral fellow at the KULTRANS research project from 2010 to 2014 and became the third supervisor of my dissertation. Helge has since become one of my closest colleagues, and his friendship, patience, and enthusiasm are warmly appreciated.

While preparing this manuscript, I also incurred a number of intellectual debts to teachers and student interlocutors in Turkey, Norway, and the United Kingdom. I thank the excellent teachers and students at the Ataturk Institute of Modern Turkish History at Istanbul's Boğaziçi University, which I attended during the autumn of 2008. I am also grateful to the Turkish scholars who helped me in my search for sources: Evren Çelik, Boğaç Erozan, Nüket Esen, Can Mutlu, Funda S. Şirin, İbrahim Şirin, and Oktay Tanrısever. My efforts have received support from several librarians in Turkey and in Norway, particularly Hazel Henriksen at NUPI and the librarians at the interlibrary loan service of the University of Oslo.

My attendance at the Harvard-Koç Intensive Ottoman Summer School in Cunda, Turkey, in 2011 proved a watershed in the preparation of this work. My roommate, Patrick Adamiak; our reading group partners, Timur Hammond and Lee Beaudoen; and our lecturers, Yorgos Dedes, Domenico Ingenito, Gregory Key, and Selim Kuru, helped make this an unforgettable experience. My grasp of Ottoman would not have been the same without them. Grappling with Ottoman and Persian translation all day long for the entire summer also gave me the experience to formulate my more general thoughts on translation.

In the autumn of 2012, I was a guest researcher at the Department for Translation and Interpreting Studies at Boğaziçi University. My colleagues there, especially Şehnaz Tahir Gürçağlar and Özlem Berk Albachten, were of tremendous help in familiarizing me with translation studies and the history of Turkish and Ottoman translation.

Somerville College and the Faculty of History at the University of Oxford, especially Joanna Innes, have my heartfelt gratitude for hosting me while I put the final touches on this book during Hilary term 2016. Louise Fawcett, Andrew Hurrell, and Edward Keene offered generous comments on the manuscript.

I cannot acknowledge all the occasions on which I have presented versions of the book's chapters and received useful feedback; however, I particularly thank the following for their extensive comments: Morten Skumsrud Andersen, Elçin Arabacı, Tarak Barkawi, Orit Bashkin, Amund Bjørsnøs, Kaja Blattmann, Kristin Haugevik, Jacob Høigilt, Rana Issa, Mana Kia, Halvard Leira, Jörn Leonhard, Brynjar Lia, Joakim Parslow, Margrit Pernau, Gabriel Piterberg, Evgeny Roshchin, Myriam Salama-Carr, Ole Jacob Sending, Quentin Skinner, Audun Solli, Ivo Spira, and Anders Sveen. Nazan Çiçek generously read and commented on the entire manuscript.

The thinking that has gone into chapter 2 was presented at NUPI in January 2013, at Oslo's Fridtjof Nansen Institute in May 2013, and at the ECPR general conference in Bordeaux in September 2013. An early version of that chapter was published as "Two-Level Language Games: International Relations as Inter-lingual Relations," *European Journal of International Relations* 21 (2): 427–50; it has been extensively revised and updated for this book. I presented an early version of chapter 3 at the Empire: Comparing the Semantics Behind Concept, Metaphor and Ideology conference in Budapest in October 2011, and it was published as *Contributions to the History of Concepts* 8.1 (2013): 44–66. A precursor to chapter 4 was presented at the Max Planck Institute for Human Development in Berlin in February 2013 and at the University of Oslo in June 2013: it appears as "The Education of Ottoman Man and the Practising of Orderliness," in *Civilizing Emotions: Concepts in Nineteenth Century Asia and Europe* (Oxford: Oxford University Press, 2015), 107–45, and is used by permission of Oxford University Press.

I am also grateful to Umut Türem of Ataturk Institute of Modern Turkish History at Boğaziçi University, who served as my opponent in a mock defense in January 2014, reading and commenting extensively on a full draft manuscript. Both Professor Christoph Herzog and Professor Patrick Thaddeus Jackson gave extensive comments and criticisms when they served as my external opponents at my October 2014 doctoral defense. The book would have been something very different without this stimulating exchange. Three anonymous readers at the University of Michigan Press and especially Patrick Thaddeus Jackson, now in his capacity as series editor of Configurations: Critical Studies of World Politics, have offered very generous comments that helped me revise and improve the manuscript. Few have helped as much as Alp Eren Topal. His generosity in providing all sorts of sources and comments on written material has helped improve this work significantly.

No one deserves more thanks than my wonderful wife and companion, Runa Gravensteen. She has not only patiently stood by me through my writing process and spent her vacations accompanying me on research trips to Turkey but also read and commented extensively on the entire volume. I am grateful to our parents and their partners for taking care of our two daughters whenever the need arises. And last but not least, I thank our daughters, Louise and He-lene, whose love for the cats and horses of Büyükada and fondness for the *teyzes* in Foça will hopefully help them overcome the hurdles presented by an agglutinative language. I dedicate this book to them.

Einar Wigen
Oslo, August 2017

Note on Transliteration and Spelling

Few things are as frustrating as trying to impose a coherent standard on Ottoman and Turkish names, concepts, and places and to translate and transliterate consistently to that standard. Not only is the Arabic alphabet, in which Ottoman was written, not compatible with the Latin alphabet, but none of the scholarly conventions for transcribing Ottoman words into Latin script give results that correspond to the words' modern Turkish spellings. Part of the problem arises from the fact that the Turkish alphabet reform (Harf İnkılabı) of 1928 adopted the Latin alphabet modified not for rendering the Arabic letters but for rendering Turkish phonemes. Turkish is more or less written as it is spoken, with one letter corresponding to one sound, and vice versa. Not all of these letters are pronounced as they would be in English. The Turkish *c* is pronounced as *j* in *John*. *Ç* is pronounced like *ch* in *church*. *Ş* is pronounced like the *sh* in *she*. *J*, which appears mainly in loan words, is pronounced like the French *j*, as in *jeune*. *Ö* and *ü* are pronounced as in German. The "soft g"—*ğ*—either prolongs the preceding vowel or (between front vowels) is pronounced as *y* in *young*.

Moreover, a great many of the concepts that appear in the Ottoman context have entered the English language with their own established spellings but with slightly different connotations. Therefore, the spelling of Ottoman and Turkish words in this work is a matter not of imposing a consistent system but rather of choosing which inconsistencies should be allowed.

For quotations from Ottoman originals in the Arabic script, I have chosen a transliteration system that is as close to modern Turkish spelling as possible but with diacritical marks for distinguishing between the various Arabic consonants as well as between short and long vowels. This system, which is used in the *İslam Ansiklopedisi* (the Turkish edition of the *Encyclopaedia of Islam*), is based on the Turkish adaptation of the Latin alphabet consisting of twenty-nine letters. (For a thorough description of this transliteration system, see Thackston 2001.)

The İslam Ansiklopedisi Transliteration System

ء	ا	ب	پ	ت	ث	ج	چ	ح	خ	د	ذ	ر	ز	ژ	س
ʾ	ā	b	p	t	s	c	ç	ḥ	ḫ	d	ẕ	r	z	j	s

ش	ص	ض	ط	ظ	ع	غ	ف	ق	ك	ل	م	ن	و	ه	ى
ş	ṣ	ż	ṭ	ẓ	ʿ	ġ	f	ḳ	k,g,ñ,ğ	l	m	n	v, ū, ō	h	y, ī

When I quote from Ottoman texts that have already been transliterated into the Latin alphabet, I have used the texts *as they appear*, regardless of which transliteration or transcription system was used.

For general discussions of concepts that are still used in contemporary Turkish (such as *medeniyet* [civilization]), I stick with the modern Turkish spelling. For those concepts that existed in Ottoman but have disappeared in modern Turkish, I use the Ottoman transcription. One example would be *'ūmrān*, another concept of *civilization* that has disappeared in that meaning but remains as a gender-neutral given name (*Ümran*) in specific discussions of Ibn Khaldun's writings.

I am studying entanglements. On the one hand, many of the concepts I study are interesting precisely because they were "originally" English or French concepts that gained translation equivalents in Ottoman and Turkish. On the other hand, many of the names for places, people, concepts, and institutions specific to the Ottoman Empire and Turkey have through entanglements acquired established spellings in English (such as *caliphate*). Because it is a methodological concern in this book that Turkish concepts have a slightly different meaning than their English translation equivalents, I have tried to keep those concepts that are central to the analysis separate in English and Turkish. The Turkish *demokrasi* means something slightly different from the English *democracy*. Likewise, although Sharia does not receive a chapter of its own, it does play a part in English political discourse in a meaning that is separate from the Turkish concept, and I have therefore chosen to keep that apart from the Turkish *Şeriat*. Such distinctions are made for methodological rather than stylistic purposes. The same point could of course be made for almost any place-name (Istanbul can also be called Constantinople or Ḳonsṭanṭīnīye, thereby drawing on different histories to give the city meaning), but where it is primarily a matter of style rather than method, I choose the *Merriam-Webster* spelling. Hence, I write *janissaries* rather than *yeniçeri*, Anatolia rather than *Anadolu*, *mufti* rather than *müftü*, and so on.

Personal names of Ottomans are transliterated with diacritical marks only when they appear in direct quotations and in the reference section, when they are given as authors of particular texts. Thus, it is Nāmıḳ Kemāl in the references but Namık Kemal in the text.

Having clarified all that, I will set to work muddling it up.

ONE

Introduction

Politics is conducted in language. International politics is often conducted in two languages or more. While the first insight is commonly acknowledged, the second has been largely ignored in scholarship on international relations. When relations take place in more than one language, they may also be called *interlingual relations*. Because all languages are different, interlingual relations typically involve more social complexity than monolingual relations. Interlingual relations involve translation, either by interpreters who are inserted into conversations between statesmen,[1] or by bilingual statesmen who negotiate internationally in one language and then legitimize domestically in another. Since no two languages are exactly the same, what is possible to argue in one language may be impossible to argue in another. While American and British statesmen can often ignore this aspect of international politics—at their peril—most of the world's diplomats and politicians cannot. Nineteenth-century Ottoman statesmen certainly could not. Their polity's survival and their own social position depended on successfully negotiating by use of a conceptual vocabulary that was fairly new to them.

As the state's relative ability to mobilize military force to ward off external threats diminished, Ottoman diplomats increasingly had

---

1. The category of people I am dealing with in this book are all those people—politicians, state leaders, diplomats and so forth—who are tasked with carrying out the actions of the state, speaking and acting in the name of the state, and thinking and writing about the concerns of the state. Empirically, the people treated in this book are by and large states*men*, but the theoretical insights would go for all statespeople, regardless of gender.

to legitimize their policies to external audiences as well as domestic ones. It was no longer enough to legitimize policies to key power brokers in the Ottoman elite (such as the Janissaries and clerics); statesmen now had to argue at European negotiating tables for the Ottomans' legitimate continuation as an independent state. To do so, they had to use not only multiple languages but multiple political traditions. Because these traditions were different, statesmen often struggled to reconcile their arguments in one language with those in another. At the same time, these statesmen started looking for ways to save the Ottoman state and to improve its ability to mobilize military forces and ward off competitors. As they did so, some of them found homologies between European states and their own and went about translating concepts from European languages. They used these concepts as tools for restructuring social relations within the Ottoman state, within its military, and between the Ottoman state and its subjects.

This book tells the story of how Ottoman and later Turkish statesmen struggled to reconcile their arguments in external language games (first mostly French, then English) with arguments in the internal (Ottoman, later Turkish) language games and in the process entangled the international and the domestic games. Moreover, the book deals with how these games structured social relations between the Ottoman state and its interlocutors, both domestically and internationally. If one takes relations to have little meaning before their expression in language, these entangled language games are the very substance, expression, and playing out of international relations. As such, they should be of primary concern for students of politics and especially for students of international relations. At stake is the validity of social theory. Scholars who take politics to be constituted in language yet ignore the interlingual aspect of international relations implicitly assume the universality of their own language.

Interlingual relations matter politically for four main reasons. First, all nonhegemonic states need to legitimize their continued sovereignty in languages other than their own. In the absence of a self-sustained overpowering military force, states' survival as corporate entities depend on legitimizing their sovereignty and actions in either the hegemon's language or that of a protector great enough to offset the military threat of the hegemon. In fact, one conceptualization of hegemony may be said to be exactly this—a situation where other polities have to legitimize *their* survival, *their* existence, and *their* actions in *your* language game, even though that language game is different from their own. Legitimizing one's existence in someone else's language demands linguistic mastery beyond the mere rudimentary level, a phenomenon that has a number of social and political consequences.

Second, when state elites consider themselves to have failed to achieve their goals in structuring relations among themselves, their agents, and their subjects, these elites start searching for both culprits and solutions. The "failure" is often said to manifest itself in relative loss of power vis-à-vis others and consequently in a loss of territory to competitors—such as the massive Ottoman losses to the Russian tsar formalized in the treaty of Küçük Kaynarca in 1774. Solutions are then sought—obviously in different ways, some of which may not exploit interlingual relations. However, when a competing polity starts seizing territory, one reaction is to try to find out what that polity does differently. If that polity uses another language, most attempts to understand the reasons for its relative success involve interlingual relations. Trying to find tools that would allow an elite to do "the same," or simply mitigate the effects of a differently organized military or state structure, inevitably involves translation. Whatever the tools may be, using tools from a different political and rhetorical tradition involves reconfiguring these tools to fit with the new context. Any imitation or adoption of another polity's state practices, which Hendrik Spruyt (1994) claims to be the origin of homogeneity in the state system, depends on interlingual relations.

While the first two points have to do with the historical emergence of international relations and the conceptualization of hegemony, the third reason why interlingual relations matter politically has to do with diplomatic negotiations in the contemporary world. When interlingual relations work smoothly, the interlingual aspect becomes obscured and scholars easily mistake them for relations taking place *in the same language*. Because of the processes of entanglement that form a key topic of this book, the existence of translation equivalents of key concepts sometimes gives the impression that translation is irrelevant. However, just as the entanglement of European and Ottoman Turkish political vocabularies is important for Turkish and Ottoman historians, so it is important for international relations scholars to understand that the interlingual aspect *has not disappeared.* Rather, although its importance recedes as a consequence of conceptual entanglement, it remains a common feature in world politics (Stritzel 2014). Translation often becomes apparent when semantic differences have clear social and political consequences—when expectations are not met because communication breaks down—as Raymond Cohen (1997) demonstrates.

Finally, in many states, especially postcolonial ones, interlingual relations are also a feature of domestic politics. Countries are typically not linguistically homogenous, and interlingual relations frequently take place in situations that cannot be said to be *international.* As a corollary, both India and South Africa, for example, use English for domestic purposes, and thus their relations with the United States may not necessarily be considered interlingual as such. An interlingual relations perspective is nevertheless useful for analyzing such states, since the actors involved use a multitude of different language games in the social field that makes up the state and its relations with different constituencies and interlocutors both domestically and externally. Thus, an interlingual relations approach is not only useful as a way of analyzing a particular type of international relations, but may also be a fruitful way to approach postcolonial politics (see Schaffer 1998).

For international relations, the Ottoman and Turkish case is well suited for theorizing how interlingual relations change over time and how the state, the language, and relations with interlocutors change in the process. Questions pertaining to the Ottoman state's *reform* project, the Turkish Republic's *Westernization* project, and the latter's *EU harmonization* project have been central topics in the history literature, in political science, and in international relations. The emphasis has been on Ottoman and Turkish *imitation* of Europe—how the Ottoman Empire "entered international society" through the appropriation of European norms that simply diffused unchanged into the empire (e.g., Naff 1984). I follow J. G. A. Pocock (1972) in the claim that at least on the collective level, one can only do what one has the language to formulate and legitimize doing. It was impossible to formulate and legitimize a collective program of "imitating Europe" in Ottoman in the early nineteenth century. The possibility of formulating a wide-ranging project of "imitating Europe" or "Westernizing" came into being only as an unintended consequence of a number of actions *intended to achieve something else.* Positing an early nineteenth-century Ottoman intention to "Westernize" is therefore indefensible.[2] This book turns its attention to the prerequisites, insisting that in principle, conceptual entanglement happens *one translation at a time,* where the use of a particular conceptual reinterpretation is always open-ended.

Having established that interlingual relations are differently configured than relations taking place "within a language" and that they matter politically, I set out to develop tools for studying how international relations are played out interlingually and how we may understand the sociopolitical transformations undergone by the Ottomans and Turks in the past two centuries by the use of these tools. Studying this political transformation and set of interactions by way of privileging concepts and conceptual change is not about "mere rhetorics" but is about the changing possibilities for legitimizing political action (Connolly 1993; Garsten 2006; Epstein 2008). Concepts are tools used to rearrange or stabilize particular configurations of social relations and are therefore tools of governance, for contestation, and for conducting politics (Jackson 2006; Nexon 2009). In this book, the relations in question are those that make up the Ottoman/Turkish state and its relationship both with its subjects and with other (mostly European) states. Both the acts of reinterpreting concepts and the use of these concepts in restructuring and stabilizing relations are political acts. In this book, theory is a means to an end, not an end in itself. The emphasis is on understanding—providing a theoretical account of—how concepts have been used in legitimizing and reconfiguring social relations specifically in the transformation from Ottoman Empire to Turkish nation-state.

Entanglement

The Turkish language of today bears little resemblance to Ottoman of the early nineteenth century. While the grammar is still very different from Indo-European languages, contemporary Turkish has

---

2. I go by G. E. M. Anscombe's (2000) use of the term *intention.*

much more semantic capacity for translating political concepts from English, French, and German. This was not the case two centuries ago. Any attempt at translating Ottoman sultanic decrees from the beginning of the nineteenth century into today's English requires no end of paratext—prefaces, epilogues, explanatory parentheses, footnotes, or running commentary—to become comprehensible. Likewise, Ottoman diplomacy with European interlocutors was rife with misunderstandings and struggles over meaning. As part of different political traditions and being upheld and imbricated in different political institutions and practices, Ottoman political language relied on a separate conceptual vocabulary to make sense of the world and to legitimize the rule of the state. It is nevertheless important to point out that I am not talking about hermetically sealed entities here. Not only did continuous if less dense interaction take place between the Ottomans and various polities in Europe, but Ottoman concept formation was heavily indebted to the Arabic scholarly tradition, which itself drew extensively on translations of Greek canonical texts into Arabic between the eighth and tenth centuries CE (Haskins 1927; Gutas 1998, 1–8, 173–75). Because much of the Greek canon was translated into Latin via Arabic, European philosophical traditions depend to some extent on the same translations from ancient Greek into Arabic that were important for the development of Ottoman as a political language (Hasse 2008). Moreover, Byzantine political tradition, which was tied to the Greek language, was clearly important for the early Ottomans (Köprülüzade M. Fuat 1931). In fact, the Ottoman Empire of the fifteenth and sixteenth centuries can in some ways be thought of as a Renaissance state that patronized some of the same artists and used many of the same military and governing techniques as its European contemporaries (Raby 1982; Kafadar 1995; Rogers 2005). Ottoman political language was not an island entire of itself.

"European" conceptual vocabulary was also no stable and coherent whole, and it would be unwarranted to juxtapose this with an Ottoman or Islamic conceptual vocabulary as if these were entities with agreed-upon boundaries and object-like qualities. Yet many more translations existed between the main European languages than between these languages and Ottoman. Whereas both Europeans and Ottomans were frequently bilingual, the languages in which they were bilingual seldom overlapped. Therefore, they seldom participated in the same language games. A denser network of individuals engaged in translation and conversation across the boundaries between what may anachronistically be called Western European languages than between Ottoman and these languages.

Wherever the Catholic Church had held sway, learned men participated in common language games that were played out in Latin up until the middle of the eighteenth century. While vernacular language games were used to legitimize political power at least from the time of the Reformations, Latin nevertheless provided a common set of references for centuries, and its legacy made for certain commonalities between the languages used by Catholics and Protestants. Conversely, no part of the Ottoman elite participated actively in Latin language games.[3] This made for a great divergence in political meaning and relatively few interlingual conversations where readers, writers, or speakers sought to reconcile these meanings.

The divergence became more poignant as semantic change picked up pace with the transformation of French political vocabulary around the time of the French Revolution of 1789. Together with the social revolution and the Industrial Revolution, the political revolutions of the late eighteenth and early nineteenth centuries made up what German conceptual historian Reinhart Koselleck (2004) called the Sattelzeit, a transitional period between early modernity and modernity. A central aspect of this transition was that new concepts were coined to give meaning to new European historical experiences. Users changed their linguistic habits in such a way that language *anticipated* change. Rather than expecting the future to largely resemble the past, this new vocabulary pointed toward a utopian future. Concepts such as *civilization, progress, equality,* and *liberty* became not only slogans but also yardsticks by which to measure history and tools for shaping the future.

This Sattelzeit vocabulary emerged *without* the Ottomans taking part in the language games that shaped it but was translated into Ottoman and Turkish after its inception. As Mikhail Bakhtin has put it,

---

3. Though Italian and Lingua Franca were important for Ottoman trade and diplomacy, primarily via intermediaries, Latin was not.

> [T]here are no neutral words and forms—words and forms that belong to "no one"; language has been completely taken over, shot through with intentions and accents. For any individual consciousness living in it, language is not an abstract system of normative forms but rather a concrete heteroglot conception of the world. All words have the "taste" of a profession, a genre, a tendency, a party, a particular work, a particular person, a generation, an age group, the day and hour. Each word tastes of the context and contexts in which it has lived its socially charged life.
>
> [...] The word in language is half someone else's. It becomes "one's own" when the speaker populates it with his own intention, his own accent, when he appropriates the word, adapting it to his own semantic and expressive intention. (1981, 293)

Having to conduct politics by the extensive use of a vocabulary that "tastes" of some other polity or context is a situation that may also be described by Antonio Gramsci's (1971) concept of *hegemony*. While words do not keep some kind of essence from their first inception, time and effort are required to populate them with one's own intonations and accents. The words by which politics is legitimized *between* states today do not generally taste of Ottoman or Turkish contexts. Words such as *civilization, empire, democracy,* and *citizenship* taste of European contexts from the Sattelzeit on and of the relations that these words entered into as the European Great Powers legitimized their globally extended rule. Any state elite that wanted to legitimize its own position vis-à-vis European encroachment had to participate in this language game, at least if it could not mobilize an overwhelming military force.

Apart from the white settler colonies, non-European polities were at a distinct disadvantage in this game. First, the political vocabulary privileged Europeans (and white Christians descended from Europe). Second, whereas most Europeans could use a language they already mastered, Ottoman and other non-European statesmen had to acquire the linguistic skills required to engage competently in this language game, usually placing them at a significant disadvantage. Moreover, networks between Ottoman and Western European elites were not very dense prior to the 1870s and 1880s, so there were few avenues of translation (Taceddin Kayaoğlu 1998). Different parts of the Ottoman state already employed specialist translators and interpreters, of course, but the work of these people was mostly directed "inward"—that is, it served as part of the internal functioning of the state rather than engaging in public discourse and hardly concerned matters of political philosophy or the principles of societal organization.[4] Thus, the use of translators and interpreters provided few new discursive elements that could serve as tools to formulate radically new policies, and their activities brought few changes in the domestic, Ottoman language game.

Early modern Ottoman diplomatic contact with European polities generally relied on exploiting preexisting connections between actors with whom the state elite had weak ties rather than on setting up an in-house diplomatic service (cf. Granovetter 1973). Diplomacy thus relied on elite liminals—mostly well-connected Christians—for its conduct of foreign affairs. The dragomans and others who served as diplomatic go-betweens usually interpreted orally and secretively, and as they were first primarily Italian-speaking[5] and later Greek Phanariots,[6] their translations had little impact on Ottoman letters or public discourse in general (Gürkan 2015). Beginning in the eighteenth century, attempts were made to translate texts for more public distribution (Taceddin Kayaoğlu 1998, 30–41). These were not primarily European texts, but included texts in Persian, ancient Greek, and Arabic. It was not until the *Encümen-i Dāniş* (Ottoman Academy of Letters) was established in 1851 that an institution attempted to systematically translate works for public availability (54–89). It has to be noted that translation was only part of their activities, and the number of works translated very limited. Another early avenue for translating foreign texts about current affairs into Ottoman was the newspaper *Cerīde-i Ḥavādis̱*, set up by Englishman William Churchill

---

4. It is difficult to argue that the Ottoman polity had a text-based "public sphere," and a clear distinction between public texts and some other category "internal" to the state's operation is obviously artificial. Moreover, there were no clear-cut distinctions between statesmen, legal scholars, scribes, and poets that would correspond to a public/private distinction. The ability to read and write was a defining trait for all of these groups, and the boundaries between them were porous.

5. That is, the members of the Genovese colony at Pera, across the Golden Horn, and their descendants.

6. Upper-class Greeks living close to the Greek-Orthodox patriarchate in Istanbul.

in Izmir in 1840 specifically to relay news about the rest of the world to Ottoman readers (Oğuz 1994).

While a handful of Ottoman diplomats learned French at the turn of the nineteenth century, not until the establishment of the Tercüme Odası (Translation Chamber) in 1821 did the Ottoman state institutionalize its training of well-connected elite Ottomans in French language for the purpose of interaction with other states (Yurdusev 2004). The immediate reason for doing so was the outbreak of the Greek Revolt (or Revolution, depending on whom you ask). The state center suspected that its *Phanariot* translators were in cahoots with the rebels and no longer dared to rely on their services (Ilicak 2011). What had been weak but positive ties had become relations of animosity that the state considered ill-suited for conducting diplomacy. This is an important change from exploiting weak ties, because by doing in-house translations, the state not only had fewer agency problems but also enabled an important element of the state elite to engage directly in new interlingual relations. Possibly as a result, the Tercüme Odası fostered some of the most intellectually innovative and politically influential Ottomans of the second half of the nineteenth century.

Prior to the institutionalization of foreign language education for Ottoman statesmen, the density of interaction across the language boundary was fairly low. Moreover, Ottoman had little vocabulary with which to explain French concepts by relying on existing links to French contexts or tradition. Translated concepts had to be explained by reference to concepts that emerged in a specifically Ottoman tradition. When such statesmen as Sadık Rıfat Paşa and Mustafa Reşid Paşa started writing about *sivilizasyon* (civilization) in the 1830s, they defined it by use of concepts that, if not *inherently* Ottoman, were embedded in Ottoman historical experience and tradition (see chapter 3).

Although I would not claim that this was the *first* Ottoman translation of concepts of *civilization*—people may have used such concepts before these two *paşas*—there is the sense that the concept was new, and as with all novel translation, it had to be translated by reference to something already known, something that readers could understand. To this end, they used Ottoman concepts that had to do with refinement, education, and urban life. When the circle to which Rıfat

Paşa and Reşid Paşa belonged was involved in the proclamation of the Tanzimat Charter in 1839, translation equivalents of *civilization* were not used in the text, despite the fact that members of the circle used it prominently in their other writings. Although this group had started using *sivilizasyon* as a word among themselves, they could probably not be confident that it would be understood outside the Ottoman bureaucratic elite.

Ottomans translated French concepts by yoking them to pre-existing concepts in the Ottoman language, and started using them to give meaning to their own situation. Maxime Rodinson (1988, 9–10) argued that explaining Muslim political institutions by equating them to Christian concepts happened in "European" texts as early as the eleventh century. These are two different phenomena, in that explaining another polity's institutions by reference to one's own is rather common, whereas introducing concepts and taxonomies from a foreign language to give meaning to one's own historical experience only comes about in very specific political contexts. As Ottoman conceptual vocabulary gained translation equivalents of many French political concepts, it became increasingly possible to retain more of the semantic connotations that French and English concepts had in the original language when translating. French political philosophy is much easier to translate if the translator does not have to digress to explain French concepts such as *la volonté générale, séparation des pouvoirs,* and *l'ésprit des lois.* A translator always has to choose between trying to convey the exact meaning or to retain the style, structure, and rhythm of the source text (Derrida 2004).[7] The more explanatory digressions and paratext a translator has to provide, the more a translation becomes an independent text and the more it constitutes the semantic field of the target language differently from that of the source language.

Having established translation equivalents for key concepts makes it easier to translate texts between languages (see Koç 2004). The extent to which it is possible to give a translation meaning similar to the meaning in the original context depends on the conceptual vocabulary in the target language having the same semantic connota-

---

7. For a discussion of "domestication" and "foreignization" as translation strategies, see Venuti 1998.

tions. The preexisting similarities of the rhetorical traditions of the two languages condition the possibility for introducing new elements from one into the other without great semantic reconfiguration. There is, however, a lot more going on than merely a translator trying to render the meaning of a text as faithfully as possible in another language. Therefore, there will never be *perfect* semantic compatibility between a source text and its translation. Translators have their faults, their agendas and their structural limitations, both semantic and institutional. Moreover, once the concept has been established in the new language, it takes on a life of its own as a rhetorical commonplace in that language. Thus, there will always be divergence, both because the reinterpreted concepts carry the marks of the history of their use in the new language and because people who use them in their proceedings in that language need not be continuously engaging in the changing tradition of their origin.

Translation, State, and Agency

This book deals with issues that are closely related to the state, both as discourses on the state and the state as an effect of certain discourses and practices of boundary making. Most of the chapters deal with texts written by statesmen or referred to by statesmen to legitimize particular decisions. As such, this work may be termed a study of the vocabulary used to legitimize the rule of a particular set of elites. It concerns the transformation of the conceptual vocabulary used to legitimize the orderings that Timothy Mitchell (2006) has called "the state effect." While not all the authors of the texts included here were statesmen or politicians, most of them belonged to an elite dependent for their status on closeness to state power, and they can to a large extent be called "intellectuals of statecraft" (Ó Tuathail and Agnew 1992).

The existing social science literature that deals with the Ottoman Empire's transformation into the Turkish Republic and its integration into a European-emergent international order rests on the assumption of the state as a unitary actor (Naff 1984; Rumelili 2007; Turan Kayaoğlu 2010; Zarakol 2010). This is a background assumption of a majority of Anglophone International Relations scholars, yet one that is seldom on display. Such an approach has the tendency to swallow individual agency, taking each person to be just another part of the social whole (Parsons 1949, 67–69). This goes for statesmen as well as commoners. Furthermore, by combining ontological individualism with a methodological desire for nomothetic generalization, as is common in International Relations (see, e.g., Keohane 1984), scholars minimize the importance of individual skills and creative agency. Although this view retains the individual as the site of decisions, the role of individual characteristics is written out of the equation. In this schema, the statesman's resources are those made available by the state, and his or her personal skills, characteristics, creativity, and flair are simply overlooked.

This is one reason why translation has disappeared from sight in social science literature. It is assumed to "just happen" because the state allocates resources so that all statesmen are equally equipped to do their jobs. Well, that simply is not the case. Language skills take a long time to develop and are highly individualized. A statesman's ability to engage in interlingual relations does therefore not only depend on the resources of the state as a collective. Furthermore, when statesmen are provided with translators or interpreters, there is no reason to assume that translators are a generic breed whose translations are homogeneous. Highly individualized, creative skills and strategies make possible highly individual courses of action. Legitimation strategies do not just come out of the blue, derived from the structural position of the statesman, politician, diplomat, or journalist. These acts of individual creativity in legitimation practices are of great significance to the ways in which polities uphold legitimacy of rule; those routes, in turn, create path dependencies for the strategies open to successors.[8]

The other reason translation has disappeared from international relations theory is the fact that a majority of IR scholars are functionally monolingual. This makes it possible for even those parts of the research collective that study international politics by privileging meaning to assume that a statement *will be essentially the same* in translation. Translation itself can thus be ignored (for exceptions, see

---

8. Few episodes illustrate this as well as the way a French translation of the Russian copy of the Treaty of Küçük Kaynarca (1774) seems to have been used strategically by the Russians to establish their "protection" of Greek Orthodox subjects of the sultan (Davison 1976).

Wescott 1990; Cohen 2001; Collin 2013; Stritzel 2014). As I will argue, translation is a *creative* reinterpretation of a statement by use of another repertoire of meaning making, thus yoking together meaning between two repertoires or languages. In other words, it is a metaphorical carrying across from one linguistic context to another, a form of code switching that ties the codes together without making them synonymous. Whether to a lesser or a greater extent, the person doing the translation must embody both of the repertoires used and engaged with. Consequently, who engages in translation and how are of great social consequence.

The state is a curious type of phenomenon since it has no existence prior to the agents acting in its name (Jackson 2006, 27). Assuming that the state is a unitary, socially coherent whole involves a leap of faith that might not necessarily be particularly fruitful for analysis of social processes that depend on highly individualized abilities. I therefore approach questions of translation in Ottoman/Turkish social transformations by dispensing with the assumption of the state as a unitary actor and analytically privileging "relations before states" (Jackson and Nexon 1999). Taking the state to be acted out by a set of individuals who are differently positioned in networks and who embody different linguistic and social skills allows me to treat translation as creative agency and avoid ending up with a diffusionist narrative of social change. Even though the scholarship on diffusion is attentive to the linguistic expression of norms, such a narrative quickly ends up ignoring the reinterpretation that occurs when meaning gets translated (Finnemore and Sikkink 1998; Acharya 2004; Checkel 2005). This in turn ignores the extent to which local agency is part of the story, as context-specific concept formation takes place through translation and reifies the narrative whereby the non-West merely imitates norms, ideas, and technologies of rule that have already emerged in the West.

Studying Ottoman Meaning after Orientalism

Semantically oriented study of Ottoman and Turkish social and political history has by and large been conducted as part of the academic field once known as Orientalism. In fact, such studies were the high points in the careers of scholars such as Bernard Lewis (1988), who wrote about "the political language of Islam" as a unitary and static entity. After Edward Said discredited this field with his 1978 classic, *Orientalism*, the concept soon became the bête noire both of anthropology and of Orientalism's succeeding incarnation, Middle Eastern studies. *Orientalism* also became used as a battle concept to delegitimize intellectual and political opponents. Said's criticism is pertinent, and the methodological, epistemological, and historiosophical weaknesses of Lewis's writings were amply illustrated. However, Said never fleshed out the "What now?" of post-Orientalist scholarship. In fact, his was a study of *European* texts and never aimed to improve on Orientalist scholarship. Said threw the baby out with the bathwater. As a result, the classic works on long-term Ottoman intellectual history written within an Orientalist tradition in the 1960s, foremost among which were Lewis (1961, 1982), Şerif Mardin (1962), and Niyazi Berkes ([1964] 1998), have not been revised or surpassed in any systematic manner.

The empirical story in this book is an attempt to move away from the Orientalist tradition while salvaging the Orientalists' interest in the specific constellations of lexis that gave meaning to Ottoman and Turkish politics *at the time.* It is therefore a study of the history of Ottoman and Turkish concepts. However, I do not take such concepts to have any kind of essential and unchanging "correct" meaning that can be found in canonical Islamic texts (though the authors of the texts I study sometimes argue along those lines). An important methodological problem of the works of Lewis and his colleagues was their acceptance of their texts' and informants' insistence on an ancient correct meaning from which any deviation is simply *wrong.*

Orientalism, like so many other contemporary Western scholarly pursuits, divided the world into modernity and tradition, where the question of *modernization* was the main topic (see, e.g., Lerner 1958).

> Under the influence of modern individualism, which was meant to free us from restrictive traditions, we have tended to equate all traditions with hierarchically structured, *closed systems* of knowledge, which are supposed to provide members with ready-made solutions to problems, not with material for arguments. (Shotter 1993, 171)

Accordingly, Orientalists tended to study semantic variation not as political and historical change *within* a tradition but as deviation from a set norm, established and guarded by religious scholars. This approach essentializes Ottoman, Arabic, or Persian meaning and consequently posits "Islamic culture"—or whatever name the social aggregate is given—as a static entity unable to change except through externally induced *modernization,* which causes individuals and societies to leave tradition behind. This is paradoxically close to the stance taken by Ottoman traditionalists, who took the "Golden Age" as their template for social organization (see Kafadar 1993). Robert Bellah et al. have argued that those who think of tradition in this way

> deeply misunderstand tradition even when they seek to embrace it. They defend not tradition but traditionalism, and, as Jaroslav Pelikan has said, whereas tradition is the living faith of the dead, traditionalism is the dead faith of the living. A living tradition is never a program for automatic moral judgments. It is always in a continuous process of reinterpretation and reappropriation. Such a process assumes, however, that tradition has enough authority for the search of its present meaning to be publicly pursued as a common project. (1985, 140–41)

Orientalist scholarship has been traditionalist on behalf of "Islamic tradition" in much the same way as have Muslim traditionalists, taking tradition to be a closed system of knowledge that provides ready-made solutions to problems (Jung 2011).

The baseline Orientalist historical narrative of the Ottoman Empire has been challenged repeatedly and quite successfully (see, e.g., Abou-El-Haj 1991; Aksan 2004; Barkey 2008). The narrative is a story of Ottoman state formation, rise, golden age, and stagnation. The way out of stagnation was supposedly through the diffusion of European ideas, technologies, and institutions into the Ottoman Empire, pointing to a nation-state future for the territories and populations of the region (Ze'evi 2004). Maurus Reinkowski's criticism of Ami Ayalon also applies to contemporary treatments of Ottoman political language:

> Ayalon, for example, intends to show how European institutions and terms were imitated by Arab intellectuals in the 19th

century, limiting his analysis to Lebanon and Egypt. Taking a one-dimensional and somewhat condescending approach, Ayalon presents Arabic as a language that has to pass from a stagnant Islamic past to the European-inspired Elysian fields of modernity. (2005, 196)

This narrative of stagnant Ottomans imitating Europe has been thoroughly and polemically addressed by Edward Said (1978), Timothy Mitchell (2002), and Dror Ze'evi (2004). I have other fish to fry—namely, how we can salvage the emphasis on linguistic, conceptual, and intellectual change in the Ottoman realms from the carcass of Orientalist methodologies and grand narratives. It is possible to study texts produced by Ottoman statesmen, bureaucrats, and intellectuals without resorting to the simple dichotomies of *progressive* and *reactionary*, *Westernist* and *Islamist*.[9] The Ottomans themselves—more precisely, Akçuraoğlu Yusuf[10] in 1904—inserted *Turkist* into something resembling the latter dichotomy, forming a conceptual tripod that has since been picked up by Turkish and foreign historians alike (Berkes [1964] 1998; Poulton 1997).

This leads me to a different matter at hand—that is, the need to detach analytical, scholarly vocabulary from the vocabulary of the texts under study. Niyazi Berkes's ([1964] 1998) adoption of the *Westernist-Islamist-Turkist* conceptual tripod as a framework for analyzing texts that rely on these concepts is a major methodological weakness of his work, yet it has set a standard for Turkish historiography. In the final analysis, detaching the analytical concepts from meaning as it appears in the sources is of course impossible. My sources inevitably use some of the same concepts I use in my analysis (or, rather, what I call *translation equivalents* of those concepts [drawing on Nida 2000]). However, every analysis needs to keep *something* stable from which to narrate. I have no other tools available to narrate the story besides the analytical vocabulary of English-language scholarship, which is not very far removed from that of European politics and European normative political philosophy. Yet I try to remain agnostic about the meaning of the concepts under study and to avoid deploy-

---

9. Maurus Reinkowski (2005) offers an eminent example of how this may be done.
10. Now better known by his post-1934 name, Yusuf Akçura.

ing them in an analytical capacity. Although lexis use is perpetually changing (albeit ever so slightly), letting all elements of the analysis float at the same time simply results either in analytical paralysis or in total narrative confusion. Each of the book's chapters, therefore, focuses on a different concept; for the sake of narrative simplicity, I have postulated continuity between Ottoman and Turkish political discourse.[11]

Historical Précis

The Ottoman polity was established by Turkic nomads in Anatolia in 1299, on the frontier between the Byzantine and Mongol empires (Lindner 2007). Through military campaigns, control of trade routes, and successful manipulation of Byzantine politics, the Ottomans gained a consolidated territory in Anatolia and an economic basis for further expansion into the Balkans in the late fourteenth century. Establishing itself as an empire around the time of the conquest of Constantinople in 1453, the Ottoman polity used an eclectic mix of elements from Byzantine and Turkic state tradition to legitimize its rule to various subjects (Kafadar 1995). From the very beginning, a central feature of its mobilization of coercive power was the promise of loot and opportunities in newly conquered lands (Lowry 2003). Moreover, the Ottoman polity tended to attract the loyalties of Greek Orthodox subjects of the Byzantine emperor because of the much lighter Ottoman tax burden. Two aspects of Ottoman legitimating practices and mobilization of resources are particularly relevant for this book: multivocal signaling as a strategy of legitimation (that is, speaking and using symbols that mean different things to different audiences)

---

11. Despite a fundamental transformation, there can be little doubt that there is continuity between the two, politically, linguistically, and in terms of personnel. This continuity makes distinguishing clearly and systematically between Ottoman and Turkish language difficult to the point of futility. There is no clear linguistic break from one language to the other that also corresponds to the name for the political entity. Since I am discussing texts both as part of politics and in the sense of the language used, this is a bit problematic. While the polity changed its name to Turkey in 1923, and its politics must be said to be *Turkish* from then on, the Arabic script remained in use until 1928, when it was replaced by the Latin script. For the sake of simplicity, I have called those texts that appear in Latin script *Turkish*, regardless of when they were originally written, and those in the Arabic script *Ottoman*.

and distributing patronage through networks of loyalty, with conquest and potential loot serving as important means of rewarding followers (Barkey 2008).

Having expanded territorially until the second siege of Vienna (1683), the Ottoman Empire first recognized the loss of a large swath of territory with the Treaty of Karlowitz, concluded with the Habsburgs in 1699. When the Russians later forced the Ottomans to sign the Treaty of Küçük Kaynarca in 1774, the Ottoman elite was ruffled. The Ottoman polity was struggling with a legitimacy crisis. Fighting a defensive war meant that there would be no new lands to loot, that there would be no new conquered territories to govern, and that the Ottoman state elite increasingly had to rely on other ways of mobilizing coercive power to fend off external threats. At the center, Ottoman military failures were interpreted as state failures and as signs of *corruption* and *turmoil* in the state order (Topal 2017b). To reverse the train of military defeats, statesmen generally argued for the need to address what they considered the root of the problem—namely, the breakdown of *order*.

During the period following the 1774 treaty, statesmen sought ways to reform the state. They found homologies in European polities and translated these into an Ottoman vocabulary. The reign of Sultan Selim III (1789–1807) is generally known for his project to institute a *new order* (nizam-ı cedid), following up on his predecessor's experiment in using French drill instructors to train "European-style" troops. These were hugely unpopular, as they challenged the position of the Janissaries. The reign of Selim III was also marked by an uneasy relationship with the French, a long-standing Ottoman ally. First the French Revolution and then Napoleon's 1798 invasion of the Ottoman province of Egypt made the relationship rather complicated. This invasion dislodged the Mamluks, who had been Ottoman clients for almost three centuries. The Ottomans did not have a navy capable of sending a sufficient expeditionary force to Egypt and thus needed help from the British and the Austrians to oust Napoleon. However, one member of the Ottoman expeditionary force was Kavalalı Mehmed Ali Paşa (Muhammad Ali Pasha), who established himself as a military leader in Cairo. Mehmed Ali Paşa soon demanded that Istanbul make his position hereditary. He also reshaped the governing apparatus in Egypt and reformed the military there by use of European (mostly French) renegades and Ottoman exiles (Fahmy 1997). His actions and a series of rebellions in the Balkans in the early nineteenth century posed a legitimacy challenge to the Ottoman center.

During the reign of Sultan Mahmud II (1808–39), the center faced an almost complete breakdown of legitimacy. Struggling to centralize power in Istanbul and increase tax collection while mobilizing a military force capable of fending off external enemies, Mahmud II faced rebellion after rebellion (F. F. Anscombe 2014). These were generally put down ruthlessly, and imperial middlemen were systematically cut out of decision making. Most of the rebellions were unsuccessful, but the Greek War of Independence (1821–29) established a sovereign state, with which the Ottomans contended for Greek Orthodox loyalties. Mehmed Ali Paşa posed a different sort of challenge in Egypt. He launched a rather successful military expedition on Istanbul: only Russian intervention stopped him after the Ottoman army had been routed at Konya and the path to Istanbul lay open in 1832. However, Mehmed Ali Paşa did not set himself up as a competing locus for the loyalties of Ottoman subjects but rather sought recognition by the Ottoman suzerain and a guarantee that his descendants would rule Egypt as Ottoman governors.

Mahmud II's ruthless campaign to centralize power by doing away with imperial middlemen alienated a great many Muslims. During his reign, the Janissary Corps was liquidated by artillery fire in 1826, an action that followed Mehmed Ali Paşa's precedent of burning alive most of the Mamluks in 1811. Having gone from elite infantry to obsolete and militarily irrelevant against foreign threats, the Janissaries supplied force for various "popular" demands on the sultan in the capital and were the main audience to whom the sultan and his statesmen had to legitimate his decisions prior to 1826 (Tezcan 2010). Having obliterated this constituency, Sultan Mahmud II and his statesmen had far more leeway to act. However, abolishing the Janissaries did not provide the Ottoman state with new coercive resources needed to discipline its middlemen and fend off external invasion. In 1828, the Ottomans suffered another military defeat against Russia. Serbia received autonomy under Ottoman suzerainty, while Russia obtained suzerainty over former Ottoman vassals Moldavia and Wallachia as well as gained territories in Eastern Anatolia and the southern Caucasus.

Sultan Mahmud's reign came to an end in 1839, and his son and successor, Sultan Abdülmecid I, soon proclaimed the époque-making Gülhane Rescript, often known as the Tanzimat Charter. The document has variously been interpreted as a program for *Westernization* or imitation of Europe, an Ottoman proto-constitution, and a sultanic legal instrument within an Ottoman tradition (see Topal 2017b, 102–5). The fact that all these claims can be made hints at the Rescript's multivocality. The Gülhane Rescript served as a legitimating device that tied rebellious middlemen to the new sultan by guaranteeing the sanctity of life and respect for Sharia (F. F. Anscombe 2014). The Rescript inaugurated the Tanzimat (reordering) period (1839–76), which coincides with the reigns of Abdülmecid and his brother, Sultan Abdülaziz I (1861–76). That era was marked by the proclamation of a large number of legal instruments and the establishment of new educational institutions.

Following the British and Habsburg intervention to fend off Napoleon in 1801 and the Russian intervention to prevent Mehmed Ali Paşa from taking Istanbul in 1833, foreign powers had positioned themselves as important audiences for legitimizing Ottoman decisions. The British were concerned that the 1833 alliance between Russia and the Ottoman Empire would threaten British naval dominance in the Eastern Mediterranean and that potential Russian territorial expansion as a consequence of Ottoman military weakness would upset the balance of power in Europe (M. S. Anderson 1966). This made the future of the Ottoman Empire an important issue for British decision makers, who referred to it as the Eastern Question (see chapter 3).

These concerns came to a head in 1853, when France and Britain intervened on the Ottoman side against a Russian military offensive. The resulting Crimean War (1853–56) brought new changes to the Ottoman Empire, as French and British soldiers fought alongside Ottomans and the whole gamut of French and British military technology was exhibited in the attempt to defeat the Russians, an effort that was coordinated by the allies in Istanbul. Although Russia formally lost the war, the Ottoman vassals Moldavia and Wallachia were granted independence. The Ottoman Empire, on the other hand, though not particularly successful on the battlefield, was given membership in the Congress of Europe, while the second major legal instrument of the Tanzimat period, the Islahat Fermanı (Reform Edict) was proclaimed, granting legal equality to all Ottoman subjects regardless of religion (see chapter 5).

When Sultan Abdülhamid II came to power in 1876, he was soon forced to proclaim the newly written Ottoman Constitution, inaugurating what has retrospectively been called the First Constitutional Period and establishing an elected Ottoman parliament. Soon, however, yet another military crisis with Russia arose, and the sultan used it as a pretext to suspend the constitution and close parliament in early 1878. Russia allied with the former Ottoman vassals Romania, Bulgaria, Serbia, and Montenegro, all of whom declared independence from the Ottomans. The Russians won a swift victory and gained new conquests in Eastern Anatolia and the northern Balkans. At the Congress of Berlin, the guiding principle was that gains by one Great Power should be offset by gains by another, and the Habsburgs and British were also given Ottoman territories. In addition, the Ottomans were receiving large numbers of Muslim refugees from the areas it had lost (Fisher 1999). In Britain, Ottoman massacres of Bulgarians were used to create outrage against the Prime Minister, leading to a change of government. The new government ended Britain's support for the Ottomans, opening the possibility of Ottoman-German cooperation. Perhaps the most transformative aspect of this cooperation was the 1883 military mission that set up a military academy on the model of the Prussian *Kriegsakademie.*

The period of Sultan Abdülhamid II's absolutist rule (1878–1908) is usually known as the Hamidian period and saw very intense state building (Deringil 1998). The Ottoman state greatly extended its reach, mobilizing resources that had previously been inaccessible to it. The legitimacy claims of the sultan also became more explicitly Islamic in that Abdülhamid II made more frequent use of the title *caliph* to strengthen ties with his Muslim subjects (and those of other imperial polities, such as Indian Muslims under British rule). With some minor exceptions, the territorial losses for the past century abated. The state went from one diplomatic crisis to another, but the sultan and his statesmen appear to have been quite adept at legitimating their position externally, as no serious military challenges arose from competing powers during this period (see chapters 3 and 4). On the domestic front, however, the situation was anything but peaceful, with pogroms against Armenians, guerrillas in the Balkans, terrorist attacks in Istanbul, a crisis in Crete, Zionists moving to Palestine, and regular crises in the Balkans and Mount Lebanon all contributing to a sense of urgency for the Ottoman state elite.

While the Tanzimat period transformed the Ottoman elite and reconfigured the relations between the state and its subjects, the Hamidian period transformed the lower levels of state functionaries through a massive expansion of education. The sons of the top officials to a greater extent used patrimonial networks to attain positions of power regardless of qualifications, making the new educational institutions vehicles for social advancement for the sons of lower functionaries. In fact, the institution building of the Hamidian period laid the groundwork for a new elite consisting of professional, Prussian-educated officers who subscribed to abstract loyalty to the Fatherland (*vatan*) rather than to patrimonial relations with the sultan. In 1908, in an attempt to save the Fatherland, these officers led a coup that has in English come to be known as the Young Turk Revolution (starting the Second Constitutional Period, 1908–13 or perhaps until 1918). Central to this revolution was the Committee of Union and Progress, which demanded that the sultan reinstate the Ottoman Constitution and call elections to reconvene parliament. Rather than saving the Fatherland, the Young Turk Revolution was seized upon by Bulgaria, which declared independence and occupied Eastern Rumelia, as well as by the Habsburg Empire, which annexed the Ottoman provinces of Bosnia and Herzegovina.

The Young Turk Revolution augured great changes to the Ottoman state and was welcomed across the Empire. Like the Gülhane Rescript, the revolution renewed the frayed bonds between a previously centralizing state and its partly alienated subjects (see, e.g., Campos 2010). The dismantling of Abdülhamid's personal network of spies as well as the creation of constitutional guarantees gave an impetus for a blossoming of civil society organizations throughout the empire. While in many ways reinvigorating social life in the empire, this process also meant that the old means of dividing and ruling the subjects became obsolete. When heterogeneous Ottoman subjects came together in a parliament, it became more difficult for those Muslims who lived far away to ascribe good intentions to the neglect of the center (Kayalı 1997, 102–6). Key developments of this period included boundary making between Arabs and Turks and the emergence of Turkish and Arab nationalism (see chapters 4 and 5).

The Committee of Union and Progress, which came to play an increasingly important role during the Second Constitutional Period, faced one military crisis after another. When Italy invaded Libya and the Dodecanese Islands in 1911, the Ottoman military could mount little in the way of a response. It lacked the naval capacity to move troops to Libya or defend the Dodecanese, and its main attempt at resistance was to direct a guerrilla war by mobilizing Bedouin tribes in Libya. The following year, Greece, Bulgaria, and Serbia attacked and easily defeated the Ottomans in the First Balkan War, depriving the empire of most of its remaining Balkan territories. The Committee of Union and Progress, whose main cadre had been educated by German officers, used the urgency of this defeat to reorganize its military and attract even more help from Germany.

No longer satisfied by the degree of control afforded by influencing elections, the Young Turk Triumvirate—Enver Paşa, Cemal Paşa, and Talat Paşa—carried out a coup d'état in 1913 and ruled as a dictatorship until the end of the First World War. By the time Grand Duke Ferdinand was shot in Sarajevo in 1914, the Ottomans were already on a war footing, having suffered defeat twice and gained a minor victory in two years and yet still trying, with German help, to reorganize their army to meet future challenges. In a way, Ottoman entry into the First World War seemed inevitable, and there seems to have been a general agreement among the elite that war was necessary for "national regeneration" (Aksakal 2004).

However, the First World War resulted in the loss of all the Arab provinces to European imperial powers, an almost complete devastation of the Ottoman countryside, and a depletion of the Ottoman population (especially men) as well as important social changes (Findley 2010, 192–246). In Eastern Anatolia, Armenians and other Christians had been expelled or massacred in what has come to be known as the Armenian Genocide. In Western Anatolia and on the coast, Greek Orthodox Christians were exchanged for Muslims from Greece (1924–26). Muslim women had been brought into the workforce to take the place of men sent to the front. The Ottoman state had taken almost complete control of the means of production, creating an economy entirely directed toward the war effort. This, along with the possessions left by Armenians and Greek Orthodox, enriched local strongmen, notables, and Muslims with political connections to the Committee of Union and Progress and later Kemalists, laying the basis for the emergence of a Muslim "national bourgeoisie."

Mustafa Kemal (later Atatürk) emerged victorious in the struggle over both the survival of a Muslim polity based in Anatolia and the legitimate control over the reins of the state. The actual fighting in this War of Independence (1919–22) pitted Mustafa Kemal's *nationalists* against Armenian, French, and Greek troops, with the British occupying Istanbul and the Italians playing third fiddle. The sultan, in whose name the nationalists claimed to fight, was outmaneuvered as a political actor in his own right through claims that he was a puppet unable to speak his mind since he lived in British-occupied Istanbul. To win both the war and the struggle for legitimacy, Mustafa Kemal relied on an alliance of Ottoman officers, the recently formed "national" Muslim bourgeoisie, and European-educated journalists and lawyers. Following the war and the Treaty of Lausanne (1923), this alliance abolished most of the central parts of the Ottoman state and sought to build a new, Turkish state in their own image. Central reference points for legitimizing Ottoman sovereignty, most notably the sultanate and the caliphate, were abolished, and the Republic of Turkey was declared (1923). All of the state—including the courts, legal system, and schools as well as the language and the state's relationship with religion—were reconfigured.

Mustafa Kemal died in 1938, but his style of rule was continued until 1950 by his close confidant, İsmet İnönü, and his reforms left path dependencies that are still part of Turkish politics today. Having received Bolshevik support against the British, the French, and the Greeks in 1920 and 1921, the Turkish Republic jealously guarded its sovereignty and neutrality until the end of the Second World War. During the war, Turkey sought to extract support from both belligerent sides while staying neutral (Deringil 1989). Near the end of the war, Turkey declared war on Germany—just in time to attend the 1945 San Francisco conference that set up the United Nations.

Around the same time, Stalin reiterated old Russian territorial claims on the Turkish Straits and on Turkey's eastern provinces, Kars and Ardahan (Coş and Bilgin 2010). Frightened by the prospect of having to face Soviet armies alone, the Turkish elite sought American protection, which it received through NATO membership in 1952, after holding multiparty elections in 1950 and contributing troops to the Korean War (1951–53). American protection and the accompanying Western recognition thus depended both on domestic reordering of state-society relations and on Turkish contribution to joint military efforts (which Western elites had seriously doubted in the wake of the country's unwillingness to heed treaty obligations to Britain during the war).

The reorganization of the state apparatus that accompanied the shift from the Ottoman Empire to the Turkish Republic marginalized large groups of people as audiences for the legitimation of state policy. Abolishing the sultanate, caliphate, religious courts, and education institutions meant that many religious conservatives found themselves cut out of the state's networks. Removed from state favor, they maintained their own networks and constituted a large section of the population. The Kemalist state limited state careers and opportunities to those who were educated like the founders, and institutionalized the domestic alliance that had led the War of Independence as the main audience for legitimizing decisions. With the introduction of multiparty elections (the other prerequisite for this dynamic, universal suffrage, was introduced for men in 1876 and women in 1934), governments now needed to seek the electoral favor of and legitimize their decisions to formerly marginalized voter groups. Yet the military set certain bounds for this legitimation, limiting the kinds of religious and ideological claims that were allowed. It was more than just a simple question of *secularists* versus *Islamists*, though analyses of Turkish politics often portray it this way. Rather, the question involved how politicians could appeal in populist terms to enough citizens to obtain political positions without being judged to be inappropriate by the military. The military thus became one of three key audiences for legitimizing political position, alongside the Turkish electorate and foreign allies. This particular configuration set the stage for the power struggle that emerged in the second half of the twentieth century. The military could easily legitimize its interventions in Turkish *democracy* to Turkey's allies as long as it could present the choices of the electorate as threatening collective *security* (see chapter 6), a characterization that applied to radical leftist, Islamist, and separatist appeals. As the Soviet threat to collective security disappeared at the end of the Cold War, the military had increasing difficulty legitimizing its role as arbiter of appropriate ways of appealing to voters and indeed its position as an appropriate audience for legitimizing decisions and political programs. Cognizant of the prestige and material benefits that would accrue from foreign recognition of Turkey's status as a fully democratic state through membership in the European Union, the military grudgingly relinquished its position as audience and arbiter of political claims. In addition, it was outmaneuvered by a government that legitimized its domestic reconfiguration of relations to foreign audiences and the electorate using concepts of *democracy*. Today, Turkey finds itself in the paradoxical situation of having democratized itself into an authoritarian state.

The Book

The historical sequence of events laid out above is largely known, and this book does not aim to add "missing parts" to that story. Nor does it take the transformation from the Ottoman Empire into the Turkish nation-state primarily to be a case of some general phenomenon about which we may derive law-like theories. Instead, I follow up on work by Patrick Jackson (2017), who calls for shifting the conversation in international studies away from nomothetic generalization— trying to arrive at "law-like causal claims" about cross-case covariation between dependent and independent variables—to causal explanations of how a specific outcome came about. In that vein, the book gives a causal account of the transformation from the multiethnic and multireligious Ottoman Empire into the nation-state Turkish Republic by showing how particular concepts were translated and used in reshaping and stabilizing social relations.

The book contributes to three different literatures: the history of Ottoman and Turkish political transformations; conceptual history; and international studies. The main and most obvious contribution is the same for all three—that is, showing that relations taking place across linguistic boundaries are differently configured than those taking place within a language. Since each of the three literatures emerges in response to a different problem situation, however, the implications are different.

The insight itself is something that all trained Ottomanists know from having grappled with translating Ottoman into modern Turkish, English, French, and other languages but that few have dealt with analytically: many of the things that can be said, written, and assumed about Ottoman history today simply *could not* be formulated as political programs or intentions at the time they are often assumed to have existed (see Mardin 2008).[12] The other implication of this insight is a shift in emphasis from that which was translated to translation as a creative and political process. The Ottoman Empire was not merely the passive recipient of ideas from Europe and a deficient imitator of European practices; rather, those doing the translating had agency. The process thus becomes more a question of pragmatics, with Ottomans and Turks *doing* things and seeking to achieve their goals by engaging in translation rather than simply receiving prefabricated ideas and practices.

In the field of conceptual history, the book answers calls by Jani Marjanen (2009) and Margrit Pernau (2012) for a conceptual history approach that does away with methodological nationalism. While the field acknowledges this weakness, it has yet to take interlingual joint action, translation, and international relations fully into account (but see Pernau et al. 2015). The book does exactly this, providing tools for conducting entangled conceptual history.

For international studies, this book implies that interpretative inquiry into interlingual relations requires a different type of sensibility than does inquiring into monolingual relations. I believe this sensibility is a fundamental point for any international studies research program with ambitions to theorize anything beyond the English-speaking world. As Frederic Schaffer (1998) has pointed out for comparative politics, it matters a great deal what concept one translates as *democracy* when comparing how "democratic" different countries are. In Schaffer's work, the emphasis is on comparison, and the interlingual aspect is primarily between the case (Senegal) or informant (Wolof-speaking) and the scholar (French-speaking, English-writing).

---

12. Holbrook's (1994) concerns are different, but her work nevertheless illustrates my point rather well.

In international studies, interlinguality is often intrinsic both to the object being studied and to the relationship between the object and the scholar, yet it has so far been forgotten (but see Stritzel 2014). For any approach that emphasizes the political importance of socially produced meaning, which includes nearly all "critical" approaches to international studies, interlinguality should be a key concern.

Chapter 2 develops an approach for analyzing international relations constituted in multiple language games and explores how these language games attain greater semantic compatibility as interaction densifies and takes place over extended periods of time. Readers exclusively interested in Ottoman and Turkish history may want to skip to chapter 3, which is the first of four chapters devoted to how the Ottoman Empire and later the Turkish Republic engaged in increasingly dense interlingual relations with European powers. These chapters amount to a history of the transformation of a semantic field that is used to give meaning to an Ottoman and later Turkish inside/outside nexus; and to ordering relationships between the polity's "inside" and the world around it.[13] Moreover, these chapters tell the story of how incompatible language games gain compatibility as the interaction in network ties that cross linguistic boundaries becomes denser and stronger. If concepts have a flavor from their previous use, there is still a set of concepts that smack as much of European high colonialism as they do of lofty European ideals.

The rhetorical commonplaces I treat here have been used both to formulate European or Western ideals (whatever those may be) and to legitimize Western domination over areas and people who allegedly do not adhere to those ideals. There is always some arbitrariness to such selection. Here I have chosen the concepts *empire, civilization, citizenship,* and *democracy* and treat each in a separate chapter before closing with a chapter on teleologies in foreign policy discourses. These are concepts on which debates about the Ottoman/Turkish polity's place in the world became centered during the nineteenth and twentieth centuries, and by the use of which the state was reified and programs for broad political change formulated. The four main concepts included here are chosen because they show how the Otto-

---

13. I retain the inside/outside and domestic/international distinctions as analytical tools to differentiate the audiences for whom the Ottoman and Turkish states legitimized their rule, not because I take them to be ontically prior to relations.

man language was transformed into a language that is more semantically compatible with English, French, and German. These concepts and their translation equivalents are not only important for the study of Turkish and Ottoman history but have gained currency in a plethora of postcolonial situations. Moreover, their translation equivalents in European languages are key concepts in political science, sociology, and International Relations. Chapter 7 examines how the teleological narrative that is ubiquitous in Orientalist and historical scholarship based on modernization theory has systematically been used to legitimize Turkish foreign policy decisions in relation to European and Western international organizations including NATO, the European Economic Community, and the European Union (EU). Contrary to the international studies literature on EU-Turkey relations, which largely accepts the narrative's premise that this is a process of *becoming*, I argue instead that this teleological narrative stabilizes the relationship between Turkey and the EU. To the extent that European identity hinges on essentialized aspects tied to geography and common historical experience, there is in fact no way of becoming European by insisting that one is Europeanizing—one would have to argue that *one has always been European* (Rumelili 2007). The final chapter then offers some concluding thoughts and implications for an interlingual approach to international studies.

TWO

Concepts

In this chapter I develop a theoretical framework for studying inter-lingual relations by way of concepts and translation, relating the tools to the Ottoman Turkish context. The "linguistic turn" in social sciences generally and international studies specifically has failed to take sufficiently into account the importance of translation for social interaction between different polities (I. B. Neumann 1999; Risse 2000; Hansen 2006; Jackson 2006; Krebs and Jackson 2007; Rumelili 2007; Wæver 1998). With the exception of translation studies, international studies shares this omission with a number of scholarly literatures. From the literature on how state elites "imitate" state-building projects elsewhere (e.g., Tilly 1992; Spruyt 1994; Badie 2000), via the literature on Ottoman and Turkish foreign policy (Hale 2000) and relations with Europe (I. B. Neumann 1999; Rumelili 2007), to Ottoman state transformation (Findley 1980; Ortaylı 1983), the importance of translation has been roundly ignored. Ottoman state elites' engagement with Europeans and European texts serve as an apt case for foregrounding processes of translation in international relations while showing how interlingual relations are a key component in the transformation of the state. While the case is used to develop a theoretical framework, I also use it to challenge the existing international studies literature on how Ottomans and Turks have "entered international society" and related to Europeans and "the West" by becoming socialized into European norms (Naff 1984; Rumelili 2007; Zarakol 2010).

Social scientists and historians who treat social interaction as constituted in language take three main approaches. The first treats language as a prism or frame that actors use to *understand* their own social reality (Shotter 1993, 22–23; Gadamer 2004). The main problem with this tack is that an actor's understanding is notoriously difficult to study: scholars cannot prove that an actor *actually* understands the world by use of a particular concept. The second approach treats language as a tool that actors use to intervene in and *shape social relations* (Skinner 1978; Shotter 1993, 116–18; Roshchin 2013). The third treats language as a device that social actors use to legitimize their positions, their choices, their actions, and their identities *in language* and contends that they need to do this in relation to audiences (Weber 1976; Garsten 2006; Jackson 2006, 16–17). We as humans use language for all three, and it is difficult to keep the functions analytically distinct. An actor may do all three at the same time or may translate a particular concept (say, *democracy*) and then use it to restructure particular relations (such as organizing multiparty elections and relinquishing government position when losing the elections) to gain legitimacy with a particular audience (such as the United States) and in turn reshape social relations with that polity (such as becoming a member of NATO). All of this may take place regardless of whether the actor in question (in chapter 6, İsmet İnönü) *understands his own social world* by using this concept as a frame, which we simply cannot know. While I emphasize the two latter aspects of language use in this book, I follow John Shotter (1993) in asserting that in terms of *understanding*, we should seek not what goes on in an actor's head but rather whether that actor can interact competently in a particular social setting by using a particular concept: that is, understanding lies in competent language use rather than in what goes on in the user's mind.

To develop these insights for the analysis of how political legitimation and shaping of social relations change in interlingual relations, I turn to Ludwig Wittgenstein, who along with Mikhail Bakhtin dealt with the dialogical aspect of language. These writers offer the basic insight that words gain their meaning in dialogue between individuals and that language cannot be separated from the relations in which it is used—meaning is imbricated in practice, and materialities have no essential meaning prior to language. The designation of a particular meaning as "essential" is *endogenous* to a language game (cf. Wittgenstein 1982, §385).[1] This is a key point when it comes to translation, as meaning does not come along when a word (or a material object) is taken from one linguistic situation and used in another. Furthermore, I use insights from Reinhart Koselleck (1982, 2002, 2004) regarding how to treat *concepts* as analytical tools in historical research. The "proof" of the analytical tools that I develop is in their utility for making a causal account of how a particular transformation took place in Ottoman and Turkish history, so rather than making this a purely theoretical exercise, I relate my theoretical tools to the Ottoman and Turkish context.

Concepts and Social Relations

A theoretical take on interlingual relations must be able to formulate how semantic variation between languages is socially and politically relevant. Many international studies scholars now recognize the importance of studying how decisions are legitimized and agreements reached in a particular language register (Risse 2000; Krebs and Jackson 2007). Although most major languages today have concepts that can translate English key concepts, such translation equivalents are likely to have different meanings in different languages or rhetorical traditions (see, e.g., Schaffer 1998).[2] As Frederic Schaffer shows, when social relations are configured differently, the concepts used to stabilize those configurations come to have different meanings, even though the words themselves have similar origins as loanwords. Yet neither international studies nor any other social science has theorized what happens when legitimacy claims are translated from one language to another nor when actors try to reach agreements across a linguistic boundary.

The validity of international studies theorizing is hampered by its lack of reflection on the central role of translation not only *in the conduct of international relations* but also in the discipline's conduct of inquiry. Anglophone meaning is neither universal nor able to capture the meaning of all human situations. (This phenomenon is not

---

1. In International Relations, Hansen's (2006, 23) argument that an armored vehicle has no *inherent* meaning as a weapon of war or a keeper of peace ties in with this exact point.

2. Some languages do not, however; see Everett 2008.

unique to English but is equally valid of any language.) Representing Turkish (or Chinese, Japanese, Russian, or Swahili) concepts in English involves a translation that is a semantic reconfiguration—meaning changes as the concept is translated from one rhetorical tradition to another. When scholars study politics taking place in another language and then write in English, their English concepts can seldom capture precisely the complexity of meaning that concepts had in the source language. Studying language across a linguistic boundary thus involves semantic reconfiguration. This is to some extent reflected in the international studies literature, with books such as *The Russian Idea of Europe* (I. B. Neumann 1996) and *Civilizing the Enemy* (Jackson 2006) amply showing how Russian or German meaning differs from the English language in which they write. Yet there is scant reflection on what happens when claims are translated between languages (but see Cohen 2001; Stritzel 2014). In a contribution closer to the topic of this book, Bahar Rumelili (2007) shows how Turks have intervened in "European" debates by challenging and changing the discursive representation of "Turkey" and "Europe," making it possible for Turkish politicians to argue that Turkey is or at least *could become* European. While Rumelili's book is an excellent contribution to the literature on relations between Turkey and the European Union (EU), it contains little reflection on which language these representations are made in or what happens when they are translated.

If social science (and more specifically international studies) is to find ways out of its current Eurocentrism (or rather Anglocentrism), it needs to recognize not only that different political traditions have different resources for giving meaning to social situations and conducting politics but also that *something* happens in the relations between individuals inhabiting different political traditions. This is both an important aspect of the social relations being studied, and of the analysis when Anglophone social scientists try to write about social and political interaction taking place in languages other than English (the reconfiguration of meaning that the writer does to present non-English material to an English reader).[3] Taking monolingual relations to be the norm is in effect to let the Anglophone countries

---

3. For Eurocentrism and Anglocentrism in the study of world politics, see Vucetic 2011; Hobson 2012.

represent the whole universe of cases—a typical case of Anglocentrism. Alternatively, one can study interlingual relations *as if* they take place in one language, thus flattening semantic variation between languages and traditions and dismissing the importance of translation for the conduct of international politics. In effect, doing so abandons to other fields the theorizing of most of the world's political relations, which are not conducted in English.

At stake here is how we understand the historical emergence and expansion of the international system and international society and the present-day consequences of how different polities have "entered" this ambiguous two-tier collective (I. B. Neumann 2011).[4] When social science deals with how polities outside Europe have been influenced by European or Western state making, there is a tendency to reify Western "models" as fungibles that can travel unchanged, displacing or marginalizing local tradition in whole or in part (Mitchell 1991; Badie 2000; Zarakol 2010). Most international relations take place in imperfectly entangled language games. The extent to which such language games are entangled is a question of degree. When language games become entangled, their concepts are established as conventionalized translation equivalents. These translation equivalents do not have *the same* meaning, but when they are lined up alongside one another, they exhibit what Wittgenstein calls *family resemblances* (2009, §§66–67). Emphasizing the translation of particular concepts, the identification of family resemblances across languages, and residual differences not only enables me to specify how the Ottoman Empire and Turkey "entered" European-emergent international society but also offers a new take on how other polities may have done so as well as tools for studying the consequences of historical entanglements for contemporary politics.

Attention to translation offers international studies a tool for specifying individual agency in the conduct of international relations. Since translation can only be carried out by individuals with competency in multiple languages, these individuals must reconcile "foreign" political meaning with "domestic" political meaning. This offers a way of moving away from grand narratives whereby the non-West is subject to impersonal Western *influence*—meaning simply moves,

---

4. For how former Ottoman subjects and neighboring polities "entered" international society, see Ejdus 2017.

and people have no role to play in reconfiguring it as it is formulated into a new political tradition (Gibb and Bowen 1950; B. Lewis 2002). Rather than "the Ottomans" blindly imitating "the West," without agency in how and why this was done, the "imitation" may in fact have represented something fundamentally new in the new context. As has been shown in other contexts, what Hedley Bull and Adam Watson (1984) termed the "expansion of international society," or non-European states' "entry into international society" may be better conceptualized as an entanglement of meaning, where individual statesmen, translators, and intellectuals have agency in reformulating the conceptual framework of what this might mean. Furthermore, these residual ambiguities and incompatibilities offer individual statesmen, diplomats, and state intellectuals ways of exercising individual agency in the conduct of their affairs.

While I criticize the "linguistic turn" in social theory for failing to take translation into account, this "turn" is by no means monolithic, and different variants offer different ways of studying the social world by privileging language. I have already outlined the three functions of language—frame, tool, legitimation—and different linguistic turn approaches generally tend to emphasize one of these functions. My grounds for privileging the latter two are pragmatic. It is not that I believe that they capture every important aspect of the use of language; rather, I can study the second and third functions, which are tied in with the public use of language, whereas the first in principle goes on in someone's head and thus cannot be observed. Rather than assuming that language is an indicator of *something else* (thoughts, motivations, or intentions), I look at how actors legitimize themselves, their positions, and their actions by using language in certain ways. The point here is to look at language in use vis-à-vis an audience and how the user tries to achieve particular outcomes (policy outcomes, for lack of a better word) by arguing for them. Likewise, what audiences *believe* is always a moot point—one that we cannot answer, because it is unavailable to the researcher. But we can look at whether the legitimizing arguments *are accepted* (Jackson and Krebs 2007). To put forward these arguments, actors use *concepts* or *rhetorical commonplaces* shared by speaker and audience.

In addition to the emphasis on the three functions of language, linguistic turn scholarship diverges on the importance it devotes to individual agency. This book is indebted to tradition of conceptual history typically identified with the work of Koselleck (2002, 2004, 2011), who takes concepts to be both indicators and factors in historical change. The gold standard in this tradition is the *Geschichtliche Grundbegriffe* (Brunner, Conze, and Koselleck 1972–97), an encyclopedic overview of long-term conceptual change in the German language, where each chapter typically starts with antiquity. Koselleck and his colleagues emphasize the collective level, more or less coextensive with the German language (though with Latin and Greek as predecessors). As such, the concepts are indicators and factors of *collective* change at the national level. This is in fact quite different from how I laid "the three functions of language" out at the beginning of the chapter, claiming that language is used by individuals as both prisms to understand social reality and tools with which they engage with that social reality. I do not disagree with Koselleck but merely place my emphasis elsewhere. Concepts are good indicators of historical change on the collective level. However, I do not believe that Koselleck and his collaborators offer an adequate take on *how* they become factors in social change. In other words, I find that Koselleck's approach tends to downplay individual agency. Because the timelines become so long, the individuals and their social contexts tend to disappear. As a consequence, the *Geschichtliche Grundbegriffe* privileges canonical texts—the likes of Machiavelli, Herder, and Kant. Moreover, this emphasis on the long term suffers from a lack of attention to the specific linguistic contexts in which these texts were written and the changing social relations in which they were used.

The other main strain of conceptual history is the approach of Quentin Skinner, who draws extensively on John Austin's (1962) theory of "speech acts." Where Austin emphasizes the kind of speech acts that were part of established usage—like making a promise, enforcing a contract, or marrying two people—Skinner (1978, 2002, 2009) has primarily studied the kind of speech acts that creates conceptual change. I believe these are two different types of speech acts. While I like Skinner's empiricist methodological position (as opposed to Koselleck's more metaphysical position), I believe he overemphasizes individual agency and downplays the importance of the rhetorical context and social relations of which utterances become part. Unlike Koselleck, Skinner tends to zoom in on a particular moment or a particular page when conceptual change happened, but he nevertheless privileges the speech acts of "great men." I believe there is much more going on in conceptual change than the speeches and texts of "great men," and I use Shotter's (1993) work to overcome the incompatibility of Skinner and Koselleck while shifting emphasis from semantics to pragmatics in a way that allows for the fact that not all individuals achieve what they intend when they try to do things with words.

While individuals have agency and intention, they are part of a context and a tradition, and they have very little control over the consequences of their utterances. Addressees or audiences misunderstand, deliberately or not. Utterances and texts become part of contexts that were unforeseen by the author or speaker. Moreover, rather than being conceived in the brain of the speaker/writer and then conveyed immaculately by way of words, meaning *is made* in the relationship between speaker/writer and audience (Shotter 1993, 79). Given the importance of this relationship, sufficient attention must be devoted to the linguistic context in which an individual speaks or writes. To study how concepts change, given that meaning is made in such relations, I emphasize how actors try to do things by use of concepts, how they legitimize their positions, draw social boundaries, and both formulate and carry out policies—in short, how actors use language to configure and stabilize social relations in particular ways. When they do this, they engage in and draw on a collective *rhetorical tradition.* Moreover, their usages leave path dependencies for what can later be argued and said within that tradition. While changing usages are part of a rhetorical tradition, it is just as important to study how the rhetorical context changes as concepts are used to reshape the social relations they are part of. Studying concepts is important not only because of their tool function in such situations but also because the reconfigured relations leave path dependencies for what can be said and argued. This does not happen with equal frequency and simultaneously in all parts of the language. Different parts of a language or a rhetorical tradition change at different speeds and at different times. While some concepts change, others remain fairly stable. To devote sufficient attention to analyzing how utterances and claims were made in a rhetorical context and how they were part of broader social relations, I have focused on periods of particularly intense conceptual change as well as periods in which concepts are used to reconfigure social relations.

In this book, the paradigmatic case of how this works is chapter 5, on *citizenship*, where I show how a particular use of categories as tools for excluding and including people in "the Turkish nation" at a critical juncture shaped and created this nation. Turkish concepts of citizenship or nationhood were shaped not so much by what a particular statesman or politician *said* in public and even less by what he *believed* (how can we know?) and more by the practical use of social categories as tools at that particular time. Once this had been done, the criteria became implicit, and there has been less necessity to spell them out when using concepts of nation or citizenship. I look at the use of concepts as tools for the reconfiguration of the social relationships in the transformation of the Ottoman Empire into the Turkish Republic, both in the makeup of the state itself and in the relations between "the state" and its international and domestic interlocutors. This is also why it makes sense to focus on shorter periods of particularly intense use of certain concepts in the reconfiguration of social relations, which then create path dependencies for the future meaning of concepts and configuration of relations. The relations and the concept are used to stabilize one another.

Translation

The academic field of translation studies emerged in the context of comparative literature and is rooted in a different kind of problem situation than political science and international studies: broadly speaking, the role of the translator and strategies of translation in the making of "world literature." When this field concerns itself with politics, it is the politics of translation (Gürçağlar 2008), which is different from my concern with the role of translation in the practice of political legitimation and governance. There are a handful of good studies of the history of Turkish translations of Western novels (see especially Albachten 2004; Gürçağlar 2008) and the history of Ottoman translation institutions (Taceddin Kayaoğlu 1998). This is certainly of relevance to Ottoman and Turkish conduct of politics, as translated novels became part of the Ottoman Turkish rhetorical tradition (Koç 2004). Holger Stritzel's *Security in Translation* (2014) is a rare attempt at applying translation studies insights to international studies questions. While Stritzel deals with how various American threat claims have been translated into German and explains their success or failure by reference to cultural and linguistic similarities and differences between Germany and the United States, the somewhat dichotomous manner in which he does this limits the usefulness of his insights for the purposes of this book.

Successful scholarly works treating translation often end up giving numerous examples seeking to illustrate that translation is in fact an extremely complex yet subtle process that covers up its own traces (Steiner 1998; Eco 2003). I take a different approach: I start out with a discussion of different theoretical insights that are useful when approaching translation, translation's importance for the conduct of politics, and how translation over time makes possible the transformation of certain social relations, institutions, and discourses. Textual statements, whether they are formulations of political or philosophical ideas, technological innovations, or diplomatic messages, are semantically reconfigured when translated from one language to another. Although their messages change, the process is more complex than meaning simply getting lost in translation. New semantic configurations also have the potential to add meaning that did not exist in the source text (Lotman 1990). For historical reasons, some languages are more similar than others. When they are similar, translation will usually entail less semantic reconfiguration of the message, but some words in one language simply do not have workable equivalents in other languages. Furthermore, since the meaning of a text depends on the context of reading and the background knowledge of the reader, no individual act of reading will produce exactly the same meaning (Gadamer 2004). While similarly socialized individuals are likely to read and interpret texts in similar manners, people brought up and educated in different social, political, and historical contexts are likely to interpret texts differently. The text remains the same, but the meaning produced in its reading changes over time and across social and political situations. Since no two language games are exactly the same, there are semantic differences between them. Depending on a number of factors, these differences can be great or small.

Translation is an act of reinterpretation by use of a different language game. The translator interprets a text in one language and then formulates a new text in another. Since the two language games are not the same, the meaning inevitably changes. The degree of this change depends not only on the difference in semantic capacity between the languages but also on the abilities and strategies of the translator (see, e.g., Venuti 1998). A translator, who is skilled in both source and target language, is in a privileged position. His or her reinterpretation involves using resources in both languages, yet the translator cannot control how a monolingual listener or reader will interpret the new message in the target language (Apter 2006). Moreover, linguistic skill is not a simple binary question where one either knows or does not know a particular language. Few translators have "perfect" mastery of both source and target language. When combining these two insights regarding a translator's partial grasp of the rhetorical situation in either language with the degree of difference between the two rhetorical situations, it becomes clear that the meaning to which a concept is put in the target language can be considered a different concept from the source language. It may be a *translation equivalent,* used in actual practice, but there is a degree of semantic difference (Nida 2000). It is impossible to compartmentalize human speech into distinct "languages" and insist on their mutual discreteness and internal coherence (Derrida 1985). Since meaning making is an individual skill that can only be used in a particular context, the abstraction that we call "a language" is a broad register that often mixes with other registers, and as not all speakers use every aspect in mutually comprehensible ways, it cannot be called internally coherent (Shotter 1993).

In addition to being a reinterpretation of a particular set of utterances, an act of translation shapes relationships between languages. It is a creative act of yoking together meaning between two different languages. There is nothing that a priori makes this or that concept inherently appropriate for translating a concept from a different language. However, as translation becomes more frequent between two languages, rules about how to translate a particular concept emerge and become part of the language game. This is what I call a process of "conceptual entanglement," which is the process that sets up conventionalized *translation equivalents* between languages. One way of looking at this at a higher degree of abstraction is by employing the metaphor of the fishing net as a heuristic device. I follow Clifford Geertz's (1973, 5) claim that culture is constituted by a "web of significance" and note that this is not altogether different from structuralist and poststructuralist approaches to language—signs take their meaning from their position in a web of meaning (Foucault 1970; Saussure 1983). Imagine this web of meaning as a fishing net: the knots are signs, and the threads are relationships between the signs. I call this "a language." Now, imagine that a bilingual person has access to two fishing nets. As long as they are separate, they may quite literally drift apart, as languages diverge when they become isolated from one another over time. However, once the person starts translating, she creates relationships between signs that "belong" to different languages, tying the knots of one net to the knots in another. Every time a translation is made, another fiber is added to the twine between the knots. Translations that happen frequently have thicker threads—more established patterns that are more difficult to rupture or change. When translation has been ongoing for a while, the two languages become entangled, and it is difficult to tell where one ends and the other begins. This does not mean that thick and durable threads connect each and every knot. Furthermore, there is nothing *inherent* in the knots of one net that makes them more apt to be tied to specific knots in the other apart from the relationships with other knots in the vicinity. The designation of a particular use as "essential" is thus *endogenous* to a language game (cf. Wittgenstein 1982, §385).

The fishing net metaphor will only get me halfway there, because it presupposes that one might know "a language." Unlike fishing nets, however, language is not made from scratch in a weaver's workshop. Instead, it comes pre-entangled, so that deciding what constitutes "a language" depends on defining certain twines as "within" that language and certain others to be linkages between one language and another. When multiple fishing nets are entangled—as human language generally is—deciding which is which becomes a matter of arbitrary choices made by someone who lacks the tools to cut the twine. As long as people keep using the signs in such a manner, the relationships between them will not respect where the linguist draws the boundary.

Speaking of language as metaphorical fishing nets easily risks reifying language—treating it as if it were an object. The fishing net can be a heuristic device for speaking about the somewhat nebulous term *semantic field,* which conceptual historians deploy when they speak about a set of concepts frequently being used together in particular ways (Koselleck 2011, 19–21). Concepts, language games, and semantic fields are all abstractions. They have no existence prior to use and are not resources that a user can access; rather, they are ideal-typical abstractions that the researcher employs to make sense of patterns of action. If language games are emergent rules of usage, then semantic fields are abstracted from those rules. Concepts are the elements that make up a semantic field, into which the researcher groups patterns of word use deemed to be similar.

Entangled Concepts

Because the meaning of a concept depends on the user's and listener's historical and cultural context, meaning is made in in what Shotter calls a "rhetorical tradition." Thus, the use of the French concept *citoyen* is not exactly the same as that of the German *Bürger,* but they are *entangled concepts,* taking their meaning from a great number of translations of political texts between French and German and from interpretations made by a large number of French-German bilingual authors (Brubaker 1990; for criticism, see Behnke 1997). Moreover, they have been established as equivalent concepts in translations of political treatises over a long period of time. Each translation of a French text into German that uses the concept *Bürger* to translate *citoyen* reinforces the conceptual compatibility between the two concepts. The adherence to the rules governing the language game of entanglement reinforces those rules. However, the existence of such rules does not make the concepts *mean the same,* because although the entanglement of concepts may create new meaning in the German tradition by reference to French tradition, it does not replace what is already there, it merely adds to the repertoire of possible concept usages or reinforces particular "French" usages in German (for culture as repertoire, see Swidler 2003). While French and German intellectuals writing on the topic may be aware that there is a difference between *citoyen* and *Bürger*, such linguistic skills are highly individualized.

While one should not make too much of mutual understanding and awareness across European languages at the individual level, there are certain family resemblances between these concepts that have to do with their history of entanglement. Even when texts have not actually been translated, many European intellectuals are and have been bilingual. This means that many of those who have written on the concept *Bürger* in German may have read French texts that use the concept *citoyen*. Such implicit interpretation is almost impossible to trace but is also difficult to rule out. Moreover, entanglement of this kind is unlikely to result in an out-and-out direct usage of the French interpretation in German, since the preconditions for the meaning made depends not only on the speaker but also on the dialogue between participants who speak, read, write, and listen. It is most likely that the German author *relates* to a French concept by adjusting her own interpretation accordingly, perhaps by contrasting her interpretation with the French. This is usually done without explicitly acknowledging the source. As anyone who has ever written anything of a certain length can attest, authors do not necessarily remember where interpretations came from even when they want to acknowledge sources. This process of relating to usage in other languages is part and parcel of the process of conceptual entanglement.[5]

In contrast to the relationship between the French and German concepts of *citoyen* and *Bürger*, the Ottoman concept *teba'a*, which is now usually translated into English as "subjects" (in the plural), was not entangled with the English concept *subject* prior to some time around 1856. It meant something else. The traditions within which the two concepts emerged were by and large politically separate. The meaning of the Ottoman concept was more entangled with its Arabic and Persian equivalents and was used in meaning making as equivalent to concepts in these languages. (It is in fact an Arabic loanword.)

---

5. This is also one reason why analyzing the interlingual aspects of the conduct of politics can only partially be informed by translation studies, where knowing a specific text as a "source text" and another as a "target text" is usually integral to the method (see, e.g., Bassnett 1990).

This made possible seamless translation between Arabic, Persian, and Ottoman. For Ottoman texts to be made available and given meaning in a European language and vice versa, additional paratext was needed. Texts could not easily be translated between these two clusters of entangled languages because the key concepts had different histories of use and thus different meanings. In addition to this conceptual incompatibility, the difference between European and Ottoman stylistic requirements (such as very few finite clauses and no punctuation) made it extremely difficult to make texts written in Ottoman legible in a European language and vice versa. In short, interaction across the Ottoman/French linguistic boundary involved a high degree of semantic reconfiguration of messages.

Jacques Derrida (2004, 427) identifies what he calls "a certain *economy* that relates the translatable to the untranslatable." First, a translation attempts to carry over "in the most appropriate way possible" the meaning of the original text. So there is a requirement that the translator should be "true" to the original text and to make the meaning of the translation as similar as possible. Second, "the translation must be *quantitatively* equivalent to the original" (428). A translation is supposed to have broadly the same rhythm, the same number of words and sentences, and the same punctuation as the original. Because the contexts differ, the translated text needs to add information about the social context with which the source text engages. The two requirements are therefore at odds. Adding paratext to maintain fidelity to the source will inevitably go against the quantitative requirement. Likewise, if one insists on maintaining the same rhythm in a target text, its meaning tends to diverge from the source text. Readers with knowledge of the source language (and for whom the translation should be redundant) will still interpret it in a way similar to that of the source, but those without such knowledge are likely to interpret in ways that diverge significantly from the source. A translation therefore tends to become part of a tradition as *a different text* from what it was in the tradition of its "original" production.

Russian linguist Roman Jakobson (2000, 114). has proposed distinguishing between *intra*lingual translation, which is "an interpretation of verbal signs by means of other signs in the same language" and *inter*lingual translation, which is "an interpretation of verbal signs by means of some other language." Put simply, interlingual translation is translation *between* languages, while intralingual translation is translation *within* a language. This is obviously problematic, since it works on the presupposition that languages are discrete entities with agreed-upon boundaries. They are not. Rather, they are ever-changing constellations of lexis that float into one another (Derrida 1985, 225). Therefore, the distinction between *intra* and *inter* is a question of degree, not a simple dichotomy. Translation—or indeed, any kind of relations taking place "within" a language—generally entails less semantic reconfiguration than those taking place across linguistic boundaries. Despite their nebulous boundaries, it may therefore sometimes be analytically useful to treat languages as if they were separate. With these caveats, the intra-/interlingual distinction may be a useful tool when studying Ottoman conceptual history and its entanglement with other languages and traditions.

Jakobson complemented his distinction with a third type, intersemiotic translation, which is "an interpretation of verbal signs by means of nonverbal sign systems" (2000, 114). Examples of this would be the instrument-based musical performance of a poem. I believe it is useful to broaden this to include translation between genres more generally and to include phenomena such as the film version of a novel. Such a "translation" involves a high degree of semantic reconfiguration, even when it takes place within the same tradition. The resulting film (say, Francis Ford Coppola's *Apocalypse Now*) may bear little relation to the original novel (Joseph Conrad's *Heart of Darkness*). While this does not precisely fit the bill, it may be a good departure point for talking about genre incompatibilities between European and Ottoman textual traditions.

The stylistic conventions of Ottoman prose texts (especially sultanic orders but also, albeit to a lesser extent, philosophical and political treatises) differed from European conventions to such a degree that interlingual translation for all practical purposes also involved translating from one genre to another—similar to translating from prose to poetry or vice versa.[6] The specific Ottoman conventions have their origins in court poetry that was composed according

---

6. Omission of passages, sentences, or details seems to have been an important strategy for dealing with the requirement of adding Ottoman poetic flourish to European political prose. For how early nineteenth-century Ottoman translators dealt with this when translating European works of history, see Strauss 1989.

to old Persian conventions and was an important way of maintaining administrative and normative continuity after the Turkic dynasties took over from the Abbasids as rulers of Iran in the tenth and eleventh centuries CE (Meisami 1987). The Ottomans upheld this tradition into the nineteenth century. By the end of the eighteenth century, divan poetry, as this genre is called, did not by any means enjoy a monopoly on text production. Rather, the genre itself receded to the margins, even as many of its stylistic and poetic conventions had become the norm for the production of other kinds of texts.

One stylistic aspect of the Ottoman poetic tradition was for an author to vary his use of vocabulary as much as possible. It was a common practice to say more or less the same thing twice in different ways. It was also a sign of great erudition to use as many synonyms as possible, and erudition was an important way to distinguish oneself socially. This emphasis on erudition made ubiquitous two practices that the literature on rhetoric calls *hendiadys* and *tautology* (Garner 2009, 899, 920–21). The rhetoric term *tautology*, which must not be confused with the homonymous term in logic, is to say the same thing twice for rhetorical effect. A common way to create tautologies in Ottoman would be to write a word in Arabic, followed by its equivalent in Persian.

Hendiadys is when two words fuse in such a way that they *together* make up a single concept. A prime example of this is the German *Nacht und Nebel* (night and fog), which was the name for the "disappearance" and internment of political activists in German-occupied territories during World War II. This is a reference to the spell of Tarnhelm in Wagner's *Der Ring des Nibelungen* but probably also alludes to the circumstances under which these prisoners were taken. It nevertheless has little to do with either "night" or "fog," nor should one necessarily assume that the Tarnhelm reference "comes with" the concept when it is used. The Ottoman concept of *din ü devlet*, which literally means "religion and state/dynasty," is an example of a hendiadys that at the end of the dynasty's rule was one of the most important concepts used in relation to the Ottoman state. This complicates the translation of Ottoman concepts into European languages, since there seldom are equivalents of such concepts, and word-by-word translations will end up creating a different meaning.

The important differences between Ottoman and European stylistic conventions meant that the degree of semantic reconfiguration in translating between French political prose and Ottoman poetry-infused political prose can be compared to intersemiotic translation. I am obviously talking not about the instrumental performance of a poem but rather about something closer to the *poetic* rendition of a political treatise that in French had been written in *prose*. This added difficulty of translation may in part explain the low frequency of texts being translated and the low degree of fidelity between European source texts and their Ottoman translations.[7] Moreover, the fidelity requirement is not necessarily shared across traditions. There is little evidence that Ottomans adhered to Derrida's normative requirements for a good translation; instead, other conventions may have been at play. As Victoria Holbrook (1994) has argued, the ideal for Ottoman poets was to recompose a known epic in such a way that it at once imitated and surpassed the great masters of Persian and Ottoman poetry. Imitation, which Orientalist scholars have considered a lack of originality and imagination, was a way to pay homage to tradition. This was, in fact, nearly a straightforward institutionalization of the maxim "imitation is the sincerest form of flattery." According to Maxime Rodinson (1988, 49–59), early nineteenth-century Orientalism emerged as a philological pursuit of *original works* that could fit into a canon of "world literature," which meant that this practice of recomposition has been systematically overlooked.

Varied practices of translation could have been a way to transcend the problem of different stylistic and genre requirements. However, the status of canonical works within the tradition did not invite extensive translation of European texts. First, untranslated European texts were by definition not canonical in the Ottoman tradition, so little prestige could be gained from imitating or emulating them until rising numbers of Francophone Ottomans increased the knowledge of and curiosity about French authors, while at the same time weakening the ideal of recomposition of great works. Second, since the faithful rendering of texts was not a normative ideal, when translation activity did increase, authors frequently included digressions and adapted the text to fit the Ottoman context. This made translations

---

7. For the "fidelity" discussion in translation studies, see, e.g., Bassnett 1990; Venuti [1994] 2008.

more clearly independent texts within Ottoman tradition. As the nineteenth century progressed and the number of translations increased, old stylistic and poetic requirements were displaced. In short, Ottoman text production increasingly became subject to European genre conventions (Koç 2004, 2). This also paved the way for more literal translations, which also became a norm in Ottoman and Turkish as part of this synchronization of genre conventions.

Language Games, Tradition, and Dialogical Thinking

My point about genre conventions, recompositions, and translations is not primarily of literary interest. Political legitimation is not conducted in isolation from other activities, as politics is embedded in a number of language games, including those of everyday life (Shotter 1993; Garsten 2006). These pursuits, which we may speak of as changing practices of legitimation and seeking out solutions to problems of governance, are two sides of the same coin. An important departure point for the literature on how social relations are constituted in language is Ludwig Wittgenstein's (1975, 2009) "language games." *Game* is here used as a metaphor for a set of norms and rules that outline what is socially acceptable to claim. These norms and rules are not objectively given but rather are intersubjectively accepted. Though the rules are arbitrary, all players must abide by them to be taken seriously. In short, "a language-game is something that consists in the recurrent procedures of the game in time," where the appropriateness of a statement is determined by the correspondence not between the statement and an empirical fact but between a statement and a response (Wittgenstein 1975, §519).

Language games are intrinsically tied to practice. As Wittgenstein (1975, §229) puts it, "Our talk gets its meaning from the rest of our proceedings." In these games, the meaning of each element depends on the meaning of others, and the relationships between them must be learned.

Children do not learn that books exist, that armchairs exist, etc. etc.,—they learn to fetch books, sit in armchairs, etc. etc. Later, questions about the existence of things do of course arise. "Is there such a thing as a unicorn?" and so on. But such a question is possible only because as a rule no corresponding question presents itself. For how does one know how to set about satisfying oneself of the existence of unicorns? How did one learn the method for determining whether something exists or not? . . .

The child knows what something is called if he can reply correctly to the question "what is that called?" (§476, §535)

Wittgenstein's language games are a way of circumventing Cartesian anxiety and countering arguments that claims to truth can (and therefore should) be determined according to correspondence theory (Jackson 2011, 128–32). The only way to evaluate such claims is the extent to which they conform to previous claims.

We do not learn the practice of making empirical judgments by learning rules: we are taught *judgments* and their connexion with other judgments. *A totality* of judgments is made plausible to us. (Wittgenstein 1975, §140)

Since such judgments are formulated in language and language is something that developed *in conversation*—that is, in language games—claims to truth are determined by their correspondence not with some external reality but with prior judgments made in language.

As Nazan Çiçek (2010) has argued, reforming and reorganizing the Ottoman state occurred as part of a set of attempts to legitimize the state elite's position vis-à-vis external audiences. The wider process of conceptual translation cannot therefore be kept separate from attempts to solve practical problems of governance. From *civilization* via *citizenship* to *democracy*, as concepts were translated, they were put to use in ways that *both* sought to solve governance problems *and* legitimize rule.

This is where Shotter's writing about *the prosthetic use of language* can be used. As Ottoman translators, authors, and statesmen alike were grappling with the problems of the Ottoman state, they tried out new concepts and found out what they could do with them. As when someone who has just had a new prosthetic limb fitted, a lot of fumbling was involved in learning to use new concepts properly. We all fumble, of course, and our language does not always achieve what we set out to achieve, but the late nineteenth and early twentieth centuries saw a lot of fumbling among Ottoman elites. The established language no longer worked to produce the intended effects.

These changes should be seen as changes in a tradition rather than the imposition, transfer, or importation of foreign elements. Just as one cannot take "a discourse" and move it from one language to another, so it is impossible to move "a concept." It simply will not mean the same in a new context. In fact, even a person who moves from one linguistic context to another is unlikely to *make the same meaning* within that new context. What one can say in a meaningful conversation depends not simply on the skills of an individual but also on the rhetorical situation in which that individual takes part. It is therefore unhelpful to think of language as a unitary structure that "comes from" the mind of a person or a structure pieced together by the scholar. Shotter (1993, 153) argues that language may be fruitfully thought of as a living tradition,

> rooted both in people's embodied knowledge and in their embodied evaluative attitudes . . . a historically extended argument, conducted both in speech and action, as to how both their knowledge and their attitudes might best be formulated.

Shotter conceptualizes tradition as a strange form of knowledge that can never be completely present in the head of any one of the individuals involved in it. It appears only in the "background" of social activities (1993, 3).

Such a view takes as its departure point that argumentation, legitimacy, and language use should not be looked at from the perspective of what ideas a particular actor "speaks out of"; instead, a more productive approach would be to look at the rhetorical situation that actor "speaks into." Since these rhetorical situations are not of a particular speaker's own making and the conversation that ensues is the result of more than one participant, one cannot reduce it to a reflection of this or that individual's mental schema. The conversation that unfolds is a process of *joint action*, with neither side's intentionality directing the conversation.

Joint action has two major features: It gives rise to *unintended consequences*, that is, outcomes which are not intended either by *you* or by *me*, but which are in fact *our* outcomes. However, as they cannot be traced back to the intentions of any particular individuals, it seems *as if* they have a "given," "natural," or "externally caused" nature, that is to say, they are *real* in the sense of being independent of the desires or opinions of any of the particular individuals involved. Also, as human activity, joint action still has *intentionality*, that is, at any one moment in time the outcomes people construct between them have a meaning or significance, such that only certain further activities will "fit" and be appropriate, while others will be sensed as unfitting and inappropriate and will be ignored or even sanctioned. In other words, as an outcome of the joint action between them, people find themselves "in" a seemingly "given" situation, an "organized" situation that has a "horizon" to it and is "open" to their actions. Indeed, its "organization" is such that the constraints (and enablements) it makes available influence, that is to say, "invite" or "inhibit," people's next possible actions. (Shotter 1993, 47)

This is a very important point of departure for how to deal with the argument implicit in Timothy Mitchell's *Colonising Egypt* (1991), where colonialism appears as the imposition of an existing European *episteme* that despite being acted upon by Europeans and locals alike was moved to Egypt as a self-contained fungible and that made itself legible by displacing the older *episteme* to the margins. Although neither the Ottoman center nor Turkey were colonies, many of the same changes took place there as in Egypt. The changes that were made resulted not from the imposition or import of an *episteme* but from dialogical joint action. Some colonial situations were more monologically constituted, but there is always some aspect of joint action as long as locals are involved in the implementation.

Since language is not a completed whole that is transmitted as abstract structures but instead a set of embodied skills that can be developed and honed differently by different people, all individuals have their own ways of expressing themselves. Even though it is fruitful to treat thinking as a dialogue and a tradition as a prolonged argument, it is important to emphasize the role of power in this equation.

> For although we all may draw upon resources (to an extent) held in common, every voice, every way of speaking, embodies a different evaluative stance, a different way of being or position in the world, with a differential access to such resources. (Shotter 1993, 15)

This means that "within" a language game, linguistic expression varies between individuals but that not all have the same ability to have their expressions accepted or repeated by others. The variation partly stems from their position in social networks in combination with their linguistic skills and ascribed attributes in the language game.

Shotter emphasizes how linguistic skill is embodied to such an extent that it is only when our language fails us that we tend to become aware of it.

> Mostly, we "see through" the language we use and are unaware of its prosthetic functioning. Only when the flow of activity between ourselves and our interlocutors breaks down, do we find ourselves confronted, so to speak, by our just utterances. To restart the flow, to clarify their meaning, they then seem to require interpretation—hence the apparent primacy of a hermeneutical account of language. But interpretation in that sense is *not* required as long as the flow is maintained. One's words are a transparent means through which one can achieve a sensible contact with those around one. Only if we switch our metaphors, only if we begin to talk of knowledge "by being in touch" do we begin to raise the kinds of questions that make contact with the issues here: to do with the rhetorical "shaping" and "moving" functions of language. (1993, 23)

This is an important point for translation. Translation is needed for maintaining the flow of activity between individuals who do not, on their own, comprehend one another. Independently of whether they "share a language," translation is primarily required when seamless interaction breaks down. It may be a patient not understanding his doctor's advice and thus not taking medicine in the prescribed manner, or it may be a diplomat trying to get the local ruler to act in a specific way. In the case of simultaneous interpretation, it is the constant reinterpretation of messages in one language game into another.

> It is in a speaker's particular use of a particular word at a particular point in time—as with the carpenter's particular use of a chisel stroke to slice off a wood sliver at a particular piece of joinery—that the speaker can sense what its use achieves in the construction desired. . . . [A] word's meaning does not inhere in the word itself, but originates *at the point of contact* between the word used and the "movements" it achieves in the conditions of its use. In this prosthetic/hermeneutical account of knowing, then, a process of "making" or construction is at work. (25)

When faced with an individual or group of people with whom we do not share a language, our prostheses are simply not adequate for the task for which we are trying to use them. This is not unique to interlingual relations in a strict sense but may also happen in a number of different instances. The foremost instance would be how concepts mean different things in different parts of a linguistic group. The second would be someone with an "imperfect" command of a language. One personal example is from the London International Model United Nations at LSE in 2003. At one point we were voting on whether we wanted to "table" a specific proposal. Those of us in favor of tabling it won the day. Yet to my dismay, it was put aside. My protestations that "Here in Britain, to *table* a proposal means to put it on the table for consideration" were not heard. In American English, it does of course mean to postpone or suspend consideration of a proposal, and this interpretation shaped the course of events. Whether this had to do with a disagreement over arenas and their attendant roles (were we in the UN or in Britain?), or imperfect English (whether the "fault" was mine or theirs, I was clearly in minority when using the phrase in this way), it serves as an apt example of how joint action can take surprising turns when interpretations diverge.

When joint action becomes surprising for one of the participants, it is an indication that his or her use of linguistic tools does not produce the expected results. Quite simply, meaning is made in a different way than the user expected, and the user needs to change his or her use of words to achieve the intended results.

Networks and Dialogues

If, as Shotter and Bakhtin claim, thinking is dialogical, then *whom* one is able to think with has consequences for what one can think, and whom one is able to converse with (in a broad sense) has consequences for how one may develop one's language game. Moreover, the dynamic of the joint action of the language game itself depends on who participates in it. This is not an easy question in contemporary society, because the complexity of the networks and multiple media involved makes it difficult to treat in a systematic manner. In a largely illiterate society without mass communication, whom one is able to think with depends simply on whom one knows and whom one encounters. This is the stuff of social network analysis, which treats individuals as nodes in a network. According to Mark Granovetter (1973, 1361),

> the strength of a tie is a (probably linear) combination of the amount of time, the emotional intensity, the intimacy (mutual confiding), and the reciprocal services which characterize the tie.

It is pretty clear that some mutually shared meaning is a precondition for creating and strengthening a tie. The strengthening may *itself* be the development of shared meaning through conversation, but shared meaning can also precede the strength of a tie. Dense network clusters are likely to function on the basis of some kind of shared meaning, but shared meaning itself does not guarantee that this will happen. I may of course *understand* a particular person without having a tie to them, but I cannot spend large amounts of time with someone or have an emotionally intense relationship characterized by intimacy, mutual confidences, and reciprocal services without sharing some kind of language for the development of the tie. While the development of the tie and mutual understanding may go hand in hand and proceed as parts of the same social interaction, mutual understanding may also precede ties. Strangers without common ties may immediately "click," in the sense that they are socialized in such a way that they are equipped to share mutual understanding before they have met. This makes for an immediate capacity for stronger ties, whereas individuals who share less meaning probably have less such capacity and need to engage in a lot of interaction in a mutual language game where they reconcile preconceptions for a strong tie to develop.

Possibly as a consequence of the low degree of mutually shared understanding, early Ottoman diplomacy was based on exploiting *already existing ties*. According to the model Granovetter lays out, exploiting *weak ties* is key to reaching a greater number of people through fewer degrees of separation. This conceptualization agrees with how the Ottomans used renegades and go-betweens with a relatively high social distance from the state center to interact with France, Britain, and Russia (Gürkan 2015). These go-betweens then exploited their own preexisting weak ties, reaching foreign sovereigns via a lesser number of linkages than the ruler could by using people strongly tied to himself.

Following successive military defeats and huge territorial losses against the Habsburgs at the turn of the eighteenth century and Russia in 1774, Ottoman statesmen of the late eighteenth and nineteenth centuries were perennially on the lookout for solutions to practical governmental problems. This was not only about legitimacy but also about the state's ability to mobilize resources and ward off competitors. Put another way, these statesmen were looking for governmental tools to stem what they considered to be polity decline. As the elite exhausted their immediate problem-solving capacities, they increasingly sought solutions further afield, mobilizing networks to a greater extent. They increasingly found homologies between European polities and their own situation and not only started using concepts developed in European historical experience to legitimize their position but put European-emergent technologies and concepts to work to solve concrete governmental problems and *get things done*.

The contact between Ottoman and European elites was not in itself new. Since the time of the foundation of the Ottoman polity in

Anatolia at the turn of the fourteenth century, state elites in the Ottoman Empire and various (somewhat anachronistically labeled) European polities were never isolated from one another. Continuous interaction took place across linguistic and cultural boundaries. Thinner networks between Ottoman elites and, say, French elites may have had as much to do with relative geographical distances as with cultural differences or reciprocal boundary making. Networks seldom tied the Ottoman state elite *directly* to its peers in polities beyond the Balkans and the Adriatic and Black Sea littorals. Yet there existed a wide network of weaker ties made up of merchants, renegades, and go-betweens (Greene 2010; Gürkan 2015). The Ottoman state elite had always exploited these ties, but what they sought and how they related to what they experienced in such interactions changed during the eighteenth and nineteenth centuries.

Social groups are upheld by strong ties between individuals within a network cluster, and tend toward conformity in socialization and experience. Bridges between network clusters are always weak ties (Granovetter 1973, 1364). As Yuri Lotman (1990) has argued, new expressions are created at the margins or periphery, from where they are picked up by the center and become dominant within a collective. "New thoughts"—if there ever were such a phenomenon— typically emerge in the dialogues that take place in conversations that constitute the bridge ties between clusters (what Apter [2006] calls "the translation zone"). Since bridges are often maintained by social marginals—centrally placed, popular people tend to integrate networks around themselves, making sure acquaintances also get to know one another—one cannot avoid thinking of Carlo Ginzburg's (1980) Menocchio, a socially marginal sixteenth-century miller with a wide network of weak ties and some pretty "original" ideas about how the universe is actually made up of cheese and worms. This book is not primarily a story of interaction between similarly socialized people; nor is it a story about social marginals such as Menocchio. Instead, it is about the relations depending on translation that involves significant semantic reconfiguration. It is about the creative tension that takes place in weak ties when differently socialized individuals engage in joint action and how the fruits of this creative tension are picked up by state elites seeking to solve problems and legitimate their position vis-à-vis outsiders.

Although the state may task particular types of people with such interactions, the ability to successfully interact across a specific linguistic boundary does not automatically come with the job. The point can hardly be stressed enough, as it goes against one of the basic assumptions of most theories of the relationship between agent and structure that are fundamental to International Relations theory, where assumptions about the state as a unitary actor tend to "swallow up the individual in a larger whole" (Parsons 1949, 52). Such an approach to states as social wholes mistakenly implies that the resources for getting the statesman's job done are simply derived from his structural position. There may be mechanisms in place to provide linguistic support, but in interlingual as well as other political situations, what can be achieved often depends upon the individual statesman, diplomat, or politician's skill set, creativity, and flair.

Likewise, the position in a network makes possible certain types of interaction, but while it may be conducive to thinking "out of the box," there is no deterministic link between being positioned at the margin between two network clusters and coming up with new ideas. One can perfectly well be positioned there without making anything interesting happen. The network only provides opportunities, but it is up to the individual what to make of them.

International Society

In the English School of International Relations, the analytical term *international society* refers to a number of states that "conceive themselves to be bound by a common set of rules in their relations with one another, and share in the working of common institutions" (Bull 1977, 13). Although my definition does not capture the whole meaning of the analytical term, I will for the purpose of this book say that international society is a number of states whose language games are so densely entangled that texts translated from one to another involve a low degree of semantic reconfiguration. Moreover, these states have each other as audiences for legitimizing decisions and accept the language game's logic of appropriateness as basis of a common normative order. This normative order is not internally coherent, but that does not mean that it does not exist.

The language games of the particular international society that the English School has theorized is played out in the cluster of languages that are largely conceptually compatible as a legacy of Latin, which was a unifying language of science, religion, and relations among the polities that were part of the Catholic Church. The literature on the globalization of international society posits the "expansion" of this society in two forms. The first (which has gained less attention) is states using European-emergent norms and practices (I call it language games) that militarily subdued many of the world's polities, which were then ruled as colonies before gaining independence from their suzerains (see Keene 2002). The second are polities that were not directly subject to European imperial rule, such as the Ottoman Empire and Japan. These were, as Iver Neumann (2011, 467) puts it, "expanded upon" by *international society* and increasingly had to legitimize their claims to rule in foreign vocabularies. At stake was their political survival. One of the key tools of international order at the time was the "standard of civilization" (Gong 1984; Koskenniemi 2010). According to European-formulated international law, any polity that did not attain this standard was a legitimate target for imperial subjugation. Successfully claiming to be "civilized" was a way of securing a ruler external legitimacy and recognition as a "sovereign state" and thus being treated as an equal within international society rather than as an apt target for colonial expansion.

When dealing with the translation of concepts that "emerged in Europe" or have a "distinctly European flavor," there is a danger of making Europe into a concrete entity, which it was not. Such an assumption is called reification, which is the fallacy of misplaced concreteness (Jackson 2006, 7). Concepts of *Europe* came to gain political currency following the Ottoman conquest of Constantinople in 1453 and siege of Vienna in 1529 (den Boer 1995; I. B. Neumann 1999, 44–45). These concepts were used to rally a common response to what was called the Turkish threat, especially across the sectarian divisions that emerged with the Reformations. One of the key origins as a political concept is in the claim that "we Europeans" ought to fight "the *Turk*" (i.e., the Ottomans/Muslims).

Despite mutual Othering, tacit alliances between Muslim Turks and Christians go back to pre-Ottoman Seljuk cooperation with Byzantine political actors and various Catholic Europeans, including the Normans. As the Ottomans lost their relative military competitiveness in the late eighteenth and early nineteenth centuries, they chose to ally with various European states in the absence of useful Muslim allies. The flip side of Europeans trying to divide and rule the Ottomans was that Ottoman statesmen tried to divide the European powers by playing them off against each other, thus ensuring the Ottoman state's survival. European states had a whole host of reasons for allying with the Ottoman Empire, the most common of which was rivalry among Christian states in Europe. The French allied with the Ottomans against the Habsburgs as early as 1536, though the geographical distances made it difficult to reap military benefits from such an alliance, primarily as a consequence of problems of coordination and logistics. The Swedes allied with the Ottomans against the Russians in the Great Northern War (1700–1721). As "the Eastern Question" emerged in the nineteenth century, European nations sought to benefit territorially from the Ottoman Empire's military and organizational weakness. British statesmen were particularly concerned that Russian southward expansion would threaten British sea-lanes to India. Moreover, the concept of "balance of power" implied that one European Great Power's territorial gains were interpreted as a threat to "stability" and "peace" in Europe (M. S. Anderson 1966).

The problem with alliances between Muslim and Christian states was originally that both parties had to deny such alliances with their respective "infidels" (Naff 1984). This taboo was overcome by a combination of the secularization of a raison d'état and the emergence of an irreligious civil sociability in Europe, with a long series of nineteenth-century Ottoman military defeats where the territorial control of the state was time and again reestablished by the intervention of European Great Powers. This was not a one-way street whereby the Europeans divided and ruled the Ottomans but rather a reciprocal phenomenon. The Eastern Question was a dialogical joint action in which Ottoman statesmen and intellectuals were among the players (Çiçek 2010). However, access to the negotiation tables where matters of international relations were discussed and often decided was largely regulated by the mastery of European aristocratic sociability in combination with the prestige of the state the statesman represented (I. B. Neumann 2012). The challenges that arose when the Ottomans could no longer mobilize sufficient military resources had to be overcome by mastery of European diplomatic practices as well as the production of cultural artifacts and symbols necessary to achieve representation in the international arena. To maintain prestige, the Ottoman state elite had to avoid being represented among the exotic objects of European rule in such contexts as the Universal Expositions and instead take part as a Great Power that puts objects on display, on par with the others. Doing so meant appropriating European scientific discourses such as racial hierarchies, redesignating various subject populations as barbarian and exotic, and putting them on display like any other colonial subject populations of the European overseas empires (Deringil 1998, 150–65).

In my conceptualization, what is in the English School literature frequently called "entry" into this international society happens when a state whose language is not part of this cluster succeeds in taking part in the language game. Attempts by such "entrants" to take part in the language games of international society are often only partially successful. Neumann (2011, 484) has suggested that

> since sticky memories may contribute to sustaining both an understanding of politics and specific policies that originally emerged within the context of a different system, an entrant into European international society may languish in the outer tier of international society for quite some time.

This is not altogether different from Bakhtin's claim that words have a taste of their prior use and my argument that much of the vocabulary used for legitimacy claims between states in contemporary international politics comes with a flavor of European dominance.

In a language game, "sticky memories" of a different way of legitimizing politics can also be said to constitute those parts of the entrant's domestic language game that are not compatible with the language games of international society. Although the set of language games that together make up international society are not a single game, among the languages that emerged entangled with Latin, few parts are sufficiently incompatible to make their mutual translation impossible or embarrassing. However, translations between recent entrants' languages and those of "core international society" frequently cause embarrassment, misunderstanding, or conflict, thus underlining the second-tier status of the entrant. If the domestic language game differs significantly from that of international society, leaders will have to engage in multivocal signaling to legitimize a particular decision or practice (Nexon 2009, 114–15; Padgett and Ansell 1993). Since meaning is made differently in domestic and international society language games, statesmen will have to legitimize decisions differently to the different audiences by using two different sets of conceptual histories. In short, they will have to say different things to different people, often in public.

Problems of public embarrassment often arise when there is a certain density of textual translations outside the state's control. If translations of the texts used for domestic legitimacy increase in number and start reaching players in the international society language game (or vice versa), statesmen and political leaders can no longer engage in multivocal signaling. The state then increasingly has to speak with "one voice" to its domestic audience and to international society, and statesmen have to anticipate that what they say will also be translated. At stake are credibility, legitimacy, and potential embarrassment. For core international society members whose domestic language game is also a language game of international society, there is seldom any potential for multivocal signaling in public because it is not facilitated by the need for semantic reconfiguration when moving between languages.[8] However, there is also less scope for embarrassment as the result of translation of domestic speeches into the language games of international society.

The degree of *entry* into international society can thus be conceived as the extent to which the domestic language game is semantically compatible with the language games of international society. However, it is fully possible for a polity to have a language that is semantically compatible with the hegemonic languages of international society without accepting the normative order, which involves those in power using rhetorical commonplaces in different ways from their hegemonic use internationally. In a sense, conceptual entanglement is a necessary but insufficient precondition for taking part in international society. Cases of this include Germany under National

---

8. Polyvalent signaling—that is, saying one thing that carries different meaning for different audiences—is still possible, as Nexon (2009, 115) illustrates using the example of George W. Bush's claim to be a "compassionate conservative."

Socialism and South Africa during the last decade of apartheid (though in the latter case, it may appear that it was international society that changed, not the Union of South Africa). These states' problems with international society stemmed not from semantic incompatibilities but from rejection of certain norms and of foreigners as an audience for legitimizing policy. Neither of these states engaged in widespread multivocal signaling by legitimizing their decisions differently to domestic and international audiences. Rather, they legitimized their decisions domestically while by and large ignoring the rules of the international society language game. The Nazis and South Africa under apartheid made few attempts to play by international society rules.

The Ottomans and the Turks, conversely, were and to some extent still are eager to engage in international society language games, and explicit rejections of international society norms have been fairly uncommon (though this is currently changing). Statesmen engage in both the domestic language game and in the language games of international society to legitimize their position as elites, their decisions on behalf of their subjects/citizens, and their state's sovereignty. Semantic incompatibilities between the language games meant that late Ottoman statesmen simply *had* to legitimize their decisions through multivocal signaling. To the extent that doing so was even possible, saying the same thing to domestic and foreign audiences could immediately undermine a decision's legitimacy among one of the audiences. The increasing numbers of French-proficient Ottomans in the nineteenth century led to an increasing density of translations outside state control. Engaging in multivocal signaling involved a greater risk of being caught out in public. Entry into international society can thus to some extent be thought of as the entanglement of conceptual vocabularies to such an extent that translation involves a low degree of semantic reconfiguration and the consequent loss of statesmen's ability to engage in public multivocal signaling.

Language Hierarchies

Relationships of conceptual entanglement are seldom equal, as entanglement usually happens in language hierarchies. These language hierarchies are connected with international hierarchies generally, but it would be too simplistic to treat them as directly deriving from power asymmetries between polities (as do translation studies scholars such as Venuti 2008, 14; Bielsa 2011, 205). Since language hierarchies are context-specific and historically emergent, they are different from hierarchies between states, as theorized in the IR literature (see Mattern and Zarakol 2016; Zarakol 2017). Language hierarchies can have two aspects, with the second following from the first. A hierarchy often emerges when the elite of a polity must legitimize their actions in a different language game from the one they use domestically. Having to legitimize one's own existence and conduct one's affairs in someone else's language game is in many ways close to Gramsci's (though not International Relations') conceptualization of hegemony (1971). In the nineteenth-century Ottoman Empire, for example, statesmen had to legitimize their policies and the empire's sovereignty by using French. Ottoman diplomats and statesmen had to *speak into* a French-speaking European diplomatic tradition (from which it was often translated into other languages, such as English for the British public), and this became a necessity for legitimizing the empire's continued survival. A hierarchy does not emerge from one such instance but comes about when such instances become a systematic feature of relations.

The second aspect of language hierarchies is that it becomes possible to use elements from one rhetorical tradition to speak into the other but not vice versa. As a hierarchy emerges between language games and the domestic language game loses its relative importance as a game in which to legitimize the state, it becomes incumbent upon statesmen to learn the foreign language game. Thus, individuals in the elite claim prestige partly by virtue of their mastery of the foreign language, and mastery of it becomes a mark of distinction. Over time, this has consequences for how one may legitimize one's actions in the domestic game. In Turkish it is now quite often legitimate to use elements from English-language tradition to *speak into* a Turkish rhetorical situation. Reverse the situation, however, and few native English-speakers will see the relevance of Turkish usage except in very specific contexts. One can seldom use elements from Turkish tradition to intervene in an English-language rhetorical situation. The practice of reinterpretation and the corpus of authoritative texts available to reference are unevenly stacked, putting the Turkish speaker at a disadvantage when engaging in such a situation.

These power relations are embedded in language hierarchies that are not straightforwardly derivable from individual states' current "hard power." While globalization is not the cause of interlingual relations as such, it is, along with European colonialism, an important factor in the emergence of the particular distribution of languages and language hierarchies that exist in the world today. Today's international language hierarchies are partly tied up with international organizations like the United Nations, which by and large emerged as the institutionalization of international power relations after the Second World War.

Japan is today economically superior to and has a military of similar size as France, yet French is a more prestigious (and useful) language than Japanese for a state seeking to legitimize its actions internationally as a consequence of institutionalization as well as of the fact that French was historically the language of important parts of the European aristocracy and of European diplomacy (I. B. Neumann 2012). However, language hierarchies are important because they provide the context for the further entanglement of languages. There are now very few situations where languages come to take on new meaning by entanglement with Japanese political concepts, while the status and practices of the European Court of Human Rights, the UN, and the Francophonie mean that French remains a reference language for dozens of states that primarily use other languages.[9]

The main European languages display a high degree of conceptual compatibility, at least with regard to political and religious vocabulary. For some languages, compatibility is a legacy of common Indo-European origins, but for languages that belong to other families, such as Finnish, Hungarian, and Basque, the causes for compatibility lie elsewhere. The role of a unified Latin-based ecclesiastical hierarchy in knowledge production and in legitimating monarchy gave European vernaculars a common set of reference points for conceptual interpretation, entangling concepts across much of Eu-

---

9. States such as Norway have a Norwegian translation of the European Convention on Human Rights, but when doubt arises regarding the interpretation of the text, Norwegian lawyers and diplomats must consult the French or English texts, which are considered authoritative and binding.

rope regardless of whether or not the vernacular in question was Indo-European. This dominance was first challenged by the use of vernacular languages for poetry, exemplified by Dante Alighieri's *Divine Comedy*, written sometime between 1308 and 1321, and Geoffrey Chaucer, writing his *Canterbury Tales* half a century later. A more serious challenge was the emergence of vernaculars as religious languages with the disintegration of Western Christendom under one ecclesiastical hierarchy in the sixteenth century.[10] Furthermore, Latin was challenged as a language for political treatises in Europe starting sometime around the publication of Niccolò Machiavelli's *The Prince* (1532).[11]

At that time, Europe was hardly the center of the world, and Latin was not a prestigious language outside Europe. Nor did French become as universal a diplomatic language as is sometimes assumed.

> To speak of the universality of the French language in eighteenth-century European diplomacy is a received idea. Yet, if it is true that French was used more often than any other language, the reality is more complex. Mediterranean diplomacy escaped the predominance of the French language. From Constantinople to Maghreb, Italian remained, until the first decades of the nineteenth century, the main language of oral communications. (Windler 2001, 85)

So, while (New) Latin only gave way to French as a diplomatic language in the eighteenth century, French was not universally used even then. Although Latin was challenged, it did not disappear entirely. Even in a Protestant country such as Sweden, the "Father of Modern Taxonomy," Carl von Linné, published his main scientific treatises, *Systema Naturae* and *Species Plantarum*, in Latin as late as 1735 and 1753, respectively. These Latin taxonomies are now used for sci-

---

10. While Martin Luther was important for the theological legitimacy and prestige of vernaculars, Nexon (2009) argues that the primary challenge to Habsburg power came from the religious *networks* that were established when spreading Luther's and Reformists' teachings. This was part of the historical constitution of territorial sovereignty, which again was a precondition for the territorialization of vernaculars as political languages: see B. Anderson 2006.

11. *The Prince* first circulated in Latin manuscript under the title *De Principatibus* (*About Principalities*) in 1513 and was published in Italian as *Il Principe* in 1532.

entific categorization across the world. Among Muslim polities, Arabic has played a similar role, though in the absence of a unified religious hierarchy (and the widespread use of Persian as a literary language outside those areas where Arabic was used as a mother tongue), its position was less monolithic than that of Latin. But Arabic persists after the importance of Latin has diminished.

For matters of state, the Ottoman language was important in the Mediterranean, largely because of the formal reach of the sultan's writ. The Ottoman Empire stretched along the entire North African coast, from Egypt almost to the Gibraltar Strait, as well as the entire Levant, the Aegean, and parts of the Adriatic coastline. Although Ottoman military and administrative control of Tunisia and Algeria was tenuous at best, the local rulers recognized the Ottoman sultan as their suzerain. Ottoman suzerainty was largely unchallenged in North Africa until France invaded Egypt (1798), Algeria (1830), and Tunisia (1881) and Italy invaded Libya (1911). Prior to this European military encroachment, Ottoman was used for interpolity correspondence between political entities subordinate to the Ottoman sultan and even among these local rulers and European states.

> In the eighteenth century, the documents of [Tunisian] beys to European powers were almost always written in Turkish [i.e., Ottoman]. The predominance of the Turkish language in documents that the bey authorized was a manifestation of the formal recognition of the suzerainty of the Ottoman sultan. The Porte only considered itself bound by the Turkish version of the capitulations. The parallel writing of treaties with the regencies in the respective languages of the parties, in which each only signed the version written in his own language, indicated that each of the interlocutors bound himself only by his own legal order. Certainly, the European powers had versions written in their own language, *but in the case of divergence it is the Turkish text that was followed.* At the end of the eighteenth century, French, English, and Spanish diplomacy was still resigned to this situation. (Windler 2001, 86–87; emphasis added)

If one is to take literally the claim that "in the case of divergence it is the Turkish text that was followed," French, English, and Spanish diplomacy did, in certain situations and for certain texts, engage in a practice of textual interpretation that treated the Ottoman language as an authoritative point of reference for a specific set of diplomatic relations. This made for a certain degree of conceptual entanglement across the Ottoman/European linguistic divide within power relationships that were completely different from the late nineteenth century.

Conclusion

Ideas and texts were not simply "circulating" and then became "influential" among Ottoman intellectuals and statesmen. Nor is it particularly fruitful to speak of the conceptual changes in the Ottoman language as a product of a diffusion of norms or a transfer of ideas or technologies. Ottoman statesmen were grappling with concrete problems involving both legitimacy and governance. These problems can be grouped together and called "modernity," "a crisis," or "decline," terms that have been used both by historians and by historical actors. The problems were not simply given, and their status as problems to be identified and solved was in itself a political phenomenon. Ottoman statesmen identified any number of problems whose homology can be found in European texts. As they exhausted possible solutions offered in Ottoman, Persian, and Arabic texts, they sought out remedies in other places. What they came up with depended on their social networks and their ability to productively interpret what they found in their readings and social encounters. The extent and uniqueness of an individual's network depends on linguistic and social skills, meaning that access to possible solutions to the problems a statesperson faces are shaped by his or her individual *social* and creative abilities. Such solutions are sought through conversations. There is no objectively given "idea" or "piece of information" that moves unchanged through a network. Individuals use what they have talked about with one person when they engage the next person, but this next encounter is a new dialogue, and the meaning may change within it. Within a cluster of similarly socialized individuals, the change may be slight, but when two differently socialized individuals engage in conversation, the potential for unexpected joint action is much greater. To speak of a concept, representation, or discourse "moving through a network" is problematic, since there is no "it" that can move (Pernau 2012). Nor can "it" change. As individuals engage in multiple traditions, practices of meaning making change; these new ways of meaning making are then used when engaging in another tradition.

In the nineteenth century, European languages were imposed as hegemonic traditions of meaning making between Ottomans and Europeans. The external aspect of sovereignty, then, hinged on claims formulated not in the language of the Ottoman polity itself but rather in the languages that were established as acceptable in the interpolity relationship. At stake was the legitimacy of Ottoman rule, which in the absence of an overwhelming military force could be bolstered only by employing concepts of rule that Europeans recognized and by engaging in practices conforming to those of "international society."

THREE

Civilization

Few concepts were as central to structuring international relations in the nineteenth and early twentieth centuries as that of *civilization*, and few were as important for Turkish and Ottoman statesmen reconfiguring "domestic" social relations as its translation equivalent, *medeniyet*. In this chapter, I deal with how concepts of *civilization* were translated into Ottoman through entanglement with existing Ottoman concepts that involved reinterpretation and new usages. Moreover, I deal with how these were used to legitimize the Ottoman state's position in the world and its rule over territories and populations, and to restructure the state center's relationship with these territories and populations. The chapter stretches from the first half of the nineteenth century and to just after the conclusion of the Second World War, when *democracy* and *human rights* gradually took their place in the language games of international society (see chapter 6).

I start out with a brief history of English and French concepts of *civilization* and how these were used in international law. I then discuss the Ottoman state's legitimacy claims in international language games and how nineteenth-century international politics were intertwined with the reforms of the Ottoman Empire and the Eastern Question. I trace a series of entanglements that illustrate my point about how concepts of *civilization* gained more generic qualities through a longer history of use and semantic struggles. In addition, I explore how concepts of civility and civilization were used as tools to reconfigure relations between state and subjects, including how the Ottomans translated particular European concepts through the reinterpretation of the concepts *ıslah* (reform) and *terakki* (progress). Finally, I show how the polyvalence in the use of *civilization* draws on its opposition to *barbarism* also when it is used in the meaning of multiple civilizations.

International Order

By the second quarter of the nineteenth century, the Ottoman state elite came to rely on the intervention of European powers to keep provincial elites in check as well as to prevent other European powers from conquering its territories and abolishing the Ottoman state itself. Ottoman statesmen furthermore had to argue *why* European powers should do so by using and speaking into various European (mostly French) rhetorical traditions. Ottoman sovereignty came to rely on legitimizing its existence and its actions to more or less ad hoc European allies to ward off Russian intervention. While much of this meant turning to British support against Russia, in 1833, Ottoman statesmen also had to persuade the Russians to provide military help against the rebellious Ottoman governor of Egypt, Mehmed Ali Paşa.

While creating a situation in which Ottomans had to legitimate their decisions in languages other than Ottoman, these interventions also placed Ottoman allies in a superior position vis-à-vis Ottoman statesmen and gave them the opportunity to engage Ottomans in conversations regarding how best to conduct their affairs and organize their state (a corollary of the Ottoman search for homologies in European states). The relationship privileged European language games, as Ottoman statesmen increasingly had to legitimize their practices in French and (to the extent that it was used) English. This process set up a hierarchy between what were largely incompatible language games. In this hierarchical language game, *civilization* and what became its Ottoman and later Turkish translation equivalent, *medeniyet*, were used not only to reconfigure relations between European states and the Ottoman Empire in an asymmetric manner but also to reconfigure relations between the Ottoman state and its subjects.

Civilization is among the more complex concepts of the English language and has been used to mean not only a social process of refining individual as well as collective mores and practices and thus *progressing* but also the historical goal of this process (Elias 2000; Bowden 2009). As a term for human collectives, it is sometimes used in the plural, often with normative connotations. This can be either for past collectives, such as "Mayan civilization," or for dividing the contemporary world into *civilizations,* most famously done by Samuel Huntington in *The Clash of Civilizations and the Remaking of World Order* (1996). When *civilization* is used in the plural in English, there is often an implicit (or even explicit) relegation of non-Western civilizations to an inferior status, either as essentially different (in racial terms and thus incapable of surmounting the threshold between "their" inferior civilization and "our" superior civilization) or as less progressed (i.e., as past incarnations of "our own" civilization, which ought to "catch up") (Fabian 1983; Rumelili 2007). Moreover, the concept is an important rhetorical commonplace for today's international law, and Article 38(1)c of the 1945 Statute of the International Court of Justice, which is generally recognized as an authoritative statement of the sources of international law, requires that the principles applied by the court are those that have been "the general principles of the law recognized by civilized nations." This is an acknowledgment that the origins of today's international law lie in the language games governing relations among "civilized nations"—that is, among the states of Christian Europe and its settler-colonial offspring.

The word *civilization* itself was coined in French and in English in the middle of the eighteenth century. According to a 1771 French dictionary definition,

> The *ami des hommes* [Mirabeau] *used this word for sociabilité.* See that word. Religion is undeniably the first and foremost brake on humanity; it is the first source of civilization. It preaches to us and constantly recalls us to confraternity, to soften our hearts. (translated by Bowden 2009, 27)

Civilization was used in the meaning of restraining passions and repressing one's beastly nature for the sake of the confraternity to which "religion"—that is, Christianity—calls "us." The word was either coined independently or picked up from French by the Scottish Enlightenment historian Adam Ferguson (1723–1816), who published his *Essay on the History of Civil Society* in 1767 (Bowden 2009, 31). The fact that it came into use in English and in French only a few years apart during the late 1750s indicates the word's closely entangled history between English and French. Not only does it have a similar origin, the history of its use has been very much entangled between British and French imperial practices, making for the kind of conceptual compatibility discussed in chapter 2. Although the two languages are different, the concept of *civilization* is so entangled between them that for the purposes of this book, I treat this concept as if there is no significant semantic reconfiguration involved in crossing that particular linguistic boundary.

Extraterritoriality

A very important context for the entanglement of Ottoman concepts with French and English concepts of *civilization* was the stigma of the "uncivilized" or "barbarian" Ottomans (I. B. Neumann 1999). Initially, the Ottomans had been represented as Europe's Other in terms of religion. By the early nineteenth century emphasis shifted toward the Ottomans being *uncivilized* or *barbarian*, although Europeans frequently equated *civilization* with Christianity and *barbarity* with its absence. As a 1795 treatise on international law put it,

> If we look to the *Mahometan* and *Turkish* nations . . . their ignorance and barbarity repels all examination, and if they have received any improvement since the days they first set foot in Europe, it is probably from their connection with people professing the very religion they most hate and despise. (quoted in Bowden 2009, 121)

Writing seven decades later, the American lawyer and diplomat Henry Wheaton claimed that

> Turks are not a civilizing people. . . . [They] are a nation of soldiers, who care little for the peaceful pursuits of trade, literature, and science; while many of their [Christian] subjects are capable of attaining to the highest forms of civilization. . . .

The governing race in Turkey has remained nearly stationary, while many of its subjects, and all the neighbouring States, have been rapidly progressing. (Bowden 2009, 121–22; Wheaton 1916 [1863], 107)

If the Ottomans were *barbarians*, it followed that it would be folly to allow the citizens of "civilized" states to be subject to barbarian laws. To "protect" their subjects, the European Great Powers imposed a system of extraterritorial courts in the Ottoman Empire. This amounted to a bifurcation of the legal system in Ottoman lands, which was legitimized by claiming an incompatibility between the Ottomans' Eastern barbarity and the civility of European subjects. This way of using the concept of *civilization* and applying its practice to the jurisdiction of the Ottoman Empire was an important way of stigmatizing the empire as a second-tier polity.

Turan Kayaoğlu (2010, 11) has argued that differences between legal systems come with asymmetries in power relations. These asymmetries are accentuated when cultural and geographic distances increase. The Ottoman legal system was in itself fragmented, and the ruler shared legal authority with societal groups and local communities. The application of Ottoman law in commercial transactions between British and Ottoman subjects initially gave the latter an advantage, but with the introduction of British extraterritoriality, this advantage was reversed. As Kayaoğlu argues,

A state's law-making and law-enforcing authority has an international dimension. Domestic legal arrangements affect transnational interactions and foreign nationals in a state. The coordination of states' legal claims facilitates transnational interactions and safeguards a state's citizens in another state. For example, transnational commercial transactions would be difficult if business groups did not know about legal and property rights in other countries. The business groups' willingness to interact will be without credible information about the enforcement of these rights. The need for legal coordination and the security of foreigners makes state rulers accountable to each other regarding their domestic arrangements. (11)

In other words, the semantic compatibility of legal vocabularies brings down the degree of semantic reconfiguration required in moving between languages, thus inviting more commercial activity.

Prior to 1825, the British Levant Company and consular courts had adjudicated disputes among the company's employees and other British citizens residing in Ottoman territories. After the Levant Company was abolished in 1825 and its legal authority transferred to the Crown, the situation remained ambiguous until the British Parliament passed an 1843 act formalizing its extraterritorial jurisdiction over British subjects in the Ottoman lands.

> The act established the legal basis of extraterritoriality by extending British legal authority into the Ottoman Empire. The Act stated that "by treaty, capitulation, grant, usage, sufferance, and other lawful means, Her Majesty the Queen has jurisdiction within diverse foreign countries." This jurisdiction authorized the British government to exercise legal authority in the Ottoman Empire "in the same and in as amply a manner as if Her Majesty had acquired that jurisdiction by the *cessation or conquest of territory*." While the Ottoman Empire had not been conquered or colonized, the British government could extend its laws into the Empire as if it had been. (Turan Kayaoğlu 2010, 44)

British subjects could expect their transactions with Ottoman subjects in the Ottoman Empire to be governed by British law and the Privy Council in London to be the final appeal court for their cases. Even though they might not leave their hometowns, Ottomans who traded with British subjects had to learn British common law or face the consequences of ignoring it (Turan Kayaoğlu 2010, 12).

Rather than decreasing the social complexity of interactions across the English/Ottoman linguistic boundary, this turned the power asymmetry between British and Ottoman merchants on its head (Turan Kayaoğlu 2010, 4, 11). Where long-distance travelers had previously borne the risks that came with a high degree of semantic reconfiguration in translation, this risk was now deferred onto the locals in the name of *civilization*. Along with a regime of unequal commercial treaties, this bifurcation created a class of "Levantines"—

people who were part of the local merchant elite but not under the jurisdiction of Ottoman law by virtue of their being subjects of European states.

Translation of a vocabulary of European legal positivism and the codification of a country's laws by the use of these translations became a prerequisite for the recognition of non-European states as fully sovereign. Until that vocabulary was made the basis for a unified Ottoman legal system and used to formulate codified laws, extraterritorial courts were "needed" to protect European citizens and their commercial interests. One may of course understand that European merchants sought to secure their property, but the way they did so was to shift the risk of litigation in an unfamiliar judicial system onto the Ottomans. Anchoring this development was the argument that one could not expect *civilized* men to be subject to *uncivilized* laws, liable to *implicit* interpretation. The claim was that *reason* was public, whereas *passions* were private. A legal system that did not have codified laws was subject to the passions of an *Eastern* judge and the state in which it operated could thus hardly be said to reach the standard of civilization. A "predictable" court system that relied on a published law code and legal positivism was an important trait of civilization and a prerequisite for acknowledging a state's sovereignty. Leaving aside the actual practice of the British legal systems, I merely note that both Kayaoğlu and his sources overstate their coherence and degree of predictability (Hussain 2003 offers a critical take). This did not stop the British from using it as a point of contrast with the Ottoman system and to use concepts of *civilization* to juxtapose the two systems.

Eastern Questions

During the nineteenth century, Ottoman domestic politics and European Great Power politics became intertwined in a set of relationships that have been called "the Eastern Question." This involved a discursive struggle over the meaning of *civilization* and the question of the Ottoman polity's civilizational status, particularly in relation to its legal practices. Most Ottoman decisions involved some kind of international aspect, as Ottoman "domestic policy" was of great concern to the European Great Powers, who simultaneously looked after the well-being of various groups of Ottoman subjects while using their privileges to increase their position in the region. The European actors, and particularly Britain, were concerned about the "balance of power" and the fear that one power would become powerful enough to dominate European politics alone through expansion into Ottoman territories. Gains made by one European power (mostly Russia) therefore had to be checked or offset by gains by the other Great Powers.

This European interest and stake in Ottoman domestic affairs meant that Ottoman statesmen increasingly needed to legitimize decisions to Europeans, where they had not previously done so. European opinions, demands and ultimatums were formulated in European languages, and this intense and prolonged interaction also entangled Ottoman and European languages. Moreover, it wasn't a simple question whereby Europeans formulated demands in their own languages, and the Ottomans then translated and implemented those demands in their process of "reform." The relationship was complex and dialogical:

> The Porte used the introduction of a European political measure or establishment of a Western institution as a forestalling precaution to ensure the quiescence and future support of the Great Powers, to distract their attention from a potential cause for friendly counselling or to gain their backing in contracting a loan in the international money market. Moreover, despite the clearly disadvantageous bargaining position of the Ottoman Empire against the Great Powers, none of the reforms championed by European cabinets was brought into being without some tough bargaining on the part of the Ottoman government. The Porte, then, acquired a less passive role in its dealings with European demands, and in its implementing of reforms than the adherents of the "external imposition and external pressure" theory had originally assumed. Although in the end it was almost invariably their will that preceded that of the Porte, owing to the dialogical nature of their relationship the Great Powers constructed their demands through their knowledge of the Porte's previous as well as the anticipated reactions. (Çiçek 2010, 19)

To understand how the English concepts of "Ottoman" and "reform" were yoked together in the context of the Eastern Question—and therefore also to understand whom the Ottomans were engaging in diplomatic dialogues on this issue—the writings of Stratford Canning (Viscount de Radcliffe), the British ambassador to Istanbul for most of the time between 1825 and 1858, are instructive.[1]

Canning was centrally placed during a period in which the Ottoman state elite had to rely on assistance from one foreign power to ward off threats from another. The Ottoman sultan had to ask for Britain's help to prevent large territorial losses after the Russo-Turkish War of 1828–29 and then from Russia to stop the Ottoman Egyptian governor Mehmed Ali Paşa (Muhammed Ali) from marching on Istanbul in 1833. In this context, a particular type of diplomatic interaction between the British and the Ottoman states emerged, and *Ottoman reform* came to be used as a tool to legitimize British support for the Ottomans to British and European audiences. Mehmed Ali was in the process of reforming his province and its army and this made him able to challenge the sultan (Fahmy 1997). Canning's importance tends to be overstated (Deringil 2012, 66–84, 244) for the simple reason that his main biographer simply took his (somewhat self-important) letters and texts at their face value. Rather than simply interpretations of events and processes in the Ottoman Empire, the contents of these texts constituted Canning's attempts to legitimize his actions in Istanbul vis-à-vis a "home" audience in Britain. As such, they are a great source for understanding how one particularly well-placed British diplomat used his language in an Ottoman context, on the one hand writing "back" from abroad seeking to legitimize his own position and actions, and on the other as tools to ward off Russian threats that could materialize if the Ottoman state were to lose to the Russians.

It is nevertheless extremely difficult to reconstruct the joint-action situation in which Canning partook in Istanbul, which involved multiple actors and was by no means the monological relationship his biographer made it out to be. Yet with these caveats in mind, it may nevertheless be useful to take a look at how Canning presented his work in an 1832 letter to Lord Palmerston from Istanbul:

---

1. Canning was posted to Istanbul in 1808, became minister plenipotentiary there in 1810–12, and later served as ambassador in 1825–28, 1831–32, and 1842–58.

The main and perhaps insuperable obstacle to the establishment of a large national army in this country consists in the
necessity of adopting at the same time a totally new system of
administration. . . . It may be true that nothing is impossible
to genius; and the natural resources of the Turkish Empire
are infinitely greater than those of Russia when Peter the
Great undertook to transform his barbarous hordes into a
civilized and powerful nation. [In the Ottoman Empire] the
despotism of the Koran is evidently yielding to the influences
of Christianity, the religion of civilization. . . . The Turkish
Empire is evidently hastening to its dissolution, and an approach to the civilization of Christendom affords the only
chance of keeping it together for any length of time. (Lane-
Poole 1888, 77–78)

Canning thus connects a "new system of administration" as the basis
for a "national army," the equation of Christianity with *civilization* and
Islam (or, rather, the Quran) with *barbarous hordes*, and the possibility
for *civilizing* the Ottomans through the influence of Christianity.

There are a number of semantic incompatibilities between the
English representations here and what was possible to argue in Ottoman language in court and intellectual circles in Istanbul at that
time. Canning presupposes the existence of an Ottoman *nation* from
which to "draw an army" and takes it to be a mere matter of *administration* to raise and support a *national army*. Speaking and writing
about the Ottoman "nation" was fairly established in English and
French, and Ottomans could do so in French, but there was no Ottoman translation equivalent for French and English concepts of *nation*
that captured this meaning.[2] Moreover, the English and French concepts of *nation* at the turn of the nineteenth century were very different from the meaning they have today. Not until seventy-five years
later did Ottoman statesmen *themselves* start arguing that a nation was
a necessary foundation for an effective army—after a translation
equivalent had become a established as a conventionalized part of
elite repertoire (see Hanioğlu 2011, 37). Canning's prescription of

---

2. Ottoman Armenian translator cum Swedish diplomat Ignatius Mouradgea d'Ohsson
(1787) used it extensively in his great work on the Ottoman state, *Tableau général de l'Empire
othoman*.

what has to be done to the Ottoman Empire was therefore a decidedly ex-ogenous discourse on Ottoman politics.

Second, the comparison with Peter the Great implies that the Ottomans were also rulers of "barbarous hordes" who ought to be brought into civilization. Third, these "barbarous Ottoman hordes" were linked to the "despotism of the Koran," as distinct from Christianity, "the religion of civilization." When Canning was sent back to Istanbul in 1842, his instructions were to "impart stability to the Sultan's government by promoting judicious and well-considered *reforms*" (Lane-Poole 1888, 79; emphasis added). What is frequently touted as the main edict of the Tanzimat period, the Tanzimat Charter of 1839, appeared during Canning's absence. In Canning's other writings he took *reform* to be an important prophylactic in preventing *revolution*, a major concern for British statesmen in the early nineteenth century (Lane-Poole 1888, 44–45). It is, therefore, not surprising that *reform* and its translation equivalents, *tanzimat* and *ıslahat*, were preferred when giving meaning to Ottoman social and political transformations.

Canning played an important role in yoking together *Ottoman* and *reform* in the British/Ottoman context of the Eastern Question (though not necessarily in suggesting, making, or implementing such reform). Furthermore, Stanley Lane-Poole's 1888 biography seems to have been formative in the creation of a narrative of Ottoman *Westernization* or *modernization* in English: Turkey marches along a path toward *civilization,* and whether it is tutored by well-intentioned or scheming European statesmen depends on who writes. "New Turkey" was a Turkey "made European," which was presented as the only alternative to dissolution (1888, 69–70).

The Concert of Europe

The practical implications of Canning's instructions to "impart stability" should be considered in a dialogical light and as forming part of a series of multiple-actor joint actions. As Candan Badem (2010, 47) has noted, "[Sultan] Abdülmecid knew some French and liked to talk about politics and life with ambassadors such as the British ambassador Stratford Canning, who had great influence in Istanbul." For the first years of Canning's 1842–58 sojourn, the promulgation of legislation seems mainly to have continued in the vein laid out by the Tanzimat Charter of 1839, in which the sultan had promised to promote "public works" and ensure the security and prosperity of his subjects. While the extent of Canning's direct involvement in the proclamation of the Islahat Fermanı (the Reform Edict) in 1856 is not entirely clear, it seems clear that he did play an important role. In fact, Lord Palmerston told Parliament after the Islahat Fermanı had been proclaimed that Canning had accepted the Istanbul ambassadorship on the condition that he get government support "to obtain that equality between Christians and Mahomedans"—something that the Edict is generally said to have done, at least in principle (Badem 2010, 344). Meanwhile, the Sultan was trying to solicit European loans at the end of the war, and was fostering close relations with the French and British embassies in Istanbul, even honoring their balls with his presence.

The Reform Edict was the second of three charter-like legal instruments proclaimed by the Ottoman sultans in the middle of the nineteenth century. The proclamation of the edict was made a precondition both for concluding the peace agreement that ended the Crimean War and for the Ottoman Empire's acceptance as a member of the Concert of Europe. The text of the Reform Edict contains a number of concepts that were new to the vocabulary of sultanic decrees. First, the word *ıslah* gained meaning as a translation equivalent of *reform* in conjunction with the edict's promulgation. Second, the edict is also the first major Ottoman proclamation to use *mütemeddin* (civilized) as a key concept. Despite the use of these new concepts, the Reform Edict nevertheless follows the stylistic requirements of the old sultanic proclamations, which makes it very difficult to translate into English. It was written in the first-person voice of the sultan and was read to the public throughout the sultan's lands. While it is commonly said to guarantee the equality of all Ottoman subjects regardless of faith (Berkes 1998, 152–53), its elliptical prose makes it difficult to claim specific rights or privileges on the basis of this text.

Despite my imperial equity-oriented wish for renewing and reiterating the new and fruitful ordering which I until now have succeeded in establishing and founding for the attainment of the perfection of the all-important condition [through] the auspicious new order in order [for the Exalted State to] take its rightful and exalted place among the civilized nations appropriate to the glory of our Exalted State, I until now have been successful in arranging and laying the foundation and the favorable and public-spirited/patriotic deeds of the masses of our imperial subjects and which is the result of the magnanimous help from the exalted states who are our special, sincere allies who glow with trust. (Gözübüyük and Kili 1982, 7–8)

Although the Reform Edict has been called "a semi-dictat of the European powers," it was formulated in a specifically Ottoman vocabulary that tied it to the Tanzimat Charter (Abu-Manneh 1990, 258; see chapter 5). This connection with the Tanzimat Charter also linked the Reform Edict with a discourse on morality and equity that in this particular context is typically associated with the Nakşibendi-Halidî brotherhood, an Islamic brotherhood with members among the Ottoman statesmen of the period (Abu-Manneh 1990; 1994).[3] Halidî discourse emphasized the importance of state *order* (*nizam*) for individual *morality* (*ahlak*); if the state were not ruled with *justice* (*adalet*), the subjects could not be blamed for being *immoral* (Abu-Manneh 1982, 14). In the Tanzimat Charter, (social) order (*nizam*) is linked to the ruler, together with *equity* (*adalet*): a virtuous ruler laid down the order, which provided the means for the attainment of individual and communal perfection.

Sivilisazyon, 'Umrān, Medeniyet

During the reigns of Sultan Selim III (1789–1807) and Mahmud II (1808–39), the solution to polity turmoil can best be described as trying to cut out middlemen, centralize power, and intensify resource extraction to raise bigger, better trained, and more costly armies. Centralization and a heavier tax burden, in combination with new emerging networks and the loss of dynastic prestige that followed military defeats, led to a legitimacy crisis for the Ottoman state, as provincial notables sought to protect their positions from centralization efforts (see Yaycioglu 2016).

---

3. Halidîs are a major branch of the Nakşbendi brotherhood, and had accumulated a strong following in Anatolia and what is now northern Syria and Iraq by the late eighteenth century. See Abu-Manneh 1982 for a fuller historical overview.

One of these rebellions became the Greek War of Independence, which lasted from 1821 to 1829. Along with Mehmed Ali Paşa's challenge in Egypt that occurred around the same time, this was one of the more momentous challenges to the Ottoman order of the early nineteenth century (Fahmy 1997; F. F. Anscombe 2014). As Şükrü İlıcak has argued, the Ottoman grand vizier Halet Efendi on the one hand sought to cut out Greek Orthodox elites from state networks and on the other sought solutions to the immediate challenge of polity decline (Ilicak 2011). The Greek Orthodox (*Phanariot*) elite had been important as governors in the Balkans and as dragomans (interpreters and translators) in the service of both the Ottomans and foreign embassies in Istanbul. The grand vizier exiled these elites to Anatolia, where there was no tradition of using Greek Orthodox middlemen and where they had few established relations.

While this move clearly ruptured many of the networks that made up the state's relations to foreign powers, my main concern here is with how a particular set of concepts were used to shape relations between the state and Muslim and Christian subjects in an attempt to strengthen the Ottoman polity. The works of Arab scholar Ibn Khaldūn were widely read, and Ottoman diplomats used his conceptual vocabulary to analyze foreign states from the second half of the eighteenth century (Ilicak 2011, 104). As Alp Eren Topal (2017a, 302–5) has shown, Ottoman scribes of this era also used Ibn Khaldūn's conceptual vocabulary and analytical setup in the literature dealing with issues of reform. In the immediate context of the outbreak of the Greek War of Independence, however, the vocabulary started being used to formulate policy and reshape relations between state and subjects, Muslims and Christians.

Ibn Khaldūn's historiography contends that ʿumrān (the totality of human habitation) comprises ʿumrān ḥaḍārī (settled habitation) and ʿumrān badawī (nomadic habitation) (Al-Azmeh 1990, 10). As this conceptual pair was translated into Ottoman, however, some curious changes appear to have taken place. Initially, settled habitation—or, rather, the qualities pertaining to settled communities—became *hadaret* in Ottoman, while its paired opposite was rendered *bedeviyet*. At some point in the 1830s, *hadaret* was replaced by *medeniyet* in Ottoman usage. There appears to have been no differentiation between the two, and the translator of the last third of Ibn Khaldūn's *Muqaddimah*

(Prolegomena, 1967) used the two in tautology: *hadâret ü medeniyyet* (see, e.g., İbn Haldun 2008, 220). The etymological origin of *medeniyet* has to do with the Arabic root *m-d-n*, from which *medīna* (city) and other words are derived. *Medeniyet* can be translated as "that which pertains to the city," "urbanity," or "city culture." Ibn Khaldūn argues that the *'aṣabiya* (community spirit) of the *bedeviyet* was superior to that of the *medeniyet* and thus that nomads are almost inevitably bound to conquer *medeniyet*, where they would become decadent and lose their *'aṣabiya*, resulting in a perpetual cycle of conquest and corruption. Nevertheless, the luxuries of *medeniyet* were necessary for increasing the prestige of the ruler and the realm vis-à-vis neighboring polities. *Medeniyet*, in Ibn Khaldūn's setup, was a necessary evil, the source of both decadence and prestige.

Because the corruption of *medeniyet* breaks down social cohesion, and a luxurious lifestyle makes men incompetent warriors, nomads will at regular intervals conquer *medeniyet*. The conquerors then enter the same cycle and become corrupted in about four generations. The word *devlet*, which in today's Turkish means *state*, is derived from the Arabic root associated with *cycle* and denotes one such cycle of conquest, rule, and demise of a dynasty. It is simultaneously the dynasty and the historical cycle during which it occupies power (Ibn Khaldūn 1967, 42–43, 91–100, 105–6, 118–20). Although the Ottoman dynasty lasted much longer than four generations, Ottoman historiography and political treatises nevertheless used a Khaldunian setup into the nineteenth century (Fleischer 1983).

'Aṣabiyet (the Ottoman spelling of *'aṣabiya*), the social glue of the Khaldunian setup, was a very problematic concept since it was particular to smaller groups. In the broader Ottoman tradition, *'aṣabiyet* stood in competition with the type of universal solidarity for which Islam called. It was not something that Ottoman elites could easily claim as a goal. Nevertheless, in 1821, Ottoman scribes explained the success of the Greek rebels by claiming that they had superior *'aṣabiyet* (Ilicak 2011, 115–16). The problem with the Ottomans, these scribes claimed, was that they had been too deeply affected by *hadaret*. In late March 1821, the Imperial Council suggested to that the sultan adopt *bedeviyet* (Ilicak 2011, 122). Within days, most Muslims were called on to abandon all luxury, arm themselves, and acquire horses. The government requisitioned weapons, and all of Ottoman

officialdom and all male Muslim inhabitants of Istanbul were soon bearing arms (130). Conversely, the Greek Orthodox population was disarmed. Unsurprisingly, having the Muslim population of Istanbul and its environs ride around on horses and bearing arms did little to stop the Greek rebellion in the Morea. Instead, this development prepared the ground for violence against unarmed Greek Orthodox subjects far away from the rebellion, thus reinforcing and politicizing the boundary between Greek Orthodox and Muslim subjects of the Sultan. The policy was soon abandoned, but not before the violence against Greek Orthodox subjects had made Ottoman claims to legitimate suzerainty more difficult to argue to Europeans.

Medeniyet as Translation Equivalent

Civilization has many meanings, and as it became entangled with translation equivalents in Ottoman, a wide range of different Ottoman words came into play. By using concepts that already had an Ottoman history of use to translate French and English concepts of *civilization*, the meaning to which *medeniyet* has been put has been at some variance with *civilization*. The example during the Greek War of Independence demonstrates not only that Ottoman elites did not use the paired opposites *hadaret/ medeniyet* and *bedeviyet* in a manner that could easily translate *civilization* and *barbarity* but also that interlingual entanglement of the concepts did not happen in a straightforward manner.

When Ottomans first started translating *civilization* from French, they linked these interpretations neither to *'umrān* nor to *medeniyet* but simply by using the French word *civilization* in the Ottoman context transcribed as *sivilizasyon* (Baykara 2007, 15). The first known textual instance of trying to explain the French concept in Ottoman is from 1834. Writing a letter from Paris, Ottoman statesman Mustafa Reşid Paşa explained *sivilizasyon* as "the education of man and a practicing of orderliness" (C. K. Neumann 1999, 176 n. 53; Baykara 2007, 29–30). From the beginning, it was tied to other commonplaces, most notably to virtues such as orderliness and education. Probably not coincidentally, this was written from Paris four years after French debates had used *civilization* to legitimize conquest of Algeria from Ottoman suzerainty (however nominal that suzerainty may have been) (Sessions 2011, 5–6, 58–59 *inter alia*). Moreover, "the Greek War of Independence" from the Ottoman Empire had been an important topic in public debates in Europe during the 1820s, and since *Greece* was being yoked to *civilization* by virtue of the canonization of Greek classics among European elites, the juxtaposition with the Ottomans, from whom the Greeks sought independence, was reinforced (Baykara 2007, 24, 26, 34–35). Halet Efendi's attempt to encourage *bedeviyet* as a way of reviving the polity in the face of rebellion appears to have gone untranslated in European texts. If European texts noted anything barbarous about the developments in the Ottoman Empire, it was the massacres of Greek Orthodox subjects, not the rejection of luxuries, riding around on horses, and bearing arms.

Three years after Mustafa Reşid Paşa penned his explanation of *sivilizasyon*, another Ottoman statesman, Sadık Rıfat Paşa, argued that a new system had been enforced in Europe since the end of the Napoleonic Wars. Sadık Rıfat called this system both *sivilizasyon* (civilization) and *medeniyet* and claimed that it was based on the determination to maintain peaceful and friendly relations between states (Günay 1992, 91; Mardin 2000 [1962], 180). According to Şerif Mardin (2000 [1962], 177–79), both Sadık Rıfat Paşa and Mustafa Reşid Paşa drew on conversations with Metternich when they engaged in Ottoman dialogues using concepts translatable as *civilization*, but they used the vocabulary of *morality*, *justice*, and *order* to formulate their arguments in ways typical of the Halidî brotherhood (Abu-Manneh 1994). They were among a handful of centrally placed Halidî-affiliated statesmen in the governments of Sultan Abdülmecid I (1839–61), and the sultan himself is thought to have been sympathetic to this brotherhood.

The way that Sadık Rıfat Paşa and Mustafa Reşid Paşa used the words *sivilizasyon* and *medeniyet* can be said to be an entangling of Metternich's discourse on the Concert of Europe as a way to secure the European "balance of power," with Halidî discourse on the importance of the ruler in imposing an equitable and moral order to ensure the welfare of the subjects and the prosperity and security of the state. According to Sadık Rıfat Paşa, peace and prosperity were mutually dependent and started with the protection of the subjects (Mardin 2000 [1962], 180–81). Underpinning this arrangement was the virtue of equity on behalf of the ruler, embedded as it was in a

"Circle of Justice," where each part of society depends on something else, but it all required a just ruler, something that was central to Halidî discourse (132). *Medeniyet* and *sivilizasyon* were used primarily in relation to the conduct of states and statesmen, and the honing of an individual's character was the road to a particular institutionalization of relationships between ruler and ruled. These terms were used in arguing for equitable treatment of the Sultan's subjects on the domestic arena, and to adhere to a certain order between rulers in external relations (132).

Progress

While *sivilizasyon* was used to structure relations between states, the discussion of Canning's reform proposals illustrates that whether *Turkey*, as he called it, satisfied the standard of civilization was related to its domestic conduct and the configuration of social relations between state and subjects. In the reshaping of these relations, Ottoman statesmen came to rely heavily on concepts of *morality*, which were later linked to *progress*. The Halidî statesmen were particularly concerned with *morality* as part of a *just order* that depended on a *just ruler* but with the morality of the subjects as a primary concern. One of the most central statesmen of the Tanzimat, Sadık Rıfat Paşa, later wrote an 1847 treatise on morality for children with an 1856 addendum for adults. These were important texts because of their wide circulation: the children's treatise was taught in Ottoman state schools for decades after its publication (Günay 1992; Karimullah 2012). In the texts, Sadık Rıfat Paşa placed particular emphasis on *morality* as proper comportment, moderation, and the exertion of the individual in useful endeavors.

Another Ottoman who used what could be called a Khaldunian vocabulary for discussing contemporary political issues of the Ottoman Empire was a reformist statesman and protégé of Reşid Paşa, Ahmed Cevdet Paşa (1822/3–1895). After translating the last third of Ibn Khaldūn's *Muqaddima* into Ottoman in 1860–61, Ahmed Cevdet Paşa started using the conceptual vocabulary in his magisterial twelve-volume *Cevdet's History* (C. K. Neumann 1999). This is a work of late eighteenth and early nineteenth century Ottoman history that went well beyond its bounds. Central to the narrative is a concept of civilization that appears as a synthesis of his mentor's concept of *civilization* and Ibn Khaldūn's concepts of *medeniyet* and *hadaret.*

Ahmed Cevdet Paşa got a chance to use this conceptualization of the relationship between the civilized and the nomadic in practice as governor of Bilad-ı Şam (Syria). These efforts were associated with the Fırka Islahiya, the Reform Brigade. In this context, *ıslah* meant the forceful settlement of nomads and their acculturation into settled life (*medeniyet*), taxing them and enlisting them into the regular army. *Medeniyet* still meant settled life, and one could not claim to be simultaneously *mütemeddin* (civilized) and *bedevi* (nomadic/barbarian). Ottoman travelers who went to places other than Europe underscored this point, equating civilization with city life (Palabıyık 2010, 213). Through translation and entanglement with European concepts, nomadism (*bedeviyet*) was increasingly represented as a way of life that belonged to the past. Bringing the periphery into the present meant settling it, which was synonymous with *civilizing* it.

As concepts of *civilization* were used ever more frequently, they became more centrally placed in the debate; in addition, their use became more polyvalent by being linked with various other important concepts. Following the early decades when *medeniyet* and other translations of *civilization* were primarily used in a meaning similar to "system of states" or as the practicing of orderliness and the education of man, the 1870s seem to have seen an increased emphasis on the *achievements* or *works* of civilization—in short, on *progresses* in the plural. Authors of this period used *medeniyet* as "a technique or as a practice, rather than a condition, a stage or a phase" (Palabıyık 2010, 171). Ottoman homme de lettres Namık Kemal (1840–1888) used *medeniyet* largely by tying it to *terakki* (promotion), which he in the process reinterpreted to become a translation equivalent of the French *progrès* (progress). *Terakki* was not used as a collective singular in Namık Kemal's texts but consisted of a number of different progress*es*—natural gas, medicine, engineering, economics, the arts, and commerce. He asks, "When will we start taking example?" (Kara and Aydoğdu 2005, 46–48).

In an essay, "Medeniyet" (1873), Namık Kemal linked *civilization* with *freedom* (*hürriyet*) and argued that civilization was fundamentally important to human comfort and happiness:

It is the right and goal of humans not only to live but also to live in freedom. But is it possible for the uncivilized nations/tribes to protect their freedom, considering the great number of civilized nations? . . . Every suffering of civilization causes a comfort, [whereas] in the state of savagery, every comfort causes a thousand torments. . . . In summary, living without civilization is like dying a sudden, brutal death. (transcribed and reprinted in Kara and Aydoğdu 2005, 360)

The civilized/uncivilized dichotomy was linked to morality in the sense of moral uprightness and an ethic that entails suffering for something good, versus licentious enjoyment of luxury now while putting off the suffering for later and thus augmenting it. Civilization gives meaning and purpose to human endeavor, and the goal of that endeavor is *freedom*. Without civilization, humans suffer pointlessly; with civilization, human suffering has a purpose.

In four articles written between 1881 and 1884, Şemseddin Sami (1850–1904) refers to canonical texts of European philosophy in discussing *medeniyet* and thus further expands the range of topics on which it could be meaningfully used in Ottoman. Rather than emphasizing technological aspects, as Namık Kemal and others had done, Şemseddin Sami argued that *medeniyet* (civilization) was a product of intellectual developments. By linking *medeniyet* to canonical philosophical texts, Sami also made possible a plurality of civilizations. Whereas technological *progress* was claimed to be linear and indivisible, each philosophical tradition had its own merits. He thus divided the world into an Islamic and a European civilization on the basis of philosophical tradition (Palabıyık 2010, 193).

This use of *medeniyet* to mean civilization as founded in a philosophical tradition centered the concept around questions of the relative merits of different traditions. Concepts of *morality* became central in this reinterpretation. One example of this is found in the writings of Fatma Aliye, the daughter of Ahmed Cevdet Paşa (Berkes 1998, 287). In a discursive move that fits perfectly with Partha Chatterjee's (1993, 6) claims about anticolonial nationalism, she divided *medeniyet* into *spiritual* and *material* aspects. Whereas the former consists of its "moral acquisitions" specific to the community, the latter is linked to industrial inventions, battleships, and sewing machines. The spiritual aspect of European civilization, she says, is "laden with innumerable shortcomings," and when she follows up by arguing that "our moral civilization is ample enough for our needs," it leaves an ambiguity as to whether she uses *moral* as a mere aspect of "our civilization" (having both a material and a spiritual aspect) or in the sense that "our civilization" is *moral*, whereas European civilization is *immoral*.

Edep, Ahlak, and a Bourgeois Sociability

European concepts of *civilization* emerged in semantic fields that have to do with the manners and comportment of European elites (Guth 2010)—the same groups of people whom European states used for diplomacy. Thus, the concepts were also used to stabilize the sociability with which Ottomans had to engage to be taken seriously in diplomatic negotiations. French-speaking Ottoman diplomats were, in a cultural sense, increasingly playing an "away game" not only in the sense of speaking a different language, but mastering other practices. They had to learn the practices of European elites to gain acceptance as a civilized state. Moreover, *civilization* was a key concept used in European Othering of Ottomans. As chapter 4 discusses, learning the ropes of a language game within which there was a conflation of the Ottomans with *barbarians* meant that it was imperative to find someone *more* barbarian onto whom that category could be transposed.

While Mustafa Reşid Paşa interpreted the concept of civilization as "education of man" (*terbiye-i nas*) and thus connected it with education, *edep* (plural *adab*) might be a more apt translation. The British lexicographer Sir James Redhouse, writing in 1890, translated *edep* as "breeding, manners, politeness . . . training, education, accomplishments, literature." Furthermore, Carter Findley (1980, 9) describes *edeb* as a

> worldly, belletristic tradition known in Arabic as *adab*, a term embracing what the Turks ultimately came to refer to as both *edeb*, "good breeding," and *edebiyat*, "literature." For this worldly literary culture, and for the official uses of the state, to the service of which the *adab* tradition is closely linked, a special language evolved: Ottoman Turkish.

Edep was, according to Findley, a concept closely tied to the specific acquisition and practice of the Ottoman language itself. Moreover, mastery of *edep* was deemed a prerequisite for entry into the Ottoman civil service. As such, it was a central part of Ottoman elite sociability.

Namık Kemal used *edep* as he divided *Avrupa medeniyeti* (European civilization) into a desirable aspect and a less desirable aspect:

> Immorality is the result not of deficiencies of civilization itself but of defects in its practice. . . . Civility [*âdâb*] and morality [*ahlâk*] can become [twisted] to the point of mischief, and there can of course not be perfection of the public order/common welfare [if they are]. [. . .] Let us suppose that civilization as it is found in Europe is brimful with a thousand types of defects and evil things. [. . . But] just as we did not for the purpose of civilization need to take up eating leech kebabs like the Chinese, we are not at all forced to imitate the dances or the style of marriage of the Europeans.[4] (Kara and Aydoğdu 2005, 360–61)

Medeniyet thus was not used synonymously with *edep*. Instead, *medeniyet* has the potential to corrupt *adab* and *ahlak*, which threatens *asayış* (public order/common welfare). However, the problem was not civilization in itself but its deficient practice if it goes against *edep* and *ahlak*. *Medeniyet*, then, was used as meaning something foreign, in potential conflict with "our" defining character.

Ahmed Cevdet Paşa (1991, 28) also linked civilization with immorality:

> While a woman has intercourse with her lover, her husband does not enter the room. . . . In the country's gardens there is plenty of entertainment. It seems that the works of civilization have started. But this civilization does not have schools as its origin. Maybe it comes from social and luscious gatherings.

---

4. This is a reference to a famous although possibly apocryphal Hadith in which the Prophet allegedly said, "Seek knowledge even unto China." The original point, according to Ben-Dor (2002, 93–94), was that knowledge should be sought even if it demands great effort, not primarily that one should accept knowledge regardless of origin.

Without *terbiye* (education) and *ahlak* (morality), the "works of civilization" consist solely of entertainment and distraction, and these distractions are detrimental to social virtues such as *chastity* (*iffet*).

The main issue was how to deal with the concepts of *medeniyet* and *civilization* and how to relate to European manners and morality (or the lack thereof). After the French language became part of elite education, adopting certain French expressions and manners also became a mark of social distinction. This was by no means static, and changed as parvenus also started adopting French customs. In short, *how* to relate to French customs and the French language became a way to show one's *edep*. This topic was treated extensively in late-nineteenth-century Ottoman literature. In fact, it would be difficult to clearly distinguish the emergence of the Ottoman novel from the literary theme of how to deal with French ways, known in Turkish as *alafranga* (only partially translatable as Francophilia).

Parallel to the emergence of the Ottoman novel in the 1860s and 1870s, a new concept appeared in Ottoman texts: the *alafranga züppe* (Francophile fop) (Moran 1977). The *alafranga züppe* was someone who did not moderate his adoption of French manners and therefore lacked refinement in how he (the main characters are usually male) related to European and French manners and customs. The *alafranga züppe* was ridiculed much as the parvenu was ridiculed in French literature.

Alafranga emerged as an antonym to *alla Turca* (in the Turkish fashion), which was an Italian expression that became part of Ottoman language as *alaturka* (Berkes 1998, 284). This dichotomy was put to use in late Ottoman literature by linking it to *edep* and *ahlak*, whereby the *alafranga* exemplified the misguided adoption of European manners and the *alaturka* was ridiculed for his traditionalism and fear of European ways. Knowing what to appropriate from European civilization and how to use the traditional Ottoman cultural repertoire in compatible ways was a mark of cultivation and refinement.

The most prolific and popular author of the 1880s and 1890s, Ahmed Midhat Efendi, did not come up with this literary theme but used it extensively in his novels (Çekiç 2009, 11–39). Largely didactic, Midhat's novels set up a neat dichotomy between Ottomans who relate to and employ European practices without sacrificing *edep* and those who do not, often by both failing to adopt modern civilization *and* sacrificing *edep*. The novels themselves can be read as guides to proper behavior that show how readers may retain *edep* and *ahlak* while taking what is "useful" from European *medeniyet*.

The immorality found in Europe had, according to Ahmed Midhat Efendi and other contemporary authors, been adopted by some of the people in Beyoğlu, the part of Istanbul where Christian minorities, expatriates, and *alafranga* Muslims lived. There is also the link between Europe and *frengi*, which meant both *syphilitic* and *European*, which comes up where Ahmed Midhat Efendi (2000 [1891], 4–5) discussed Émile Zola's literature:

> [One would assume] that there was no trace left of human virtue in . . . that part of the world called France and especially that section of France called Paris. There, the general activity of humanity consisted of fornication; venereal diseases intermingled with political animosities; murderous skills [were refined]. [. . .] Emile Zola and his like see almost no one there other than whores, those who almost idolize them, and the wretches who are content waiting for a daily meal while drinking a bottle of wine, cognac, or rakı purchased even at the expense of their wives', daughters', or sisters' chastity and who do not give up their laziness even though they have nothing to eat for dinner.

Frengi's ambiguous meaning was here used to link France to moral degradation, drunkenness, and wanton fornication. The general lack of *ahlak* (morality) in French society becomes the source of Parisians' suffering. Syphilitic sexual intercourse also becomes explicitly linked to the conduct of political affairs, and they become two different expressions of the same underlying problem: the French are unable to control their passions as a consequence of insufficient morality.

Despite his misgivings about the immorality that resulted from *medeniyet*, Ahmed Midhat expounded the virtues of organizing one's private life by use of a set of practices that outsiders would recognize as a European bourgeois sociability. One such issue was his description of the ideal dwelling, where the points of reference were on the one hand how things were done in Europe and on the other how best to preserve the "good name" (*namus*) of the family (Çekiç 2009, 70–97). *Namus* was (and to some extent still is) that part of family honor linked to the protection of women and their chastity (*iffet*) (A. Parla 2001; Kogaciolu 2004). It is not literally a "female honor" but instead is honor in relation to how men protect their women. For women it is linked to virtues such as *chastity* and *modesty*. For men, it is a matter of warding off threats to these virtues in the family. This is different from the "male" honor or glory that may be won on the battlefield (*şeref* and *şen*).

Where the old house had been divided into a *selamlık* (where guests were received) and a *haremlik* (the preserve of the family), the new house was supposed to have a different layout, with a *salon* for social intercourse between people of either gender, a *boudoir* where the women received their intimate female friends, and a *cabinet du travail* where the man of the house worked and received business acquaintances (Çekiç 2009, 70–97). There were also separate bedrooms for each family member (though it is unclear whether husband and wife ideally should have separate bedrooms). Thus, single-purpose rooms would differentiate social relationships. Differentiation also made it possible to have certain types of relationships between the sexes without jeopardizing *namus*, although this concept was reinterpreted in the process. Preserving virtues while making sure not to offend guests constituted an important part of *savoir vivre cosmopolite*. Teaching Ottomans this concept was Midhat's explicit purpose in writing his *Avrupa Adab-ı Muaşereti yahut Alafranga* (Çekiç 2009, 77; Ahmet Mithat [1896] 2016).

Social Darwinism and Educating the Nation

Ahmed Midhat also started using Ottoman discourse in ways that resemble British philosopher Herbert Spencer's writings, arguing that human progress was the result of rivalry between human beings always seeking to be better than their peers (Doğan 2006, 158). Ahmed Midhat's works on proper conduct and comportment should be read within this context. Virtues such as moderation, honing one's comportment, and showing restraint were all tools to be employed in a rivalry between human beings and between societies. Yet this was not a matter of life and death on the battlefield. During the Ottoman

Second Constitutional Period (1908–18), these concepts were used in ways that bear family resemblances to what has been called Social Darwinism, which took history to be a struggle for a survival of the fittest among *races* rather than a (more amicable) competition between *nations* (Aksakal 2004). The difference was that in the former context, passions needed to be restrained and moderated at all times, while in the latter, passions must be nourished and directed at the enemy.

Whereas *terbiye* (education for the sake of attaining *edep*, cultivation, rather than technical skills) had previously been linked to upper-class refinement, it was increasingly argued to be the key to success in the survival of the fittest and should therefore be spread to all parts of society. Leading Ottoman authors of the Second Constitutional Period consistently argued or merely assumed that the strength of an army depended on the level of education and vitality of the society it represented. Thus, the state had a duty to both harden and educate the masses so that the army could protect the state (as well as possibly the masses) from external threats.

> The army may try as hard as it wishes to improve a society's military strength. The army's officers may be the most skilled in the world, but if the society's material and moral standards are low, the army will certainly enter the battlefield in a deficient and disorderly manner and quickly meet with defeat. (Aksakal 2004, 525)

Order depended on education and morality and was the key prerequisite for victory. The problems of the Ottoman army, according to this author, were those of Ottoman society itself. In an immoral society, the army itself would become disorderly. Only by educating and improving society could one strengthen the army.

The Committee of Union and Progress, the dominant organization in Ottoman politics during the Second Constitutional Period, frequently used this Social Darwinist discourse. Its members were clearly aware of such writings as Ludwig Büchner's scientific materialism; Auguste Comte's positivism; and the racial theorizing and civilizational hierarchization of Herbert Spencer, Arthur Gobineau, and Gustave Le Bon as well as of Ernest Renan's attack on Islam, which became part of Ottoman repertoires of political references following the 1908 revolution (Hanioğlu 1995, 32). Ottoman statesmen of the post-1908 period formulated their policies using Social Darwinist discourse: they did not consider themselves to have a choice between living in peace or fighting a war; rather, their choice was whether to fight for the nation's life or accept its death. "Living means struggling. Absence of struggle can only be found in cemeteries. Only the dead are without struggle" (Aksakal 2004, 523).

Large demonstrations in support of the Balkan Wars in 1912–13 were accompanied by headlines such as "Either Honor or Death," which appeals for a fight to the death for the *namus* of the *vatan* (motherland/fatherland) (Arıkan 1989, 172–73, 176). As Mustafa Aksakal has pointed out, international law was argued to offer no viable platform for countering the external threats to the empire. The Izmir newspaper *Ahenk* argued, "We must now fully realize that our honor [*namus*] and our people's integrity cannot be preserved by those old books of international law, but only by war" (Aksakal 2004, 516). This was a marked contrast to Metternich's and Sadık Rıfat Paşa's discourse on civilization and the balance of power as the guarantee for peace and prosperity. Here, survival depends on fighting.

Few Ottoman intellectuals of the Second Constitutional Period have enjoyed as wide a reception as Ziya Gökalp (1876–1924). Writing during the Balkan Wars, Gökalp ([1923] 1968, 22) translated the German *Kultur* by linking to the Arabic word *ḥars*, which had not previously been put to this use. In Arabic, *ḥars* quite simply means *culture* in the sense of *agriculture*, with no sociopolitical connotations (Wehr 1976). Gökalp used *hars* extensively in his writings, claiming it as the source of national strength, whereas *medeniyet* (civilization) was a mere bonus. Building on the organic metaphors to which *Kultur* is frequently linked, Gökalp claimed that *hars* was natural while *medeniyet* (civilization) was artificial. The Ottoman language belonged, according to Gökalp ([1923] 1968, 23), to the sphere of *medeniyet*, whereas the Turkish language was part of *hars*. This differentiation between culture and civilization was used in a Social Darwinist discourse with a peculiar twist: *hars* would always trump *medeniyet*, so that a culturally strong but civilizationally weak nation will always defeat a nation with a weak culture but a strong civilization (31).

Gökalp ([1923] 1968, 33) did not use a simple civilizational dichotomy of East = Asia = Islam versus West = Europe = Christianity; instead, he reinterpreted these concepts and put them to use in a way where he could argue that Turks were *really* Western while the Arabs, Greeks and Ottomans were Eastern:

> Eastern civilization is not really Islamic civilization, as some people think, but rather owes its origin to Byzantium. Similarly, Western civilization is not Christian civilization but an outgrowth of Roman civilization. . . . The Turkists will succeed in their efforts . . . because they want to discard entirely the Byzantine civilization of the East and adopt Western civilization in toto. Turkists want to enter Western civilization completely and unreservedly while remaining Turks and Muslims.

However, Gökalp was not specific as to what kind of manners and mores were natural and which were superficial. There is little in this text that clearly distinguishes what it means to behave as a "Turk" rather than as an "Ottoman" or what behavior was to be considered artificial and what was natural. The text nevertheless helped delegitimize certain interpretations of proper behavior as *Eastern* and *corrupt* while legitimizing others, thus changing what was possible to claim by using these concepts. This configuration of meaning is something that cannot easily be translated into other language games, as these usages imbue the concepts with meaning specific to Turkish. Despite all the entanglement, some meanings still do not easily translate.

European Civilization

By the time the Ottoman Empire surrendered to the Entente powers in the First World War, *medeniyet* was increasingly used in the plural. In his book *Üç Medeniyet* (Three Civilizations), Azeri émigré intellectual Ahmet Ağaoğlu (1869–1939) claims that

> to say civilization [*medeniyet*] is to say "way of life," except that one should take the concept of life in its widest and most encompassing meaning. All the manifestations of life and its material and spiritual events ought to be put into this concept. (Ağaoğlu 1972 [1927], 3–4)

According to Ağaoğlu (3), the world has three civilizations: the Islamic civilization, the Buddha-Brahma civilization, and the European or Western civilization. He calls the first two "defeated civilizations" and the latter a "victorious civilization" (9–10). Those tribes/races/nations (*kavim*) that belong to a defeated civilization are forced to follow the path taken by the victorious civilization (3). Ağaoğlu argues that the Islamic civilization is the least important in terms of both its population and its history (4). Ağaoğlu's discourse reifies *medeniyet* as an entity with object-like qualities, yet he does not treat civilizations as essentialized or impermeable objects. Civilizations change, and nations change. Although he uses *civilization* in the plural, he combines it with *civilization* as practice. In other words, there are different ways of being civilized, but a hierarchy clearly exists between them, and this hierarchy is susceptible to change. Polities may climb the hierarchy by reconfiguring relations between subjects and state elite and by changing collective practices—a topic familiar to international studies scholars (Turan Kayaoğlu 2010; Zarakol 2011).

Ağaoğlu's work implies (though it never explicitly states) that civilization is connected to religion, since he shapes the boundaries of his three civilizations by reference to religious collectives. Moreover, in his illustration of how it is possible to change civilization, he uses *religion* as a key marker of civilizational identity: all nations, "even the Arabs," change religion from time to time. Ağaoğlu also insists that change is a normal part of social life. One cannot assume that just because "we" are changing, "we" are losing our identity (Ağaoğlu 1972 [1927], 14–15). Those who ask "What will our national character be?" are reminded that "Only stagnation kills the national character" (13, 17). Using a slightly different concept than *corruption* or *turmoil*, Ağaoğlu picks up on conceptual usages of the literature on *reform* that had been an important part of Ottoman political writing for a century (see Topal 2017b).

According to Ağaoğlu, stagnation leads to *defeat*, which has the same two aspects as Fatma Aliye's *civilization*: material (*maddî* and spiritual (*manevî*). Material defeat is so obvious to Ağaoğlu "that it cannot have escaped anyone." (He was writing from his exile in Malta in 1922, during the time when the British still occupied Istanbul and the Greek invasion of Western Anatolia was ongoing.)

What is defeat? Is it not to accept someone else's personality and to be subject to his will? This acceptance and subjection is a defeat, regardless of whether it happened by wish or by force. From this perspective, both the Islamic and the Buddha-Brahma civilizations have been defeated, and they have been forced to accept the personality and characteristics of Western civilization and to be subject to its will. . . . Look at all of the Asian societies of today: everywhere you see the domestic struggle between two currents. The proponents of European civilization clash with the civilization that relies on the local old traditions. It is a struggle of life and death that is going on. (1972 [1927], 9–10)

Ağaoğlu claims that the struggle between old and new, local and European, is common to all Asian societies. Ağaoğlu subtly shifts from using *civilizations* to using *continents* as his structuring concept. Whereas he includes Africa in Islamic civilization, when he writes of the Buddha-Brahma civilization and Islamic civilization collectively, they become *Asya* (Asia), thus excluding Africa. It is also quite clear that this is a struggle between old and new, where *Asian, local,* and *traditional* are linked with *old*, while *European, Western, modern,* and (later in the text) *scientific* are linked with *new*. This sets up a series of dichotomies that align history along both a *forward/backward* axis and a geographic *east/west* axis.

Do we or do we not accept and admit Western civilization's superiority and victory? If we do, we should not ascribe that supremacy only to arts and sciences and to certain political and social institutions; we should link ourselves to the totality of that civilization, to its mentality, its way of seeing, its spirit, its mind, its brain, and its heart. Western life has conquered our way of life in its entirety. Because of this, if we want to save ourselves, live, and continue our existence, we need to adjust ourselves to it with all the aspects of our life, our heads, our hearts, our ways of seeing, our mentality—not only our clothes and some of our institutions. There is no other salvation than this. (13)

The argument is that all societies, and most specifically the Ottoman, face a choice between accepting the superiority of Western civilization and ending up trampled by the civilized.

Nationalist leader Mustafa Kemal (later Atatürk) used this type of representation in a speech some years later:

> It is necessary to deepen and strengthen the foundations of the reform [*inkılap*] every day. Esteemed inhabitants, let us not fool each other. The civilized world is far ahead. We have to catch up with it and get inside the sphere of civilization. Questions such as should we or should we not wear hats are meaningless. [Just as] we shall wear hats, we shall take every type of works/artifacts of civilization that the West has. Gentlemen, the humans who are not civilized are bound to end up under the feet of those who are. (Kemal 1952, 226)

This quotation is exemplary of the early Kemalists' use of *civilization* and how they linked it with concepts of *reform* (*inkılap*). As in Ağaoğlu's interpretation of the concept of *civilization* and its importance for human progress and thus also survival, there is no choice but to accept all aspects of *civilization*. Although *civilization* is not in itself essentially Western, "the West" or Europe is the general geography where one finds the most refined civilization.

Medeniyet remained a key concept of Kemalist discourse also after Mustafa Kemal died in 1938. Turkish theater critic and columnist İsmail Hakkı Baltacıoğlu (1886–1978) started an essay collection by assuming the existence of a consensus that "we all want to be Europeanized." This, he claimed,

> is to break with culture and traditions, isn't it? This is the question that every nation and state that wants to Europeanize and does become Europeanized first has to ask and provide a reply to. Where are we in the matter of Europeanization? There are none left who say, "Is it right or wrong to go West?" No one tires his head with this question any longer. Everyone from greenhorns to the most mature knows that it is necessary and good to go West and to Europeanize. But wanting to go West

and knowing how to get this right are two different things. (Baltacıoğlu 1945, 7)

Baltacıoğlu insists that *civilization* is about *methods*, not about content. In using the concept in this way, he implicitly links it to the *alaturka/ alafranga* dichotomy, actualizing a debate about imitativeness and what it means to be *truly* rather than *superficially* civilized.

> The idea of civilization is more than anything the idea of objective knowledge. When we say European civilization, the first that comes [to mind] is its science. In our minds, the thought of [being] European is the thought of being knowledgeable. There is a European civilization. There cannot be any doubt that the foremost foundational elements of this civilization are its knowledge and its machines. (75)

Civilization or *Western civilization*—terms that Baltacıoğlu used largely synonymously (48)—applied *methods* to produce knowledge, while the East relied on "subjective knowledge" that was produced without methods, merely "what comes to one's mind" (75–76). Note the similarity with European statesmen's objections to the Ottoman legal system as uncodified and hence detached from reason and liable to *subjective* interpretation rather than objective legal criteria. Baltacıoğlu appropriated a distinction between *civilized* and *uncivilized* that hinged on the concept of *reason* and objectivity:

> Societies that [base their] way of life on knowledge derived in the latter manner exist everywhere. But knowledge that one reaches by *objective* methods exists only in societies whose civilization has progressed [*medeniyeti ileri olan topluluklar*]. [The kind of] knowledge that is the fundamental element of civilization is *methodical knowledge*. (75–76)

Methods have to do with the application of *reason* in the pursuit of knowledge. Being *European*, being *Western*, meant being *civilized*. And being *civilized* was to apply certain methods. This is clearly a practice definition of *civilization*, which renders a particular civilization open to new members who learn the proper practices.

To Europeanize [*Avrupalılaşmak*] in the affairs of knowledge does not mean to learn, cram, move, and purvey what the Western intellectuals/scientists know; it means to do what the Western scientists/intellectuals do; instead of reading and learning knowledge, it means to create knowledge, to assimilate the creative process, not the products of knowledge. (113)

This is use of a Turkish concept of *Europe* that links it to certain practices rather than to essentialized aspects of European identity (such as geography, "inherited religion," or race). Becoming European means applying certain European practices (see Rumelili 2007 for the theoretical insight). Baltacıoğlu's point is that one should not imitate a particular European nation, but should relate to European universalism in the same manner as *other Europeans*.

Here is the crux of Baltacıoğlu's writings, namely the argument that civilization is a framework for the display of what is national. He argues not for an essentialization of the national but rather that "we" should have "our theater" by displaying "our experiences" while using Western techniques (1945, 105–6, 116). Moreover, "Western theater is [also] in search of itself. To move west in theater is to take part in this search" (117).

What does it mean to Europeanize? To Europeanize means to go to Western civilization. Going to Western civilization means going to Western techniques. If this is so, the correct meaning of the slogan "To the West" is "To the Western techniques." To fully Westernize it is necessary to fully techniqueify [*teknikleşmek*]. (14–15)

This fits quite well with Benedict Anderson's (2006) argument that the nation-state involves the compartmentalization and celebration of "unique" contents in a fairly uniform manner and the placing of the national within a universal framework (see also Meyer et al. 1997). *Europeanization*, in Baltacıoğlu's discourse, means exactly this—fitting the Turkish nation-state into an international order where its "national" experiences are compartmentalized but where national artists take part in a universal endeavor to create "great works" and "classics" that have an appeal beyond the national audience

(Baltacıoğlu 1945, 109). Becoming Western or European is to take part in the creation of works that can appeal to all humans universally and to do so by employing methods and techniques that are distinctly European and that denigrate other forms of knowledge production and art techniques as *subjective*.

Conclusion

After *civilization* was established first as the historical goal (telos) for "Ottoman reform" in English-language discourse, *civilization* later became translated into Ottoman by entanglement with *medeniyet*. While the two language games started out using these concepts in ways that conveyed only partially the same meaning, there is a sense of convergence over time. By the 1920s, *medeniyet* became the explicit historical goal of the Kemalists. Yet as the Turkish national anthem attests, some ambiguity remained in the usage of this concept. One line of the song celebrates how *medeniyet* is like "a toothless monster," no longer invoking fear. As such, it is presented as an Other associated with the Great Powers. However, this anthem was composed and adopted in 1921, *during* the War of Independence, while Britain was occupying Istanbul—before the proclamation of the Turkish Republic (1923) and certainly before the formulation of a republican project of *reform*. If there is one common denominator to state discourse in the pre-1950 Turkish Republic, it is the emphasis on *reform* as *inkılap*—rather than *ıslah* or *tanzimat*, concepts that had become associated with the specific changes of the mid-nineteenth century—for the sake of attaining *civilization*, reaching *the level of civilization* or becoming part of *Western civilization*.

The semantic field relating to *civility* and *civilization* that came into being through translations and reinterpretations during Ottoman times was used as the basis for the conceptual vocabulary of the Turkish Republic that was founded in 1923. With the Turkish Language Reform, started in 1931, the words began to be changed, and with them, old interpretations and connotations disappeared or concepts were divided up. *Uygarlık* became the most important neologism that was supposed to take over for *medeniyet*. As was so often the case with the Turkish Language Reform, however, the new word did not succeed in replacing its predecessor but instead came to have a slightly different interpretation. In this case, *uygarlik* either carried connotations of being *modern* as a person or became used as a word for *civilization* in the archaeological or historical sense of the word (G. Lewis 1999, 122).

There is a very subtle and sometimes floating distinction between *civilization* in the singular and *civilizations* in the plural. While these two interpretations are indistinguishable at the level of everyday language use and are frequently left ambiguous, the difference has wide-ranging implications for how policies can be argued. *Civilization* in the singular is a concept interpretation that emphasizes practice rather than essentialized qualities of a society. It is a matter of dressing in a certain way, adhering to certain rules and norms, following certain practices, and adopting certain institutions. In principle, according to this interpretation, anyone can become civilized, unless the concept is combined with explicit racial hierarchization by reference to quasi-biological differences. Although these two representations do appear together, biological-racial hierarchies are not a necessary part of concept usage.

When concepts of *civilization* are used in the plural, there is often some essential quality that makes it difficult for a society to transcend the intercivilizational barrier. This may be "race" or some conviction that is so deeply held or trait that is so ingrained as to be nearly impossible to change at the aggregate level. This interpretation often implies *civilizations* as reified entities with object-like qualities rather than as sets of practices that can be universally adopted. The best-known contemporary example of this is of course Huntington's *Clash of Civilizations and the Remaking of World Order*, but his discourse has a long prehistory. How the world is divided depends on the main concerns of the author. While *civilization* in the singular is usually contrasted with *uncivilized* (or the cluster of partially synonymous concepts, *primitive, savage,* and *barbarian*), the counterconcepts to *European civilization* in the plural setup are often *Islamic civilization* and *Chinese civilization*. This relationship was usually asymmetric in the sense that *European civilization* was privileged in English-, German-, and French-language discourse and was frequently given a monopoly on the positive qualities associated with *civilization*.

The Kemalists deployed concepts of *medeniyet* in such a way that *advanced civilization* meant a set of practices and artifacts found in

Europe but not essentially European. To paraphrase Forrest Gump, "European is who European does."[5] Moreover, hegemonic Turkish discourse links "European civilization" not to religious practice but to practices associated with secular modernity. In the 1980s, 1990s, and 2000s, Turkish anti–European Union discourse depended on attacking this representation using essentializing counter-discourses where "being Turkish and Muslim" is incompatible with "doing European."

As both the telos of Ottoman and Turkish history and a community to which the Ottomans aspired to belong, *civilization* became the key concept of both the late Ottoman Empire and the early Turkish Republic. However, as chapter 6 discusses, the concept lost some of its currency in European languages around the end of the Second World War, with concepts of *democracy* taking its place as the *standard of civilization*. Although there is a great degree of ambiguity, a democratic state belonged to "the Free World" rather than to "a civilized family of nations."

For all these entanglements and reconfigurations of Ottoman social relations, little change appears to have occurred in how Europeans evaluated the *civilizational* position of the Ottomans (I.B. Neumann 1999, 39–63). The general discursive setup involved debating whether the Ottomans had *the capacity* to reform or civilize, not whether they had already done so. This approach contains some elements of the European debates about Turkey's potential to become part of the European Union: the debate concerns Turkey's capacity for change, not its actual achievements. Some, such as the followers of David Urquhart, considered Ottoman *reform* undesirable, instead taking a Romantic view of Ottoman institutions (Çiçek 2010). The European "side" of the dialogue and debate about Ottoman reform was too complex to sketch out here, but as Chase Gummer (2010) has argued, the arguments often seem to be part of intra-European (e.g., Germany versus Britain) or even intra-elite (Gladstone versus Disraeli, Kaiser Wilhelm versus Bismarck) power struggles more than they concern the actual restructuring of Ottoman social relations. This feature of European debates persists to this day.

---

5. Rumelili (2007) has called this the "inclusive" or "practice-based" aspect of identity, as distinct from essentialized traits that are used as stigmata even after a change of practice.

FOUR

Empire

In this chapter I trace the entanglement of concepts of *empire* and later *nation* with their emergent Ottoman and Turkish translation equivalents. Although these are closely connected phenomena, the emphasis here is on the legitimating aspect, leaving much of the reconfiguration of social relations that was done by the use of concepts of *nation* and *citizen* for the next chapter. If we are to understand the emergence of a Turkish nation-state and its integration into an international society, Turkish concepts of nation-state must be understood in relation to their paired opposite, *empire*. Empire has a much longer history as a concept in English and in French than its translation equivalent does in Ottoman, and was used to legitimize French and British rule and dominance over a major part of the world in the nineteenth century. By claiming to be *empires*, these polities also staked claims to prestige and leadership and to setting the standard for others to follow. This became known as the standard of civilization (see chapter 3).

Since the Ottoman polity has become known as the Ottoman *Empire* in English, it is noteworthy that no Ottoman translation equivalent was fully compatible with such a concept while the empire existed. I therefore start by exploring the "absence" of a concept of *empire* from the Ottoman language, and the various concepts that instead were used for the Ottoman polity. Moreover, I analyze how translation equivalents emerged for *empire* in Ottoman/Turkish and linked to the Ottoman polity as a rearguard action that legitimized the position of the "Turkish nationalists" and constituted a Turkish nation-state by delegitimizing the Ottoman state and associating it with *the past, the East,* and *imperialism.*

In the case of *empire,* there are clear semantic incompatibilities along both the synchronic axis (between Ottoman and nineteenth-century French) and the diachronic axis (between nineteenth-century Ottoman and present-day Turkish). Both nineteenth-century French (Empire Ottoman) and modern Turkish (Osmanlı İmparatorluğu) have a concept of what is known in English as "the Ottoman Empire," and all three have now become entangled. Ottoman, however, had no concept that made a similar meaning. The polity existed—of course there can be no doubt about that—but the concepts that were used to give meaning to it at the time did not involve *empire.*[1]

Concepts of *empire* first came into use in Ottoman claims to prestige vis-à-vis European states in the seventeenth century. These claims were formulated in European languages and embedded in the names by which the Ottoman polity was known in European languages: Ottoman Empire, Empire Ottoman, and Osmanisches Reich.[2] Although these emerged as European rhetorical commonplaces, Ottomans also sometimes used them to legitimize their polity to outsiders. By the time a concept of Osmanlı İmparatorluğu emerged in Turkish as a calque translation of the French and English concepts after the First World War, the international language games had fundamentally changed. Shoring up claims to prestige by using *empire* was no longer possible. Rather, the concept *Osmanlı İmparatorluğu* was coined as a counterconcept to the *Türk milleti* (Turkish nation) and *Türkiye Cumhuriyeti* (Turkish Republic) in the discursive and military struggle over the legitimate rule of Anatolia that followed the First World War. The English-language international context was dominated by Woodrow Wilson's Fourteen Points, which made *popular sovereignty* a discursive high ground that could be claimed vis-à-vis imperial polities (Manela 2007; Palmer, Colton, and Kramer 2002, 687–96). Furthermore, in 1920, Turkish nationalists elicited support—gold, weapons,

---

1. On the altogether different discussion of the analytical purchase of the concept of *empire* for studies of Ottoman history, see Barkey 2008. For a theoretical take on what constitutes *relations* as imperial, see Nexon and Wright 2007.

2. These terms were frequently used interchangeably with *Turkey, Turkish Empire, Turquie, l'Empire Turc,* and *Türkei* in their respective languages.

and ammunition—from the Bolsheviks in the struggle against the *imperialist powers*. Not only did it then become easier to claim the right to sovereignty on a basis of the Turkish *nation* than by reference to imperial descent (see chapter 5), but this particular claim allowed the nationalists to solicit material support that would have otherwise been difficult to legitimize to the Bolsheviks.

Endogenous and Exogenous Concepts

Just as words have a particular flavor associated with their history of use, a choice of names and concepts may as readily identify the speaker as describe the object that is spoken of. The Italian city known in English by the name *Naples* is known in Italian as *Napoli*. The former is an *exonym* (a name not used by native speakers), while the latter is an *endonym* (that by which native speakers call the city). They may be different names for the same city, but they are also concepts embedded in different rhetorical traditions. The semantic connotations of *Napoli* in Italian are different from the connotations of *Naples* in English.[3] Differences between closely entangled traditions may not be great, but they nevertheless exist. In the same manner, exogenous and endogenous concepts have diverging conceptual histories and thus different meanings, even though they may be used by the same people.

An interesting case for the entanglement between endogenous Ottoman concepts and exogenous French concepts is Ottoman bank notes, which in the nineteenth century carried the title of the issuing bank in both French and Ottoman. The context in which they were used can hardly be divided into separate French and Ottoman spheres, even though most users likely understood only one of these names and ignored the other. Nevertheless, the two names were entangled through their synonymous use. In French, the issuing authority was called Banque Impériale Ottomane (Ottoman Imperial Bank, 1863–1924) (Eldem 1999). The Ottoman name for the bank was Bānk-ı

3. In a situation where a conversation takes place between an Englishman and an Italian, there would of course be entanglement between the concept of *Naples* and that of *Napoli*, as the Italian would in all likelihood bring to bear his or her own connotations of *Napoli* and imbue *Naples* with some of that meaning. This is again a case of what Gadamer (2004) describes as one language establishing itself as the primary medium of understanding.

'Osmānī-i Şāhāne (most appropriately translated as the Royal Ottoman Bank). *Şāhāne* is an adjective derived from the Persianate title *şāh*, in English typically written *shah*, meaning "shah-like" or "of the shah." The Ottoman state's exogenous self-representation was as *impériale*, but its endogenous self-representation was *şāhāne*. If meaning depends on context, then in the immediate context of the banknote being used, these concepts have more or less the same meaning. Detached from the particular context, the separate conceptual histories of *impériale* and *şāhāne* come into play to a greater extent, thus making them more apt for diverging usages and interpretations.

Conceptual historians' first impulse is to reach for etymologies. However, in the absence of an Ottoman concept of *empire*, a search for what may broadly speaking be called synonyms is a more fruitful pursuit. While a semasiological investigation of a concept traces the changing meaning of individual words, onomasiological investigation traces different words that have previously been used in a similar meaning or in competition for the same meaning (Koselleck 2004, 87). Claims to political legitimacy come in different variants. I do not deal with all of them systematically here; I merely note that rulers make a particular type of legitimacy claim that is based on universalist notions of rule and is not territorially delimited. I call this type of claim, which can come in different forms with or without religious foundations, an *imperial* claim to rule. This way of categorizing particular *legitimacy claims* as imperial differs from calling particular types of *relations* imperial, as do Daniel H. Nexon and Thomas Wright (2007). Imperial claims do not necessarily deploy concepts of *empire* or *imperial*. The context in which a ruler may credibly make such an imperial claim seldom arises, and when it does, it usually depends on a claim to succession to an earlier polity. If no succession can be invoked (or created), imperial claims are likely to fail.[4] The Ottoman dynasty asserted three *translationes imperii* (claims to imperial succession), deployed according to context and audience. The first was to

---

4. Conceptually, the British Empire tied its claim to empire to the fact that the ruler was emperor or empress of India. The British rulers lay claim to a *translatio* from the Mughals, who in turn claimed *translatio* from steppe empires. Claims also need to be tied to military capacity and international prestige and in their absence can fail spectacularly. For example, in 1976 Bokassa declared himself *empereur* of the Empire Centrafricaine, the Central African Empire.

the imperial title of the steppe,[5] often associated with such rulers as Attila (the Hun), Genghis Khan, and Tamerlane. This claim was first taken up by the Ottoman dynasty around the time when the Turko-Mongol conqueror Tamerlane invaded Anatolia in 1402 and the Ottoman dynasty needed to secure its legitimacy vis-à-vis the nomadic tribes who formed the bulk of the Ottoman armies during the early period of its existence (Lowry 2003, 31, 78–79). This *translatio*, and the attendant titles *han* and *hakan*, were used until the fall of the Ottoman dynasty in 1923.

The second claim was the *translatio imperii* from the Roman Empire. It was first included in the dynasty's conceptual repertoire of legitimation after the conquest of Constantinople in 1453 as an attempt to create continuity between the Roman and the Ottoman Empires via the Byzantines (whose empire, in their own discourse, *was* the Roman Empire) (Greene 2015, 49–54; Kafadar 2007). The third claim to *translatio imperii*, which is the best known to Europeans, was that from the caliphate. This built on the historical legend that the last ʿAbbasid caliph had bestowed the caliphate on Sultan Selim I (the Grim) in 1517, when he conquered the Mamluk Sultanate and hence also the ʿAbbasid Caliphate, which had stood under Mamluk "protection." While the legend of actual bestowal does not fit with historical events (Holt 1984, 507), the fact of military conquest remains, and the legend was an important legitimizing claim made by the Ottoman dynasty and its statesmen starting around the time of the Treaty of Küçük Kaynarca in 1774 (Katz 2016, 18).

Sultan Süleyman I (the Magnificent), who is often seen as the embodiment of the so-called Golden Age Era (ca. 1451–1566) of the Ottoman Empire, used all three of these *translationes imperii* in legitimizing his rule (as well as the Persianate title *şah* [*shah*], later to give way to *padişah*).[6] In an inscription at the Castle of Bender (in present-day Moldova), which Süleyman conquered in 1538, he is attributed the following description of himself:

---

5. These come in variants *Hakan, Khagan, Qağan, Khan,* and *Han,* depending on transliteration and tradition of use.

6. While the title *shah* (most frequently in the form *padişah* or, rather, *pādişāh*) was used by the Ottoman dynasty, it was not accompanied by an elaborate mythmaking that sought to draw a lineage back to a Persian origin. Therefore, it does not quite qualify as a *translatio imperii*, as there was no claim to imperial succession to the empires of Iran. See Babinger and Bosworth 2013.

I am the slave/servant of Allah and the Sultan of the realms
of this world
The beloved of my all-compassionate [i.e., Muhammed] has
made me the trustee of Muhammed
Because the grace of God and the miracle of Muhammed are
my companions
I am Süleyman [in whose] name the Friday sermon has been
read in the Holy Places
I run the ships on the seas of Firenk [i.e., the Mediterranean],
Maghreb and India
I am the shah of Baghdad in Iraq, the Kayser of Rum and the
Sultan of Egypt
I am the Sultan who took the golden throne and seat of the
King of Hungary
[And gave] them to a lowly subject of mine
. . . I am the conqueror of the cities of Moldavia
. . . I am Süleyman bin [descendant of] Osman, and made this
castle and wrote history. (Çulpan 1966, 882)

And in a 1526 letter to the French king, Süleyman's wrote,

I am Sultan Süleyman Han, son of Sultan Bayezid Han, son of
Sultan Selim Han, the Sultan of Sultans, ruler of the *hakans*,
bestower of the crowns of monarchs on the face of the Earth,
the shadow of God, the Sultan and Pādişāh of the Mediterranean and the Black Sea, of Rumelia and Anatolia, and Kara-
man and the province of Zulkadir, and of Diyarbakır and Kurd-
istan and Azerbaijan and Damascus and Aleppo and Egypt and
Medina and Jerusalem and all the Arab lands and Yemen and a
lot of other lands, which my noble forefathers and exalted ancestors (may God have mercy upon them) conquered with
their overwhelming power, and which my own noble majesty
has conquered with my flaming sword and my victorious sabre.
(Jouannin 1833 [1526], 4–5)

Sultan Süleyman here uses the concepts *kayser, sultan, han, hakan,*
and *shah* to legitimize his rule. Though he used almost every imperial

title he could credibly use, he did not refer to the Ottoman state as an "empire." Indeed, there is no reference to "the state" at all, only to the ruler and his possessions. It would be tempting to argue that a claim to being a "kayser" implied ruling an empire, as both concepts can be etymologically traced to the Roman Empire (Imperium Romanum), whose ruler was titled *caesar*, from which *kayser* is derived. Moreover, in the fifteenth century, Sultan Mehmed II (the Conqueror) frequently employed the Greek term *basileus*, which was the translation of the Latin *caesar* in the Greek-speaking half of the Roman Empire (where the empire was called "Ἡ Ῥωμαίων βασιλεία" [hē rōmaiōn basileia]) (İnalcık 1994, 26). None of these titles, however, appear in Süleyman's honorifics, and the titles do not seem to have been linked to a concept of *empire*; rather, they were prestigious titles in and of themselves.

Concepts of State

Not only was the Ottoman polity not called the Osmanlı İmparatorluğu, as it is today, but no single institutionalized and generalized Ottoman concept captured the state, the collective subjects, and the territory. Different aspects of the state-population-territory tripod later known by the unified concept Osmanlı İmparatorluğu were known as Devlet-i ʿAlīye-i ʿOsmānīye (the Exalted Ottoman State/Dynasty) or Āl-i ʿOsmān (the Family/Dynasty of Osman), *tebaʿa* (subjects/flock), and Memālik-i Maḥrūse (the Well-Protected Domains), respectively. The meaning of these concepts shifted over time, and there were a number of overlapping and competing concepts as well as *hendiadys* and *tautologies*.

In accordance with the importance that the Ottomans placed on poetic flourish and erudition for claiming social prestige, they referred to the state and the sultan's realms by use of a variety of concepts that had partially overlapping meanings. Devlet-i ʿAlīye and Memālik-i Maḥrūse were the most frequently used (Deringil 1998). Another central concept was *dīn ü devlet* (religion-and-state/dynasty). In the earlier centuries, the Ottoman dynasty was for the most part called the Āl-i ʿOsmān, which was replaced by the Devlet-i ʿOsmānīye (the Ottoman State/dynasty; *devlet* can be translated as both state and dynasty) around 1876 (Findley 2005, 72). Furthermore, the state was also called the Devlet-i Ebed-Müddet (the State/Dynasty of Eternal Duration or simply the Eternal State/Dynasty).

All of these concepts seem to imply that claims to legitimacy in Ottoman state discourse were all about the ruler, the dynasty, and his or their possessions.[7] As Marinos Sariyannis (2013, 96–97) writes,

> It was Rifaat Abou-El-Haj who first stressed that the term *devlet* had neither "the connotation [nor] the denotation of the modern nation-state" but rather (conveying a definition by Andreas Tietze) meant up to the seventeenth century "the decision-making power of the legitimate head of state as well as to whom he had delegated this power." Recently Nikos Sigalas studied the semantic development of the word, showing that it only acquired the modern sense of "state" toward the end of the seventeenth century. Following his analysis, the term (which started its political career, so to speak, in the Abbasid period with the sense of "luck, good fortune") meant clearly "power" or "dynasty," with strong overtones of "divine favor," in the text of Aşıkpaşazade, for instance, and it continued to be structured around the divine charisma of the ruler throughout the sixteenth century. Sigalas finds that in Mustafa Ali's texts, almost a century later, the *devlet* is a power particular to the Prince or Sultan, which cannot in any way be delegated; in contrast, from the beginnings of the eighteenth century onwards (more or less just after the Treaty of Karlowits, which marked the first official recognition of a loss of Ottoman territory), the use of the term *devlet* for other states of Europe marks the "desacralization" of its notion.

A closer inspection of the use of the term *devlet* seems to corroborate Sigala's conclusions. In fifteenth-century texts "state" (in our sense of the word) is usually rendered as *saltanat*, and always with a highly personal connotation, as identified with the ruler's household and palace.

---

7. This is not at all unique: Great Britain, for example, still has "God Save the Queen" as its national anthem, a remnant of a similar way of privileging the ruler.

Differentiating between the dynasty and the state and using *devlet* for European states was an important development. The latter came about with the emergence of more entangled language games in which the Ottomans were increasingly recognizing European states as peers and with increasing differentiation of the Ottoman scribal service into what may somewhat anachronistically be called a bureaucracy. Sariyannis's point should not be read as an argument for a radical break; when used in the context of the Ottoman *devlet*, the concept still smacked of its association with the Ottoman dynasty until the end of the Ottoman polity.

There is a much stronger case for arguing that the concept of Osmanlı İmparatorluğu either did not exist in the Ottoman language or was relatively unimportant prior to the establishment of the Turkish Republic, than the case for arguing that a translation equivalent of the more generic concept of *empire* was entirely absent. It is also much easier to search the relevant sources. There are a number of examples in which names other than Osmanlı İmparatorluğu were used for the Ottoman state. It is more difficult to comment on the absence of a generic concept of *empire*, as it is not clear where to look. Moreover, since translation equivalents are not always calques or loanwords, it is not even certain what to look for. A cursory search of the Prime Ministry Archives (Başbakanlık Osmanlı Arşivleri) in Istanbul indicates that to the very limited extent that *imparatorluk* was used in the nineteenth century, it was primarily in relation to European polities such as Napoleon's France and tsarist Russia as well as to Japan.[8]

In an 1829 Ottoman translation of a French history work on Empress Catherine II of Russia, the Ottoman translator explains the concept *empéreur* by the digression "the meaning of the word *imparator* is to say *emir*." He then gives a history of the word before explaining that "the word *kıral* [king] has become the term for

8. See, for example, Başbakanlık Osmanlı Arşivleri (Prime Ministry Ottoman Archives), İstanbul. Hatt-ı Hümayūn Tasnifi, 31, 1483, 29 Muharrem 1218 [21 May 1803] and Başbakanlık Osmanlı Arşivleri (Prime Ministry Ottoman Archives), Istanbul. Hatt-ı Hümayūn Tasnifi 31 1448F, 18 Muharrem 1220 [18 April 1805]. Renée Worringer (2001, 167) also references an 1897 newspaper article, "Devlet-i 'Alīye-i 'Osmānīye ve Jāponyā İmparāṭōrluğu," in which the concept of *imparatorluk* was used, but not in reference to the Ottoman polity [*Mālūmat* 1897]. Ottoman statesman Sadık Rıfat Paşa used the more Arabic-sounding *imparatoriye* in a 1834 letter from Paris (Baysun 1941, 33).

melik [ruler], while *imparator* has become the term for *melik ül-müluk* [ruler of rulers]" (Strauss 1989, 253) This is exactly the kind of paratext that is introduced by a translator to adhere to what Derrida identified as the qualitative requirement of translation. It furthermore indicates that there was no established Ottoman translation equivalent for the French *empéreur* at this time and that the translator could not assume that Ottoman readers would understand the French word. Furthermore, Ottoman had no established concept that could be used in a similar way as the French. This example not only illustrates the relatively unentangled situation but is in fact itself an instance a conceptual entanglement that establishes a relationship between a French concept and possible Ottoman translations, and introduces the loanword *imparator* into the Ottoman language game by reference to *melik ül-müluk* and *emir.*

It is clear that *imparator* was not an important concept in Ottoman. Although the absence of a concept can never be fully illustrated, a brief excerpt from a late-nineteenth-century text discussing the Ottoman sultan, dynasty, and polity would likely have used *imparatorluk* (empire) or indeed *imparator* (emperor) if these concepts were necessary for Ottoman authors when discussing matters of state:

> The august person the *pādişāh* is heir to the noble dynasty, which the Ottoman family established by protecting religion. It was thanks to this fact that they became the cynosure of the people and the caliph of Islam. (Nāmık Kemāl 1327 [1911], 173; originally published in 1869)

This excerpt also raises the issue of semantic reconfiguration between the Ottoman original and my translation, since my translation smooths over the fact that nineteenth-century Ottoman vocabulary and twenty-first-century English vocabulary fundamentally differ.

L'Empire Turc

The concept *imparatorluk* gained currency in Turkish in the twentieth century through a complex process of entanglement and international political contestation. The Empire Ottoman first appeared as an exogenous concept—an external, French designation for the Ottoman polity, but one that Ottoman statesmen engaged in discursive struggles over; then it became part of the Ottoman language as Ottomans carried across some of that meaning, expanding their repertoires of legitimacy claims by translating from French. This process brought with it an increasing semantic convergence between French and Ottoman meaning through a series of entanglements made possible by the Turkish nation-state's claim to a "modern" if not necessarily "Western" identity. This claim was made primarily through delineation vis-à-vis "Eastern," "backward," and "disorderly" populations to Turkey's east and south and vis-à-vis Istanbul-based "old" and "Eastern" competitors to the Ankara-based Turkish leadership.

Sixteenth-century French writers usually referred to the Ottoman sultan as *le Turc, le Grand Turc,* or *le Sultan.*[9] In 1544, French explorer Jean Alfonse wrote that Cyprus was a "seigniory of Venice, which is a tributary of 'le grand Turc'" (Alfonse 1559, 46 recto). Concepts for the Ottoman polity are not used—merely the ruler of the polity. This depiction contrasts with the Ottoman texts from the same era, where Sultan Süleyman enumerates his titles (which in the absence of a conventionalized single concept of the Ottoman Empire constitutes the endogenous concept for the head of the polity). *Le Grand Turc* was an exogenous French concept, while the long list of terms that would probably be shortened to *padişah* in less formal circumstances constitutes the endogenous concept. The lack of reference to an Ottoman *state* in the French texts of the time is probably connected with the simple fact that the concept of state (*état*) as separate from the ruler had not emerged in that meaning in French at the time, just as it in Ottoman had no clear meaning detached from that of "dynasty" (Skinner 2009).

In the Ottoman case, "the Porte" or "the Sublime Porte" often appears as a conventionalized English shorthand for the Ottoman

---

9. See, e.g., J. Marot (1977 [1526], 41), who lists "le Turc" alongside popes and kings, using it more like a title than an ethnicity or political collective. For other examples, see C. Marot 2005 [1538], 204; Alfonse 1559, 44 recto–47 recto. For "le Sultan," see, e.g., Balzac 1631, 327; Le Moyne 1653, 10 (book 1); Tristan L'Hermite 1975, 775, 794. Maréchal (1971, 128, act 2, scene 3) lists "le Sultan" as one ruler among "l'Empereur, et les plus grands Monarques."

government. In 1577, the *court* of the sultan is mentioned in a book on the demise of "l'Empire Grec" (the Greek [i.e., Byzantine] Empire) as "the porte (thus they call the Court of the Turk)" (Chalcondyle 1577, book 2, chapter 1, p. 78). This is a reference to the endogenous Bāb-ı ʿĀlī (sublime/exalted gate/porte, the Ottoman name for the Ottoman privy council) being *calqued* by the French into *porte*. It was probably translated into English from French or Italian and has become conventionalized to the extent that Ottomanist scholars now speak of the Ottoman government, or rather the office of the Grand Vizier, as the Sublime Porte. *Ottoman* and *L'Empire Ottoman* appeared in French during the seventeenth century (see Racine 1886, 496; Fontaine 1991, 386; Robert and Rey 2001, book 6 [Lim–Oz], 1014), but they probably did not become conventionalized as French concepts for the Ottomans and their polity until the 1730s.[10] In English, the main name for the Ottoman polity seems to have been *Turkey*, although it was not uncommon to use *Turkey* and the *Turkish Empire* interchangeably throughout the nineteenth century.

The Emergence of France as a Reference Society

Ottoman-using elites had long prized knowledge of Arabic and Persian and could avail themselves freely of commonplaces in these languages. This was mostly a semipermeable boundary between traditions, whereby Ottomans could use Arabic concepts without necessarily partaking in the Arabic or Persian joint action and changing these traditions yet could expect Ottoman listeners or readers to interpret these statements in a way that drew heavily on shared meaning. In short, an Arabic concept used in an otherwise Ottoman language game did not necessarily change meaning in the Arabic language game, while the use of the Arabic concept could change once it had become part of Ottoman.

In the late nineteenth century, French increasingly became a similar source of "outside" resources and tools that could be used in Ottoman. Johann Strauss (2003, 42) has argued that French even attained the status of a semiofficial language in the Ottoman Empire,

---

10. For the 1730s, it seems to start with Jean-Baptiste Dubos *Histoire Critique de l'établissement de la monarchie françoise dans les Gaules*, (1742 [1734]) and Jean-Baptiste D'Argens *Lettres juives ou Correspondance philosophique, historique et critique* (1738).

used between educated speakers of different linguistic communities. This was a relatively new phenomenon. Knowledge of French or other languages spoken in Europe beyond the Balkans was more or less nonexistent among the Ottoman state elite until the early nineteenth century. When a course was instituted at the Ottoman school of mathematics for the navy in 1784, French instructors taught cadets via Armenian interpreters. The cadets were not obliged to learn French. In 1792, Sultan Selim III instituted new military and navy academies, to which French officers were recruited and where learning French became a requirement for all students. The choice of French as the first and main foreign language Ottoman officers should learn had to do with the traditionally good relations between the Ottoman Empire and France (which had been allied against the Habsburgs on and off since 1536) and with the rising status of French as an important language of European diplomacy.

The Ottoman court rarely sent its own representatives as envoys to other polities and to a great extent relied on renegades and couriers for letter exchanges (Kürkçüoğlu 2004; Gürkan 2015). For the production of the letters that constituted their main interaction with European polities, the Ottomans traditionally depended on dragomans (translators) and rarely learned European languages.[11] European ambassadors residing in Istanbul also for the most part communicated via dragomans, allowing them to more or less monopolize the actual practice of direct interlingual relations with other polities. When the Ottomans established their first resident ambassadors in London, Berlin, Vienna, and Paris in the 1790s, the ambassadors took with them "young secretaries, whose duty it was to study the languages of Europe—and especially French—and to learn something about the ways of Western society" (B. Lewis 1953, 112). Thus, when these individuals started returning to Istanbul around 1800, Ottoman diplomacy had only a handful of statesmen proficient in French and with some acquaintance with European high society.

After the declaration of an independent Greek state in 1822, the Ottoman state removed Greek Orthodox dragomans from service

---

11. Many statesmen were multilingual, knowing a combination of Albanian, Georgian, Greek, Arabic, Armenian, Kurdish, Persian, and Slavic languages. None of these languages, however, were particularly well suited to communicating with people beyond the immediate frontiers of the Ottoman Empire and certainly not with elites in Western Europe.

(part of the process discussed in chapter 3) and established a Ter-cüme Odası (Translation Bureau) manned by Ottoman Muslims. Along with the 1820 establishment of the Medical School (Tıbbiye) in Galatasaray (Galata Palace), where French was taught, the systematic efforts at training the Ottoman Muslim elite in European languages were expanded to include statesmen and the civilian elite as well as military officers (B. Lewis 1961, 85). In 1868 the school at Galatasaray was reestablished as a French-language high school, now known as the Galatasaray Lisesi. Staffed by French teachers, this institution started producing a Muslim Ottoman intelligentsia that was knowl-edgeable in French and that had received an education independent of the religious establishment.

Although all layers of Ottoman society, if not all individuals, were to some extent polyglot, knowledge of French was almost uniquely the preserve of the administrative elite, officers, and merchants whose networks stretched westward, most of them Christian or Jew-ish. The social and intellectual importance of the French-proficient Ottoman elite outstripped their small number. Many members of this elite were either journalists and authors or involved in running the state, or both. This made them important interlocutors in this inter-lingual game. Their readings in and knowledge of French became part of how they conducted their affairs as statesmen, thus making French conceptual tools part of state practice (see Çiçek 2010).

The heavy predominance of French texts as sources for Ottoman translations in all fields apart from religion indicates the French lan-guage's importance in the late Ottoman Empire. While French was still the preserve of a select few, proficiency in Persian and Arabic was the norm for all educated Ottomans until those languages were re-moved from secondary school curricula in 1928. Since Persian and Arabic texts were accessible to Ottomans without translation, the greater number of French translations does not demonstrate that French was more important than Persian and Arabic. Nevertheless, 59 percent of all translated books published in the Ottoman lan-guage between 1729 and 1875 had French as a source language, while English and German represented 7 percent and 5 percent, respec-tively (Berk 1999, 21). Even though percentages do not necessarily correlate with importance, it seems likely that at least until the 1880s,

French was more important than any other European language and quite possibly as important as all other European languages combined. As Bernard Lewis (1953, 111) puts it:

> The result of all this was to create a new social element [in the Ottoman Empire] familiar with some aspects of Western civilisation through study, reading, and personal contact, acquainted with at least one Western language—usually French.

Whether or not his description of a "new social element" is apt, the fact remains that at the margins of the state elite there emerged a set of individuals who were tasked as interlocutors with European counterparts using the French language. Whether France can be called a "reference society" for the Ottoman elite is not entirely clear. What is clear is that these statesmen used French to engage in dialogues beyond the Ottoman polity, and most of their engagements with European writings occurred in French. In a sense, French became a means for exploring the world beyond one's immediate environment.

While the scholarly literature on how Ottoman intellectuals debated the Ottoman and Turkish language and judged its merits against the French is quite voluminous, the literature on how they *used* French in combination with Ottoman is not (B. Lewis 1961; Moran 1977; Berkes 1998; Mardin 2000 [1962]). In most of the major languages in the Ottoman Empire, diglossia was the norm—each language had a spoken vernacular form and a written high language often associated with religion (Strauss 2003, 42). This practice excluded a great many language users from their respective written languages, not only because they did not have the specific skill of reading and writing but because the vocabulary and grammar used in written language were largely unrecognizable without a proper education. As was argued at the time and is commonly repeated today, diglossia detached the intellectual elite from the rest of society (Strauss 1995). The elites' emerging ability to engage in dialogue with French sources and French-speaking individuals further reinforced this tendency and to some extent set them apart from those intellectuals within their respective language communities who did not know French.

Temporally Othering the Empire

Much of the Ottoman/French conceptual entanglement in the nine-teenth century involved Ottomans relating to European Orientalist discourse. This discourse was typically used by a European subject speaking both *about* and *for* "the Orient" and "the Oriental" and thus also about "the Ottoman" (Said 1978; I. B. Neumann 1999, 39–63). This was a type of objectification that muted *the Orientals* as speaking and acting individuals. Ottoman engagement in such language games can to some extent be seen as a contradiction in terms. The Otto-mans employed three main strategies for managing their stigma as Orientals in this type of linguistic situation (comp. Zarakol 2011). The first, "self-Orientalization," implies the acceptance of Western Orientalist representations of the Oriental Other as *true* and thus as a fair description of who "we" are (Kirecci 2007, 26–27). Such an ac-ceptance comes with the implication that "we" have to change. Sec-ond, the strategy of speaking back is exemplified by how intellectuals Namık Kemal and Jamaladdin al-Afghani defended *Islam* against the accusations put forward in French scholar Ernest Renan's 1883 lec-ture, "Science and Islam." This strategy entailed telling Europeans that they were misrepresenting "us." The third strategy, "passing the buck," involves appropriating the discourse but finding someone "more Eastern" or "more traditional" and constituting oneself as *modern* and in some cases *Western* by comparison (see Neumann 1999, esp. 183–206). So rather than accepting that *I* am "Oriental," this strategy entails the appropriation of the Orientalist discourse to dis-tinguish oneself from others in the same society, on its "eastern" mar-gins, and further east. This strategy did not dispel the stigma from the Self but reproduced it in relationships first between groups within the Ottoman Empire and later within the Republic of Turkey.

While the first two strategies have generally received the most at-tention in the literature, the third strategy came to dominate how the late Ottoman elite legitimized their position not only vis-à-vis Euro-pean audiences but also within the Ottoman elite itself. The basic setup was to differentiate an Ottoman metropolitan Self that was *or-derly, civilized,* and *modern* from Ottoman peripheral Others: Arabs (basically Bedouins) and Turks (country bumpkins and nomads), who were *disorderly, barbarous,* and *backward* (Herzog and Motika

2000; Deringil 2003, 311–12; Reinkowski 2005). As Ussama Makdisi (2002, 768) explains, "In an age of Western-dominated modernity, every nation creates its own Orient. The nineteenth-century Ottoman Empire was no exception."

> [T]he Ottoman elite conflated the ideas of modernity and colonialism, and applied the latter as a means of survival against an increasingly hostile world: "Within its remaining territories, the Ottoman state began imitating the western colonial empires. The state consolidated the homogeneity of the core region, i.e.—the Anatolian peninsula and the eastern regions of Thrace . . . even as it pushed the periphery—principally the Arab provinces—into a colonial status." (Deringil 2003, 312)

Exogenous claims to *empire* had to be anchored in practices that were used to anchor *empire* in French and English discourse, and an important part of this process involved having colonies and a civilizing project (Deringil 1998; Minawi 2016; for anchoring practices, see Swidler 2001). Civilizing the Ottoman hinterland also involved reifying it as an object toward which metropolitan Ottoman goodwill and governmental efforts were directed. By doing so, it was constituted as different from the metropolitan Self. The periphery was already an important opposite to the metropole in the Khaldūnian setup, although in that conceptual pair, the two elements of humanity were in a more symbiotic relationship. The nomads were not represented through negative stereotypes, and the center's main relationship with the periphery was one of a duty to protect it against external encroachment. What was new about the Othering that was translated from French was the form it took. With the translation of European Orientalist discourse, the relationship between center and periphery was structured in a very particular manner, much in the same way as that between "old" and "new" parts of towns in Timothy Mitchell's *Colonising Egypt* (1991). The nomads on the Ottoman periphery, who had previously been represented as brave, well-organized yet uncouth, moral, and so on, were now represented as disorderly, fanatical, backward.

After what later became known as the 1908 Young Turk Revolution, the dichotomy between old and new was given a particular political slant: the old was discursively tied to despotism (*istibdād*) or oppression (*ẓulm*) and the new was tied to liberty (*hürriyet*). The 1908 revolution was in fact known at the time as the İlan-ı Hürriyet (the Declaration of Liberty). These dichotomies of old/new and despotism/liberty were then used to give meaning to the difference between Sultan Abdülhamid II and the Committee for Union and Progress, whereby state intellectuals associated the Committee with all that was positive and Abdülhamid's regime with all that was negative (Brummett 2000). From the Constitutional Revolution of 1908 until the Arab Revolt of 1917, these dichotomies were tied to qualities that had newly been ascribed to the relationship between Ottoman center and periphery, civilized and barbarian. Moreover, these dichotomies were in Ottoman discourse increasingly linked with a dichotomy of Turks versus Arabs, where the Arabs were ascribed the string of negative qualities inherent in the Orientalist discourse: backward, corrupt, Eastern, uncivilized, and so forth. The essential difference between Arabs and Turks became established in discourse, and the two identity concepts were increasingly constituted in opposition to one another during the 1910s and 1920s (Kayalı 1997).

Arguments for securing the survival of the nation by "returning" to some essential core of Turkishness—what may be interpreted as an argument for becoming a nation-state—engaged with many of these concepts. Writing in 1913 under the pen name Habil Adem, Ottoman author Naci İsmail employs a translated conceptual apparatus for analyzing Ottoman history and society. By claiming that his text was in fact the translation of something written by an Englishman, Naci İsmail argues that the Ottoman elite should consolidate the state's attention on the "true nation" consisting of Turks: "Turkey in Anatolia" (*Anadolu'da Türkiye*) (Aksakal 2004, 519). He explains this by saying that intermingling with non-Turks had caused the Turkish *race*'s plight. In a manner that sets up some of the discursive preconditions for a Turkish nation-state, he divides the Ottoman Empire into "the real Turkey and colonial Turkey (*hakiki Türkiye* and *müstemleke Türkiyesi*, respectively)" (519) and returned to his argument that Turkey must free itself of its *colonies*, which were only a drain on the state's resources.

Becoming a nation-state is as much about writing a history of the past in a certain way and Othering or erasing other parts of the past as about imagining a future collectively as a nation. In the Turkish case, becoming a nation-state was to some extent about Othering the Ottoman Empire and its leaders while celebrating a pre-Ottoman Turkic past. This rearrangement of narratives was used to legitimize the renegotiation of the polity's position vis-à-vis Europe as well as to marginalize certain institutions and leadership rivals. Such representations gained importance in the discourse of the Kemalist Republic during the 1930s (see chapter 5).

Turkey the Ottoman Empire

When the Ottoman state surrendered to the Entente powers in 1918, the international political and discursive context was shifting. The end of the First World War changed international (European) discourses in three ways. First, the Russian Revolution of 1917 involved increased struggle over concepts of *people*, which became major battle concepts for the revolutionaries. The Treaty of Brest-Litovsk had given the tsar's former lands in Eastern Europe independence on the basis of *national sovereignty*. Boundaries were being redrawn, with European *empires* dismantled and their remnants made into nation-states and republics. Furthermore, Woodrow Wilson's Fourteen Points tied political legitimacy to the concepts of the *nation* and the *people* while delegitimizing *empire*. According to Point 12,

> The Turkish portions of the present Ottoman Empire should be assured a secure sovereignty, but the other nationalities which are now under Turkish rule should be assured an undoubted security of life and an absolutely unmolested opportunity of autonomous development.[12]

The Fourteen Points use *nation* and *people* interchangeably and assert that the Americans "feel ourselves to be intimate partners of all the governments and *peoples* associated together against the *Imperialists*" (emphasis added). Here, we see the delegitimation of *imperialism* as a rhetorical commonplace that can be used to claim legitimacy in in-

---

12. President Wilson's Message to Congress, January 8, 1918; Records of the United States Senate; Record Group 46; Records of the United States Senate; National Archives. https://www.ourdocuments.gov/doc.php?flash=false&doc=62# (accessed 26 Jan. 2018).

ternational society language games. To successfully claim to be a *nation* and a *people*, the elite of the nascent Turkish Republic had to distance themselves from the concept of *empire*.

The political claims formulated by the use of *halk* (people) and *millet* (people/nation/congregation) emerged in what the Turks have called the War of Independence (İstiklal Harbı) or National Struggle (Millî Mücadele). The power struggles between the elite in Ankara and those in Istanbul during the National Struggle were embedded in the wider international context. A key part of this context was obviously the recently concluded First World War (or the Great War, as it was then known in English), its stated objectives, and the meaning that its protagonists gave it. Part of the legitimizing argument that the Entente governments gave President Wilson for a U.S. entry into the war was the dismemberment of the Ottoman Empire:

> "The Entente objects of the war are well known," they insisted, and then went on to list the points that "the civilized world knows that they imply." Among these were "the enfranchisement of populations subject to the tyranny of the Turks" and "the expulsion from Europe of the Ottoman Empire, decidedly alien to Western civilization." (Katz 2016, 1)

The Fourteen Points were later proclaimed in this context, becoming both the foundation for the postwar international order based on "national sovereignty" and a key legitimation for Armenians', Greeks', and Kurds' territorial claims in Anatolia. Intertwined with the military struggle in Anatolia was the rhetorical contestation over the definition of the "Turkish portion of the present Ottoman Empire." Now, if the Turks were a *people*, they could still claim, according to the Fourteen Points, "absolutely unmolested opportunity of autonomous development," language that was taken to mean rights of national self-determination. Moreover, the opposition between "governments and peoples" on the one hand and the "Imperialists" on the other was particularly productive when it was translated into the Turkish language because it could easily be used to legitimize the (Ankara-based) nationalists' rule in the power struggle with the Ottoman dynasty in Istanbul and its entourage. If *empires* and *imperialists* were the constitutive Other of this new international order, surely a Turkish *people* would have better chances of international legitimacy and thus survival as a political unit.

This process delegitimized certain parts of the Ottoman elite, thereby strengthening the hand of the part of the elite leading the "National Struggle" from Ankara. This is how the Turkish Republic came to use the Ottoman Empire qua empire as a constitutive Other. The Ankara elite seized the discursive high ground by physically retreating to what had recently been represented as *hakikî Türkiye* (real Turkey) in Anatolia and fighting against those who were represented as imperialist great powers and infidels.[13] It consolidated power by representing the individuals immediately close to the sultan in Istanbul as corrupt, Eastern, cosmopolitan, imperialist, and ultimately responsible for the polity's economic decline and military collapse. Such legitimacy struggles were part and parcel of what came to be known as the Turkish War of Independence or the National Struggle.

The current conceptual relationship between Osmanlı İmparatorluğu and Türkiye was established around the time when what in English is called "the sultanate" was abolished.[14] Osmanlı İmparatorluğu came into use as a name for the *past* incarnation of the polity that the Ankara-based elite was claiming to rule. During the first three years that the Grand National Assembly met (1919–22), the concept of Osmanlı İmparatorluğu was hardly used in the debates. The few times it *was* mentioned, the emphasis was not on the concept of *empire*. The phrase appears three times in the transcripts of the Turkish Grand National Assembly for 1920 but not at all in 1921. In two of those three instances, the specific usage was "Türkiye Osmanlı İmparatorluğu" (Turkey 1336 [1920]a, 14). It was not Turkey *or* the Ottoman Empire; it was "Turkey the Ottoman Empire." We here see a case of the *tautologies* that were ubiquitous in Ottoman political writing. The two were one and the same (Turkey 1336 [1920]a, 14; Turkey 1336 [1920]b, 118).

This particular combination of concepts may be seen as an indi-

---

13. Ankara was particularly well suited for a defensive war, out of reach of most seaborne invading forces and centrally located to direct battles on multiple fronts given its railway connections and geographic position.

14. While in English *sultanate* is commonly used to mean "rule by a sultan" and tied to a specific kind of Islamic monarchic tradition, in Ottoman *saltanat* had more generic qualities, and could also be used to mean *sovereignty* or *rule*.

cation that there was no clear-cut distinction between Türkiye and Osmanlı İmparatorluğu. The concept of "Turkey" (Türkiye) did not at this point take its meaning by differentiation from the "Ottoman Empire" in the same way it did only a few years later. Moreover, this phenomenon attests to a political maneuvering that was necessitated by a duality in political legitimacy—the nationalists were explicitly fighting to save the *vatan* (fatherland) and *millet*. In the conceptual apparatus of the time, the *devlet* was the protector of both. Whatever the statesmen "intended" to mean by *devlet*, they spoke into a rhetorical tradition in which *devlet* still smacked of dynasty. Saving the nation meant saving the state, and to claim to be saving the state without at the same time arguing for saving the dynasty required further shifting the rhetorical commonplace.

After being used in compound with other concepts for the first few years of the meetings of the Grand National Assembly (Büyük Millet Meclisi), Türkiye became differentiated from Devlet-i ʿAlīye and Devlet-i ʿOsmānīye at approximately the same time as the concept of Osmanlı İmparatorluğu emerged. In terms of official political discourse, a 1922 debate in the Grand National Assembly on the previous year's Law of Constitutional Organization seems to have been an important moment in distinguishing between the two:

> Therefore, from [the proclamation of the Law of Constitutional Organization], the old Ottoman Empire [Osmanlı İmparatorluğu] was assigned to history and in its place a new and national State of Turkey [Türkiye Devleti] [was established], actually from that time imperial rule [*padişahlık*] was abolished and the Turkish Grand National Assembly [Türkiye Büyük Millet Meclisi] took its place. (Turkey 1338 [1922], 313)

Conclusion

As the Ottoman polity became ever more engaged in a dialogical relationship with European polities through European involvement in the Eastern Question, Ottoman statesmen started establishing translation equivalents for European concepts. In the nineteenth century, the French name of L'Empire Ottoman prevailed as an external self-representation, but there was no perfectly corresponding concept in Ottoman.

With an increasing number of people becoming bilingual in Ottoman and French through the nineteenth century and more texts being translated from French into Ottoman, concepts were established as conventionalized translation equivalents. Through such processes, the Ottoman language became increasingly entangled with French and thus also more conceptually compatible with it. While this process of entanglement is important, as Jörn Leonhard (2013, 5) points out,

> There is rarely a deeper reflection on the diachronic change and synchronic variety of meanings which stand behind different uses of "empire" and imperial pasts: "imperium" is not "empire" in English is not "empire" in French is not "Reich."

Nor is the Turkish concept *imparatorluk* precisely synonymous with these. Moreover, it is important to avoid jumping from an onomasiological investigation to a semasiological conclusion. That is, just because one may analytically argue that the Ottoman Empire *was* an empire, one should not blindly translate the concepts the Ottomans used to describe their polity as *empire*. As European exogenous concepts relating to the Ottoman Empire became translated into Ottoman, Turkish Republican discourse started detaching "modern" Turkey from the "backward" Ottoman Empire in terms of temporality and "Western" Turkey from the "Eastern" Ottoman Empire in terms of geography. Osmanlı İmparatorluğu is primarily meaningful in the Turkish language as a counterconcept to a Turkish nation-state—in historical fact the Türkiye Cumhuriyeti.

FIVE

Citizenship

This chapter explores the constitution, homogenization, and disciplining of parts of the subject population of the Ottoman state into an entity onto which politics is inscribed and, in time, an audience to whom policy is legitimized. Where chapter 4 dealt primarily with the legitimacy aspects of the use of *empire* and *nation* in entangled language games, I here deal with how concepts were used as tools to reconfigure social relations and how this reconfiguration was used to anchor claims to legitimacy as a Turkish nation-state. I do so by integrating conceptual history with an analysis of the processes of migration and what is euphemistically called "demographic engineering"—massacres, expulsions, and population exchanges—that resulted in the present ethnic and religious composition of the nation-state of Turkey and its neighbors. This chapter shows how the historical taxonomies categorizing the population into Muslim, Greek Orthodox, Armenian, and so forth on the basis of religion have shaped and stabilized social relations and in the process laid the foundation for possible conceptual use and interpretation of *vatandaş* (citizen) in the Turkish Republic. Furthermore, this chapter shows how particular concepts shaped social relations and how the stabilization of this new social configuration shaped the future meaning of these concepts.

During the legitimacy crisis that marked the passage from Ottoman imperial polity to Turkish nation-state, the boundaries of appropriate concept use narrowed significantly. At stake was survival, both individual and collective. The narrowed usage laid down the terms for the practices of inclusion and exclusion that marked the boundaries of the new Turkish nation-state. The concepts were used as tools to delineate who was permitted to live, who was left to die, and who was actively killed; who was included in the Turkish nation-state, who was expelled to Greece, and who was deported from Anatolia to Syria. The earlier principle of segmenting the Ottoman population according to religion, without an expectation that the subjects were to share the religion of the ruler or inhabit religiously homogenous areas, came under increasing pressure. Starting in the seventeenth century, the neighboring states increasingly organized themselves according to principles such as *cuius regio, eius religio*. Although it is possible to question the extent to which this principle was practiced, in theory, the religion of the ruler should also be the religion of the ruled. Beginning in the nineteenth century, secessionist movements that defined themselves by religious affiliation and claimed to act on behalf of *millets* started emerging in the Ottoman Empire (F. F. Anscombe 2014). This was partly a consequence of Ottoman policies that ruled religious communities autonomously through their "internal" hierarchies, a process that strengthened those hierarchies and cemented group cohesion by making religion the prime identity marker in relations between subject and state. As the *millets* gained secessionist aspirations and established states with support from one or more of the Great Powers, the Ottoman state became increasingly distrustful of the remaining religious minorities.

When the Turkish Republic was established in 1923, its population had already gone through a two-century-long process of homogenization of populations based on religious affiliation. This process culminated in the population exchange with Greece in 1923–27. Given this situation, it is not surprising that religion retained a social role even after the governing Republican People's Party became nominally secular in 1931 and the state did so in 1937. Herein lies a paradox. A secular state should in principle be blind to religious distinctions, but religion nevertheless became an important social marker in the new Turkey and remains so today. Religious affiliation was until recently indicated on all identity papers, and at birth, Turks automatically assume the same religion as their fathers (Çağaptay 2006, 65–81).

Religious affiliation is a public matter in Turkey, even though religious practice is supposed to be private. Although how the state relates to religious practice has often breached this principle, especially over the past decade, this is an important distinction. At least in principle, the state does not interfere in whether one practices the religion one belongs to; nevertheless, there is no category for "nonpracticing," "agnostic," or "atheist" in state documents. Soner Çağaptay (2006, 83, 92, but see 75–77 for more complexity) argues that the Turkish state considers religious affiliation an inherited trait, so that converts to Islam continue to be categorized according to their fathers' religion when it comes to matters of state security (although women are less important in these matters, since the principle of patrilinearity is strongly institutionalized). The main issue for the state is whether the members of one's family were categorized as loyal Muslims at the time of the collapse of the Ottoman Empire.

Until the early twentieth century, the Ottoman state and its functionaries dealt with the majority of the population by use of concepts that denoted explicitly hierarchical relations, such as *teba'a* (subjects; singular, *tābi'*) and *re'āyā* (flock). Following the establishment of the Turkish Republic, the population was known primarily as *vatandaş* (citizen), *halk* (people), and *millet*.[1] While the first two were relatively new, the concept of *millet* had a long history in Ottoman, and was also used to delineate the boundary between the Turkish nation-state's inside and its outside.

A three-pronged transformation occurred. First, the population was homogenized according to religious affiliation through practices of demographic engineering. Second, the religiously homogenized subjects were disciplined into *makbul vatandaş* (accepted, or perhaps rather proper, citizens). Finally, they became legally equal in their relationships with the state and with one another. These developments did not occur sequentially but temporally parallel and with overlaps. However, I separate them for the purposes of analysis. All three aspects of this transformation happened through entanglements with European concepts of *citizenship* (most importantly *citoyen*, *citizen*, and *Bürger*) and *nation* (primarily the French *nation* and the German *Nation* and *Volk*). Despite these entanglements, however,

---

1. A number of competing concepts have also been used. One is *ulus*, which translates almost exclusively the French conceptual usages of *nation* based on loyalty to a state; others include *soy* (stock); *ırk* (race); and *milliyet*, which is derived from *millet* but has less emphasis on religious connotations and is probably closer to a German concept of *Nation* linked to *Kultur* and *Geist*.

Turkish concept usage retained a significant degree of context-specific meaning. Subjects who were not part of the "Turkish *millet*" could never be properly Turkish regardless of how they acted. Moreover, a person who was part of the *millet* had to act as a *makbul vatandaş* to be accepted as an integral part of the body politic. As analyzed by Füsun Üstel (2004, 69), a key element of the disciplining effort that sought to create *makbul vatandaş* was the civic education course instituted in Ottoman schools immediately after the 1908 Constitutional Revolution. The authors of the books used in these courses drew strongly on the French body of literature that sought to replace religion as the main social bond with a bond based on civic education that instilled *patriotisme*. While the movement of people between the late nineteenth century and the 1920s relied on quite narrow interpretations of *millet* as religious affiliation, the education of the *teba'a* into *vatandaş* relied on a concept of citizenship that retained a much more complex meaning (where attachment to the *vatan*—the Ottoman translation equivalent of the French *patrie*—was a core element).

The common denominator of the population of the Turkish Republic was originally that most of it shared *Islam* as *religious affiliation*, not that it shared a language, a fact that was impossible to ignore even as the Kemalist state elite in the 1920s and 1930s started using a discourse that used concepts such as *race, blood, language,* and *culture* to denominate the collective. The fact that the population of the emerging nation-state had been shaped by concepts of *millet* was an important aspect of the rhetorical context that into which the early republican elite spoke. All of the members of this elite knew from personal experience that when the chips were down and the state's survival was at stake, it was in the final instance a religious definition that had been employed to sort individuals into categories of "loyal" and "disloyal," "citizens" and "foreigners," or "Turks," "Armenians," "Greeks," and "Bulgarians." When collective survival is at stake, conceptual ambiguity becomes a threat, and the state seeks to impose a singular operationalization of key concepts. In such situations individuals are, as Slavenka Drakulic (1993, 50–52; see also Brubaker 1996, 20) has phrased it, "pinned to the wall of nationalism." As the threat receded, ambiguity was reintroduced, but it was used in relation to a population that had recently been categorized as either *in* or *out* on the grounds of religious affiliation and was thus homogenized according to a single criterion.[2]

Askerī and Re'āyā

Rather than having an "official" religion, the Ottoman state was so inextricably linked to Islam that the expression most commonly used for the state/dynasty was the hendiadys *din ü devlet*—"religion and the dynasty/state."[3] *Din ü devlet* is therefore not a mere listing of different entities, as if any and all could be added to the list. The two were linked in such a way that religion gave meaning to the dynasty, and vice versa. The dynasty ruled by divine grace and at the same time protected the religion.

Although the Ottoman state/dynasty was inextricably linked with religion, it did not have as a governing principle that its subjects should be homogenously Muslim. Instead, it governed through the *millet* system, each religious group was ruled autonomously by its religious leader without a corresponding territorial jurisdiction (Ursinus 2014). The Greek patriarch was the most important of these religious leaders because of the large number of Greek Orthodox subjects, ranking just below the grand vizier (prime minister.) Various other religious minorities were over time governed as *millets*, with Armenians and Jews the other most important groups. Recognition was afforded on the basis of religious belonging, and the state made no assumptions regarding equality between religious groups. While one should be careful not to reify the *millet* system as a timeless arrangement, the basic premise was that each *millet* was treated as a collective and given privileges and punishments according to the conduct of its members. This way of ruling subjects through middlemen quintessentially typifies relations as *imperial*: the various groups were involved in unequal and heterogenous contracting, and political contact between the groups typically was limited (cf. Nexon and Wright 2007; Barkey 2008).

---

2. This process was not complete, as there were still the Greek Orthodox *Rum* in Istanbul and the islands and the Armenians in Istanbul, but they were considered marginal remnants of an old order rather than an integral part of the new.

3. The bond was made explicit in Article 11 of the Kanun-ı Esasi (Constitution), which was proclaimed in 1876. This article states, "The religion of the Ottoman state/dynasty is Islam" (Gözübüyük and Kili 1982, 28).

Other concepts central to how the state divided its subjects were *askerī* and *reʿāyā*. These concepts have a dynamic history and have had several other meanings, but they may crudely be translated as "military class" and "commoners." *Askerī* were not necessarily particularly far up in the hierarchy, but belonging to the military class meant belonging to the state. According to the logic of the steppe nomads, from whom the Ottomans drew part of their political tradition, the *askerī* were those allowed to take part in sharing the spoils of war (I. B. Neumann and Wigen 2018).

These two concepts did not originally have religious connotations, although Muslims constituted a majority among the *askerī* and Christians were overrepresented among the *reʿāyā*. Within a few generations after the conquest of Constantinople (1453), access to *askerī* status was closed to non-Muslims (Lowry 2003, 56–57, 64). Although this development has not been studied in depth, Turkish historian Baki Tezcan explains that the distinction between *askerī* and *reʿāyā* became synonymous with that between Muslim and non-Muslim at the beginning of the eighteenth century. The transformation of the concept of *reʿāyā* into a synonym for Christian paralleled the informal enfranchisement of parts of the Muslim population through the institutionalization of the Janissaries as power brokers in the capital. The Janissaries guarded their privileges by claiming to safeguard the Muslim population and made sure that the sultan's actions did not exceed certain informal boundaries that they set. At the same time, non-Muslims were increasingly marginalized in public life and from the Sultan's favor (Tezcan 2010, 235–36). In Tezcan's view, this was one of the key developments in the emergence of a distinctly Muslim political identity in the Ottoman Empire.

This dichotomy seems to have been the baseline for how relations between state and subjects were configured by the nineteenth century. At the turn of the twentieth century, lexicographer Şemseddīn Sāmī (1317 [1901–2], 666) defined the concept of *reʿāyā* as

> 1. Enclosure, an enclosure [where] animals are being pastured, the animals being tended by a shepherd. 2. People/commoners being subject [*tābiʿ*] to the rule and administration of a ruler and giving their duties of allegiance [or "duties as commanded" (*tekālif-i ʾamīrīye*)], subjects/inferiors, [a] subject

who finds himself under the protection of a state [but] who is not among the men of the sword.

While Tezcan argues that *ra'iye* (that is, one of the *re'āyā*) was used to mean "Christian" from the early eighteenth century onward, Şemseddīn Sāmī simply defines *re'āyā* as "commoners subject to the rule and administration of a ruler [who] are not among the men of the sword." "Men of the sword" (*ehl-i seyf*) is thus used as a conceptual antonym to *ra'iye*. The relationship is one of subordination, as these "common folk" are said to be "subject" (*tābi'*) to a ruler. The concept has certain similarities to the Christian pastoral concept of "the flock" tended by a shepherd and is still used among Arabic-speaking Christians in the meaning "parish" or "parishioners," with no negative connotations. In the Ottoman language, however, this distinction was not between the one and the many (between Jesus and his followers or between a priest and his parishioners) but rather was between those who took part in war and those who did not. It is important not to overstate the significance of the fact that the same word was used for commoners who did not fight wars or take part in administration and animals tended by a shepherd, but the relational aspect is nevertheless difficult to miss. The agency of these people was not considered relevant to the conduct of state affairs, and members of this group need not be consulted when making political decisions.

Subject or Citizen?

Today's established translation of *citizen*, *vatandaş*, differs etymologically and semantically from the European concepts that it is used to translate. First, it is not derived from any word for *city*, unlike the French *citoyen* and the English *citizen*. Nor is it related to *castle*, such as the German *Bürger*, which originally meant castle dweller (from *Burg*)—that is, someone who lives within the city walls and therefore enjoys certain privileges (Koselleck and Schreiner 1994). Rather, *vatandaş* is derived from the concept *vatan*, the translation of which is most precisely *patrie* (with which it was entangled in the 1870s), or *fatherland*. Before its reinterpretation through entanglement, *vatan* meant a person's native village, city, or province, detached from any political connotations (Haarman 2014).

According to Şerif Mardin, Namık Kemal popularized the concept as a translation equivalent of *patrie* in an 1873 article, "Vatan,"
and in his enormously popular play, *Vatan yahut Silistre* (Fatherland
or Silistria), which was first performed the same year. In the former,
he argues that *vatan* "is not composed of the vague lines traced by the
sword of a conqueror or the pen of a scribe. It is a sacred idea resulting from the conglomeration of various noble feelings such as the
people, liberty, brotherhood, interest, sovereignty, respect for one's
ancestors, love of the family, and childhood memories" (Mardin
2000 [1961], 327). Likewise, the 1886 Ottoman translation of Prussian general Colmar von der Goltz's hugely influential *Das Volk in
Waffen* (The People in Arms) used *vatan* to translate the German
Vaterland (fatherland).

The Turkish suffix *-daş* that became attached to *vatan* denotes a
form of fellowship, as in *kardeş* (literally "fellow wombsman," meaning sibling). *Vatandaş* therefore "originally" meant something closer
to *compatriot*—someone who shares the *patrie*. This is based on horizontal relations between nominally equal individuals. The way that
this concept is composed emphasizes the community that lives in and
has a certain emotional attachment to the *vatan* rather than bonds of
obligation to a ruler.

Vatandaş came to be used in place of two concepts that were used
to give meaning to relations between commoners and the military
class— *re'āyā* and the more encompassing concept of *teba'a* (followers, subjects). Şemseddin Sami's dictionary (1317 [1901–2], 370) indicates that *tābi'* (the singular of *teba'a*) is also premised on *being led*,
with connotations of hierarchy and an emphasis on obedience and
compliance:

1. Someone who follows another. Who follows [*tab'iyet*] and
imitates: those who have come to follow the great [religious]
scholars and imams of [one of the four orthodox] schools of
Islam. 2. One who submits and complies. Someone who is obe-
dient/compliant. Who is being led. The Kingdom of Bavaria is
the subject [*tābi'*] of the Empire of Germany [Ālmāniya
Imparatorluğu].

In 1901, the Kingdom of Bavaria occupied an inferior position within the German Empire. Wilhelm I of Prussia and of the German Empire was *Kaiser* over all the constituent parts of the empire, while King Otto was merely the king of Bavaria. The relationship is that of a subordinate to a suzerain, and this hierarchical relationship appears to be the point of using it as an example. *Tābiʿ* thus meant the inferior party in a hierarchical relationship, obedient and compliant and someone to consult when making decisions. In short, they were *subjects*.

Legal Changes

Contrary so many narratives that posit a stasis prior to the proclamation of the Tanzimat reforms in 1839, the relationships within the Ottoman ruling elite were changing through the seventeenth and eighteenth centuries. The Tanzimat reforms did not disrupt some ancient and untouched traditional order. Nevertheless, with the Tanzimat reforms, the relationships between ruler and ruled were changing in such a manner that the meaning of subjecthood itself was starting to change. Üstel (2004, 25) has argued that these reforms as well as three other law codes laid down the foundation for what she calls a "vatandaş topluluğu"—a community of citizens.

Be that as it may, both the Tanzimat Charter (1839) and the Edict of Reform (1856) spoke of the *welfare* of the *tebaʿa* (subjects) in ways that are reminiscent of the Circle of Justice, which was of utmost importance to traditional Ottoman political and philosophical writing (Mardin 2000 [1962], 95–101; Darling 2013). According to the Circle of Justice, justice brings security, and security breeds prosperity, which in turn is a prerequisite for subjects' loyalty and devotion to the ruler (Abu-Manneh 1994, 196). The Tanzimat Charter set a precedent by using the concept in a slightly different meaning:

As is known to all, the Quranic and [other] Islamic laws have been obeyed to perfection since the coming into being of our Sublime State. While the power and the might of our exalted sovereignty and the welfare and security of all its subjects have reached an extreme degree, there have been one hundred and fifty years when, because, owing to successive difficulties and reasons for mourning, neither the honored Şeriat nor the illustrious Kanun [laws] were obeyed or conformed to, the earlier power and security was turned into infirmity and poverty, and [because] it is manifestly evident that a country that has no one on its throne to administer the rules of Sharia will not be everlasting. Since the prosperous day of our imperial enthronement, the beneficial thoughts will by our regal foundation bring purer improvement of the country and regions and prosperity to the inhabitants and the poor. Despite the fact that efforts were made over five to ten years to provide the necessary means for public works according to the circumstances of the geography of the possessions of our Sublime State, the fertility of the land, and the people's ability and aptitude, [this was] destined to fail in producing the exalted shapes that were desired. (Gözübüyük and Kili 1982, 3)

The charter claimed that because the Sharia and Kanun laws had been unenforced for a century and a half, both the survival of the state and the welfare of the subjects were imperiled. The new sultan promised to work to *improve* the country, increase his subjects' prosperity, and "provide the necessary means for public works." While previous scholarship has tended to view the Tanzimat Charter as an effort to impose European models on the Ottoman subjects, it has recently been reinterpreted as an effort to reassert the sultan's authority, to centralize power by reintroducing and reestablishing the *adalet* (justice) of the Circle of Justice (Abu-Manneh 1994).

The displacement of the concept *teba'a* took decades, during which time it was far from clear that *vatandaş* would become accepted as the main alternative. Moreover, in some of the constitutive texts of the nineteenth century, *teba'a* itself seems to have been becoming entangled with the French concept of *citoyen*. It is difficult to understand the edict that followed up on the Tanzimat reforms, the Reform Edict, which made all imperial subjects formally equal in the legal sense, without an interpretation of *teba'a* that ties it to *equality*, which in English and in French constituted a central aspect not of subjecthood but of citizenship. As discussed in chapter 3, the Reform

Edict (or Islahat Fermanı) was introduced as part of intense negotiation over the protection of religious minorities at the Paris Conference that ended the Crimean War (see Özsu 2015). Equality of imperial subjects seems to be a contradiction in terms[4] but did not prevent the Ottoman state from using this particular concept when granting its subjects formal equality in 1856:

> I have until now been successful in arranging and laying the foundation and the favorable and public-spirited/patriotic deeds of the masses of our royal subjects . . . and through this in this age herald the beginning of a beneficial time for our Exalted State and internally augment the strength and power of our illustrious sovereignty and to [secure] the occurrence of the complete felicity of condition of all classes of my royal subjects who are tied to one another by the heartfelt bonds of compatriotism [*revabıtı kalbiyeyi vatandaşî*] and who are equal before my merciful eyes filled with justice. (Gözübüyük and Kili 1982, 7–8)

I have translated the word *vatandaşî* (in compound with *revabıtı kalbiye*) as "bonds of *compatriotism*"—a horizontal bond between subjects. This word is an adjectival form of *vatandaş*. However, in this text it is not the bond between the citizens that forms the primary bond of loyalty. The primary bond of loyalty was supposed to be between subject and ruler, with the horizontal ties between subjects a secondary matter.

Demographic Engineering

The overt politicization of categories broadly corresponding to *Muslim* and *Christian* and the emergence of a distinctly Muslim political identity came about during a period when the Ottoman Empire first started losing large swaths of territory. The current composition of the population of the Turkish nation-state is the result of how the concepts under study here were used in the inclusion of refugees and

---

4. Moreover, formal equality did not bring about equal treatment, primarily because Ottoman Christians objected to taking on military duties, and hence did not want equality with Muslim Ottomans (see Davison 1963).

of mass expulsions, mostly ending in 1927. Thus, the pre-nation-state categorizations and usages of concepts of "citizen" or "subject" had an important bearing on how the concept of *Turk* and that of "citizen of the Turkish Republic" came to be used.

The great territorial losses that the Ottoman Empire suffered at the hands of the Habsburg Empire in 1699 in many ways began a process that over the years led to increasing correspondence between religious affiliation and territoriality in the Balkans. This was in line with a practice that emerged in the Holy Roman Empire in the mid-1500s and became known as *cuius regio, eius religio.* Though it hardly attests to a blanket application of the principle, the Habsburgs' expulsion of some one hundred thousand Muslims from the recently conquered territories gave the principle its first indirect bearing on Ottoman state-subject relations (Kasaba 2009, 57).

The other main Ottoman source of Muslim refugees, imperial Russia, also came to use *cuius regio, eius religio* in organizing state-population relations but this did not have much bearing on the Ottoman Empire until it lost Crimea to Russia in 1774. Russia annexed the peninsula in 1783, and significant numbers of Muslims started fleeing to the Ottoman Empire. This increased with the Turkish-Russian War (1828–29) and peaked following the Crimean War (1853–56), when Muslims were systematically expelled from Russian territories. Up to nine hundred thousand Muslims were driven from the Crimea and Russian-controlled Caucasus in the eight years following the Crimean War (Fisher 1987, 356).

Since an inhabitant's potential loyalty to the state was largely judged by religious affiliation, Sunni Muslims, whose religion was the same as that of the state, were considered reliable by the Ottoman state. Shi'a Muslims, who had the same religious denomination as the Ottoman archenemy to the east, Iran, as well as heterodox Alevis whom the Ottoman state considered akin to Shi'i, were frequently deemed potential traitors. They were among the very few groups who were subject to direct politico-religious persecution in the Ottoman Empire in the sixteenth and seventeenth centuries. Following 1774, the Russian Tsar claimed spiritual overlordship over the Greek-Orthodox on the basis of a particular translation of the Küçük Kaynarca Treaty (Davison 1976), and used this to frequently intervene in Ottoman affairs. After 1820, the newly-declared Greek state to the west also made claims on Ottoman territory and subjects. The Catholics in the empire (among them Catholic Armenians) as well as the Maronites in Lebanon came under France's protection. The British protected the Protestants and the Druze. As foreign powers pressured the Ottoman Empire to give economic or political privileges to themselves, which they then extended to "their" minorities, these minorities increasingly came to be represented as the extension of an external enemy. Worst hit by this conflation were the Ottoman Armenians, who in the decades before their extermination in 1915 were claimed to be potentially treacherous because their presence in Ottoman realms could be used to legitimize Russian expansion.

The stigmatization occurred on the basis of privileging religious affiliation as a collective identity marker. Belonging to the collective identity *Armenian* was determined by religious affiliation and was not directly tied to language or actual religious practice. It was possible to be a religiously indifferent Turkish speaker and still be considered Armenian by the Ottoman state (Dündar 2008). Thus, the Ottoman state's taxonomy of subjects was based on categories of religious community, which the neighboring states in the Balkans also used. In Serbia, Bulgaria, and Greece, subjects were considered "Turkish" if they were Muslim, regardless of language. Muslims were accordingly persecuted and sought refuge in Anatolia, the part of the Ottoman territories that increasingly became represented as "real Turkey" (see chapter 3).

In the same way although to a lesser extent, Christians were driven from Ottoman territories to the neighboring states. This trickle did not become a flow until the Ottoman state security apparatus began the systematic expulsion of Christians from their homes on the Aegean Coast during the summer of 1914 (Dündar 2008, 175–248). These homes were then taken over by Muslim refugees or local notables. The process came to a head with the mass killing and expulsion of Armenians in 1915 and the population exchange between Greece and Turkey in 1924–27. According to the Treaty of Lausanne (1923), concluded by the Turkish nationalists with Britain and its allies after the Turks had defeated the Greek expeditionary force in Anatolia, nearly all Greek Orthodox Christians (with the exception of those in Istanbul and on the Turkish islands in the Sea of Marmara and Aegean) were sent from Turkey to Greece, while all Muslims (except those in Eastern Thrace) were sent the other way. This "solution" came about through dialogues with the high commissioner for refugees, Norwegian Fridtjof Nansen (Özsu 2015, 1–3).

The collectives known as *halk* (people) and *vatandaşlar* (citizens) thus came into being through state practices of inclusion and exclusion where statesmen and their agents used the above concepts to categorize individuals. According to Kemal Arı (1995, 18), some eight hundred thousand people entered Turkey as immigrants in the period 1923–39. The proportion of non-Muslims in the Ottoman Empire, which had stood at approximately 20 percent before the First World War, fell to 2.5 percent after the population exchange (Keyder 1989, 67). Even as the population exchange with Greece was concluded, the Turkish state continued to consider Muslim communities in the Balkans as potentially loyal members of the Turkish nation, accepting Muslims from Bulgaria, Romania, Serbia, and Crimea while rejecting the Turkic-speaking, but Orthodox Christian, Gagauz of Moldova (Çağaptay 2006, 78–83).

Religious affiliation and *loyalty* to the Ottoman state (primarily applied at the group level) constituted the main criteria for inclusion into the community of Turkish citizens (İnce 2012, 54). Population groups that had rebelled against the Ottoman state, such as Albanians (1912) and Arabs (1916–18) were excluded on grounds of disloyalty despite being Muslims.[5] Collective disloyalty to the Ottoman state prior to the nationalist rebellion in 1919 did to some extent lead to the exclusion of Albanians from the Turkish national project. Albanians were said to be insufficiently attached to Turkish culture (İnce 2012, 54). This also went for the individuals who had gained citizenship other than Turkish. Disloyalty to the Ottoman state before the "National Struggle" or War of Independence led to outright exclusion from the nation-state collective, while later disloyalty generally triggered the repressive organs of the state, although "traitors" were and still are represented as external to the Turkish body politic. Individuals or groups disloyal to the state were represented as *foreign* or as simple and backward people being led astray by foreigners (Poulton 1997, 120).

---

5. When the Turkish Republic sought to claim and integrate the Arabs of Antakya following the annexation of this province to Turkey in 1939, the claim was that they were "Hittites"; see Çağaptay 2006, 116–18.

Demographic engineering did not end with inclusion/exclusion on the basis of religious categorization. Which language an individual or group spoke was used to determine where in its territory the Turkish state settled immigrant populations and where groups considered potentially dangerous to state unity were resettled. This was not unique to the Eastern Provinces, where the policy was largely directed at Kurds. However, the policy of forceful disciplining and resettlement of Kurds fostered a Kurdish political identity, which has made it a particularly pertinent issue. Although Kurdish sheikhs had been part of Mustafa Kemal's movement during the War of Independence (1919–22), Kurds rebelled in 1925 (the Sheikh Said Rebellion), 1926–30 (the Ağrı/Ararat Rebellion), and 1936–38 (the Dersim Rebellion). These uprisings did not necessarily involve "the Kurds" acting as a political entity or even identifying as Kurds and resisting the imposition of Turkish nationalism. Rebellions were directed by former imperial middlemen in the Ottoman Empire, such as tribal chiefs and religious sheikhs, whose political position was challenged by the nation-state governance that at least in principle depended on direct bonds between individual and state, thereby eliminating the need for middlemen. The tribal chiefs and religious sheikhs used the emotional attachment to the sultanate and the caliphate to rally their supporters against the state that abolished these institutions in 1923–24. The coalescing of a politicized Kurdish identity was likely the *result* rather than the *cause* of these rebellions (Yeğen 1996; 1999).

The early republican elite was particularly concerned with controlling the movement of nomads and dispensing with imperial middlemen. Only this way could they establish direct links with individual subjects in all their heterogeneity and discipline them into Turkish citizens. However, the extensive armed resistance by Kurdish tribes made this difficult. Following the Ağrı rebellion, the government promulgated a new law to forcefully assimilate these populations. This law sought to "secure" what were considered sensitive areas. Kurds were transferred to western provinces or resettled in other parts of eastern Turkey. The Kurds inhabiting the mountainous areas of Dersim (renamed Tunceli after the 1936–38 uprising) were forcefully relocated to the Elazığ plain (İnce 2012, 56). Officials sought to transfer disloyal or unreliable elements from places they found hard to control to areas that were easier to exercise authority over. Conversely, the government also deliberately settled Turkish-speaking immigrants in the eastern provinces to "Turkify" the region. The government was, however, careful to prevent the transfer of non-Turkish-speaking immigrants to the east (İnce 2012, 56).

Rather than excluding *Kurds* from the Turkish nation-state project, the state represented the matter by use of the stigma management technique I, in the previous chapter, called passing the buck. What foreigners often call "the Kurdish issue" has in hegemonic Turkish discourse been represented as an issue of reactionary politics, tribal resistance, and regional backwardness, a position that implies a *mission civilisatrice* of the *civilized, modern,* and *progressive* Turkish metropole (Yeğen 1996, 217).

> In Turkish state discourse, the Kurdish question was identified with "the past" (of which the Caliphate and the Sultanate were the representations) in opposition to "the present" (for example, the Republican regime); with "tradition" (autonomous political structures, for instance) in opposition to "modern" (centralist republican politics); and with "the political and economic resistance of the 'periphery' (smuggling and resistance to taxation and military recruitment)" in opposition to "national integration" (an integrated national market economy). (226)

This temporal Othering invoked European categorizations of materialist dialectics, where the "Kurdishness" of the issue was denied while concepts such as "reactionary," "backward," and "the past" were used to speak of those who rebelled (see chapter 3). As the chairman of the Independence Tribunal that sentenced the leaders of the 1925 rebellion formulated the issue,

> Your *political reaction* and rebellion were destroyed immediately by the decisive acts of *the government of the Republic* and by the fatal strokes of the *Republican army*. . . . [T]he young *Republican government* will definitely not condone any cursed action like incitement and political reaction. . . . The poor people of this region who have been exploited and oppressed under the domination of *sheikhs and feudal landlords* will be freed from

your incitements and evil and they will follow the efficient path of *our Republic which promises progress and prosperity.* (Aybars 1995, 325–26)

This links together *feudalism, oppression,* and *reaction,* with *disloyalty* to the Turkish Republic and uses them all to label those who rebelled. In contrast, the Turkish Republic was represented as the guardian of *freedom* and *progress* and as *young* in contrast to the old feudalism.

Türk

It is impossible to treat Turkish concepts of citizenship without also dealing with the concept of *Türklük* (Turkishness) in relation to the concepts *Türk* (Turk) and *Türkçülük* (Turkic-ness or Pan-Turkism), which together constitute an important part of the semantic field used to give meaning to Turkish citizenship. The concept *Türk* was used in the 1924 constitution in places where one might expect to find "individual" or "citizen." Constitutional rights were granted qua *Türk* rather than qua citizen or individual. Article 68 states that "Every Turk is born free," while Article 69 declares that "All Turks are equal in the eye of the law," and according to Article 10, "Every male Turk has the right to choose a deputy" (Gözübüyük and Kili 1982, 112–13, 128). Not all *citizens* are equal, but all *Turks* are equal. This is an important distinction, and must be viewed in light of the population exchange that was taking place as the constitution was being drafted.

Two different categorizations were combined in the concept of *Türk.* The centuries-old *Turk as Muslim* of European languages was combined with the categories used in the emergent field of Turkology, which was oriented toward the racial, cultural, and linguistic commonalities between the peoples descended from the steppe nomads and speaking what came to be known as Turkic languages.

The word *Turk* in its many variations (*Tork, Türk, Törk,* and so forth) has an obscure etymological origin and derives from a nomadic steppe empire called the Türk Khaganate (552–744 CE) in a less than straightforward manner. According to the main authority on ethnogenesis on the steppe, Peter Golden (1982, 40),

The ethnonym Türk was originally associated with a small tribe headed by the Ašina clan. With the foundation of the Türk Empire in 552, this ethnonym was politicized and became, as H. Ecsedy has phrased it: "co-extensive with the area of their political and military superiority rather than their actual ethnic sphere. The name was borrowed for and by other components of the empire too, in a simplificatory way as well as in consequence of the name's authority."

Prior to the spread of this catchall phrase for nomads, the preferred self-designation of steppe nomads may well have been "those who draw the bow," indicating that their identity was tied up with their way of life and the way they waged war more than with a specific language (Golden 1992, 3). The spread of the word *Türk* is the result of how people outside the polity—Arabs in particular—needed to make sense of a category of humans who did not behave as outsiders were used to (Golden 1982, 41; Barthold 1962, 34). *Türk* was then taken over as a self-designatory concept after some of these tribes converted to Islam.

The division between Turk and non-Turk was initially one between nomad and sedentary, regardless of language. This division remained, at least in the Ottoman lands, until *Türk* was appropriated by the Young Turks of the early twentieth century. *Türk* denoted if not necessarily a nomad someone very rustic. Turkologist Fahir İz got into a conversation with a local shepherd outside a provincial town in Anatolia during the Second World War. Socialized into the contemporary nationalist Turkish discourse as he was, İz talked of "We Turks," to which the reply was "Lord have mercy! *I* am a Turk; Your exalted person is Ottoman" (G. Lewis 1999, 22). In rural Anatolia, *Türk* still implied a country bumpkin, which the well-educated İz was not.

The matter of how the ethnonym *Türk* changed and came to be used as a political marker in the late nineteenth century is a rather complex affair (see Landau 1995). In short, the re-definition as a political marker resulted from the confluence of three distinct developments. First, scholarly interest in the history of the steppe peoples resulted in a vast increase in philological and linguistic writings on the topic. Second, Europeans had frequently used *Turk/Turc/Türk* in the meaning not only of the subjects of the Ottoman sultan but as a generic category for Muslims, thus establishing it as an exonym for *Ottoman*. For example, the English phrase "turning Turk" meant converting to Islam (see, e.g., Daborne 1612). With their language becoming ever more entangled with European languages and exoconcepts such as *Turk* legitimating their own group identity, certain Ottoman elites—most notably, intellectuals coming as refugees from the Russian Empire and particularly Crimea—appropriated *Türk* as a positive self-identification (Arai 1994). This marks the third of the three conceptual changes.

The most famous among those who appropriated Türk as a positive self-identification was Akçuraoğlu Yusuf (1876–1935), now best known as Yusuf Akçura. In *Three Types of Politics*, Akçura discussed the relative merits and strategic implications of various subject populations, one of which he based on Osmanlılık (Ottomanism), one he based on *Islam* (expressly linking this to the French concept of *pan-islamisme*), and finally he formulated "a political Turkish *millet* based on race [*ırk*]" (Akçura 2005 [1904], 35). Ottomanism was, according to Yusuf Akçura's formulation, based on the political equality of all citizens of the Ottoman state and territorial claims coextensive with the area the Ottoman Empire already possessed. Akçura wrote that these subjects inhabited the Ottoman *vatan* and linked this political option with France as a political ideal for the organization of state-society relations (42–43). The second alternative, which has been translated as *Islamism*, appears in Akçura's writings as a secular policy option that emphasizes the solidaristic bond of religion rather than its role as relating to divinity. It does in fact not entail anything religiously specific except relying on *all the world's Muslims* as the subject population for the Ottoman state. He rejects both of these options on the basis that they would bring the state into conflict with *all* the European imperial states, since the former would mean trying to hold on to a territory that the Europeans already coveted and that experienced frequent rebellions while the latter would also involve irredentist claims on the colonial possessions of France, Great Britain, and Russia. The third option, *Turkism* or *türkçülük*, was a new interpretation and use of the concept of *Türk*, made by yoking it to both *millet* and *race* (*ırk*).

While it may be possible to see similarities with German Romanticism in Akçura's conceptualization of the nation, Akçura's main way to legitimize *Türkçülük* is that it would bring the Ottoman state into conflict with the fewest Great Powers while claiming the greatest number of subjects, since only Russia was imperial overlord over Turkic speakers (Akçura 2005 [1904], 60–61). He argues that the Ottoman state could expect an alliance with the British (the French were considered weak and therefore militarily unreliable after the 1871 defeat by Germany as well as too friendly with Russia). The main arguments he makes against the two other options are that they would bring the Ottoman Empire into conflict with Britain and France in addition to Russia.

Five important assumptions underpin Akçura's text. First, "we" is more or less synonymous with the Ottoman state elite. Second, the author reifies a collective he calls the "Ottoman Turks" and includes the group in the project under all three strategies (Akçura 2005 [1904], 47–48). Third, the Ottoman state should seek to have a subject population suitable for a Great Power, and the core group of Ottoman Turks would on its own be insufficient for the preservation and glory of such a state. A small state consisting only of "Ottoman Turks" is not even mentioned. Fourth, there seems to be no assumption that there needed to be a preexisting emotional bond between "the nation" and "the state." Having picked an appropriate subject population, the state could create such an emotional bond if it was needed at all. Fifth, the main consideration when a state "chose" a population is whether it would be able to govern that particular population and the geopolitical implications of these ambitions. The strategies were evaluated purely in terms of their likelihood of success, not in terms of their moral correctness. These assumptions illustrate that Akçura's "*Kultur*-based nationalism" was nothing of the sort but was, rather, an instrumental evaluation of the relative merits of various subject populations that primarily took into account the concerns of the state.

In state documents such as the 1924 constitution, the meaning of *Türk* and its linkages with other concepts were kept relatively open. The discursive struggle over how to narrow these concepts down and define them more clearly therefore came about in the formulation of practical policy. An important occasion for such a discursive struggle arose when the Turkish Grand National Assembly debated a 1924 law to protect "Turkish" companies. The debate was centered on the appropriate meaning of the concepts *Türk*, *Türkiye*, and *vatandaş* (İnce 2012, 45). Asked whom this law concerned, one legislator declared, "We mean whatever the laws understand from the words *Turk* and *Turkish companies*" Another member then asked, "Are we calling the Armenians and the Greeks Turkish?," prompting a third representative to conclude, "They have never been Turkish" (Çağaptay 2006, 69). Political and administrative practice had a rather narrow scope for what was appropriate use, equating Turkishness with being a Muslim loyal to the state. The debate about this law set the standard for the relationship between the Turkish state and its religious minorities. Turkishness remained tied to religious affiliation even after religious minorities received full de jure citizenship rights.

While the principle of *cuius regio, eius religio* had been the basis of much state-subject relations in Europe for centuries, "the Turks" created a religiously homogenous population for their state precisely as major actors using English, French, and German emphasized concepts of *race* and *blood*. Partly on the basis of the nascent European interest in Turkology, the early Turkish Republic started creating what outsiders often consider rather fanciful myths of origin that tie together diverse discursive elements and link them to the subject population of the republic. The two most important examples were the Turkish history thesis and sun-language theory. Proposed at the time of the First Turkish History Conference in 1932, the Turkish history thesis held that

> Although the Turks had left the Palaeolithic Age by 12000 BC in their homeland, Central Asia, the Europeans were saved from this stage only 5000 years later. While people in other parts of the world were still living in trees and caves, the Turks had already created a wood- and mineral-based civilization; they domesticated animals and had begun cultivating the land. Many Turkic tribes began to migrate due to grave natural transformations that took place as a result of the receding glaciers at the end of the Ice Age, which coincided with the Neolithic Age. In this manner, after scattering from Central Asia, the Turks, who had brought forth agriculture and pastoralism as

early as 7000 BC and who had conquered bronze, tin, and iron, diffused the first civilization in the places they went and thus founded the bases of the Chinese and Indian civilizations in Asia; the Hittite civilization in Anatolia, which they adopted as their holy homeland; Elam and the Sumerian civilization in Mesopotamia; and finally the Egyptian, Mediterranean, and Roman civilizations and saved Europe, whose advanced civilization we appreciate and pursue today, from a life in the caves. ("Maarif Vekili Esat Beyefendinin Açma Nutku" 1932, 6)

The Turkish history thesis is a narrative that legitimized Turkish possession of Anatolia on the one hand and "borrowing" from Europeans on the other. It systematically deploys concepts of *civilization* and the claim that the Turks made the *first progress in human technologies* and then imparted those developments to the rest of mankind. The Turks were the origin of civilization, and therefore every product or practice associated with civilization is inherently Turkish. Using European technologies was simply a matter of benefitting from something that had been set in motion by the Turks themselves.

People and Nation

Concepts of *citizenship* are used in relation to other concepts such as *nation* and *people*. In most European languages, the concept of *people* gained importance as it was consistently used by individuals and groups claiming to speak on behalf of the ruled vis-à-vis the ruler or ruling elite and the concept underwent a continuous transformation as new groups claimed to speak on behalf of "the people" (Foucault 2003). Crudely put, first the aristocracy used it against the sovereign, then the bourgeoisie used it against the aristocracy, and then the working class used it against the bourgeoisie.

Halk became a key concept for the early Turkish Republic, frequently used by Mustafa Kemal and the nationalists to legitimize their claim to rule in a power struggle with both the Ottoman dynasty and external powers. The use of *halk* was by no means unique to Mustafa Kemal, but his reliance on it as a battle concept had great importance for closely linking the Turkish *halk* to the concept of *Türk*. First, Mustafa Kemal and the nationalists used the concept to legitimize their position vis-à-vis the sultan and various institutionalized power hierarchies such as the *ulema* (religious scholars). The principle of *halkçılık* (populism) was a way to outcompete the nation as *ümmet* (*Ummah*), which through its overt religious meaning was linked to the state as the protector of Islam and the sultan and caliph. *Halkçılık* is enshrined in the Six Arrows of Kemalism, which were the axioms by which the Republican People's Party claimed to rule. (The arrows were adopted by the party in 1931 and included in the Turkish Constitution in 1937 but were then removed when the Demokrat Parti came to power in 1950.)

Central to the emergence of *halk* and *millet* as translation equivalents of *people* and *nation* was the shift in various European discourses on the international level—that is, after the Russian Revolution of 1917 and the publication of Woodrow Wilson's Fourteen Points in 1918, *imperialism* and *empire* were no longer unequivocally positive concepts (see chapter 4).

> With the Treaty of Alliance of 1921, Russia abolished its extra-territoriality [in Turkey]. The treaty depicted the Bolsheviks and the Turkish nationalists as a unified front by "the common struggle undertaken against imperialism," and called extraterritoriality an imperialist tool incompatible with national independence and sovereignty. (Turan Kayaoğlu 2010, 132)

Political legitimacy could in this rhetorical context be better argued by using concepts such as *popular sovereignty* and *nations' right to self-determination*. However, "popular sovereignty" also depended on the concept of *civilization*, as only those peoples were deemed civilized were considered fit for self-determination (Turan Kayaoğlu 2010). The concepts of *millet* and *halk* were thus placed in the teleological narrative that posited *medeniyet* (or, rather, *muasır medeniyetinin seviyesi* [the level of modern civilization]) as a goal. As Mustafa Kemal himself stated as early as 1921,

> Gentlemen, I count myself fortunate that I have succeeded with all of these observations of mine to enlighten a truth and a doctrine. This truth is that the nation [*millet*] has chosen with great success the path that it is taking and that at the end of this

path one can see the shining sun of felicity in all its clarity (applause). This nation will reach that sun. And there is not a power that can stop it (heavy applause). (Kemal 1945a, 214)

Freed from the fetters of *imparatorluk* and given self-determination, the *millet* could set out on a path toward modern civilization.

The Millet in Arms

Among the key actors in the contestation over political power in Anatolia and Thrace in 1913–24 were officers graduated from the Ottoman War Academy (Mekteb-i Erkân-i Harbiye). This cohort of officers had also quite literally been the key movers in the 1908 Constitutional Revolution. Their position as officers and members of the Committee of Union and Progress (CUP) was also the basis for their rise to prominence during this period. Until the so-called Young Turk Triumvirate seized direct power in 1913, the members of the CUP remained somewhat withdrawn from actual political decisions and instead played kingmakers of Ottoman post-1908 politics: rather than running for office, they coerced people to vote for their candidates. From the arrival of the German military mission in 1883, the Ottoman War Academy was modeled on the Prussian *Kriegsakademie* and staffed by Prussian officers. While earlier armies such as the Janissaries had over time become an integral part of Ottoman society, the new academy-educated Ottoman officer corps became what Şükrü Hanioğlu (2011, 37) calls a "cloistered elite" that "stood apart from the masses—pretentious, Westernized, and overweeningly ambitious." These officers educated at the War Academy were the most important not only among the Young Turks in the CUP but also among the nationalist elite who established the Turkish Republic, including Mustafa Kemal Atatürk himself.

Few people were as central in shaping how late Ottoman officers conceptualized politics and fought wars as Prussian general Colmar von der Goltz, who led the German mission to reorganize the Ottoman military from 1883 to 1895 (Kreiser 2008, 43; Hanioğlu 2011, 35). Of particular concern was the reorganization of the Ottoman War Academy, where he added a year and shaped the curriculum. Goltz's writings are therefore important points of reference when analyzing legitimation strategies in Turkish politics of the early twentieth century. As he set out in his 1883 book, *Das Volk in Waffen,* war was inevitable in the modern world and involved not only armies but entire nations or peoples (Goltz 1914, 2). Moreover, the military elite had a duty to go beyond their traditional role of simply fighting wars. Military commanders ought to be more than loyal servants of the state, assuming the full responsibility thrust upon them by virtue of their "superior position in the state" (Hanioğlu 2011, 34). Goltz's book appeared in Ottoman translation as *Millet-i Musellaha* (The Armed *Millet*) as early as 1886 and soon became one of the key texts taught at the Ottoman Military Academy (37).

Goltz (1914, 2) equated the nation/people[6] with the army in the sense that the military *is* "the nation [or rather *people*] in arms." Wars may be started by *empires*, but they are fought by *nations/peoples* (*Volk/millet*). Wars are fought in a manner that is *total,* and at stake is the survival of the fatherland (*vatan*). The only way to compete in the Social Darwinist struggle that this implies is to "completely fuse military life into the life of the people, so that the former may impede the latter as little as possible, and that, on the other hand, all the resources of the latter may find expression in the former" (4–5).

Since the nation/people depends on its army for survival and to protect the *fatherland,* the officers have a particularly important duty that can only be upheld if they also received a socially privileged position in society as a whole.

> Influence over the soldiers must be gained in time of peace by a proper application of the superior qualities of intellect and character, in training and in leading them. . . . The officer must not spare his life. Only in order to urge on his troops, he must frequently expose himself more than the ends of battle would otherwise at the moment demand. By thus showing himself unusually fearless and self-sacrificing, he awakens noble impulses in the soldier's breast, for only by these can great deeds be done. To the officer-class there is, accordingly; due of internal necessity, a more favoured position in the state. *Noblesse oblige.*

---

6. *Volk* in the German, *millet* in the Ottoman translation, and *nation* in the English translation.

> He who is accustomed to regard himself as belonging to a spe-
> cial class will also, in war, consider himself bound to do some-
> thing special. (Goltz 1914, 38)

This is duly contrasted with those who occupy a socially inferior position, and Goltz concludes that "slaves are always cowards" (24). It is
imperative for the survival of the nation that this officer class upholds
its position in society. As its members cannot devote themselves to
amassing wealth and can never be sure of their survival, the officers
as a class should receive social privileges, distinctions and honors.
"Without social privileges, the class must of necessity soon sink down
to a very modest *niveau*" (40).

Not only was it important for the performance of the army that
the officers enjoy a privileged social position, but Goltz also quoted
Rüchel approvingly: "The soul of the Prussian army is in its officers"
(28). But Goltz's officers are not an aristocracy of inheritance but are
what he calls "the aristocracy of the people . . . this means the aristocracy of education" (37). This assessment sums up the CUP officers
more than any other characterization (and more than the Prussian
officer corps), since the members of the CUP were the first cohort of
academy-educated Ottoman officers, recruited from among the sons
of lower state functionaries rather than from among the sons of the
upper echelon of statesmen who had sworn personal loyalty to the
sultan (Göçek, 1996, 68–86). Furthermore, Goltz (1914, 28) claims,

> The officer-corps alone forms the nucleus. It hands down tradi-
> tions. Through its hands passes, year by year, a new class of re-
> cruits. The whole nation in arms is subordinated to its influ-
> ence. The alterations that great thinkers and great eras have
> wrought in the army can only be passed on to future genera-
> tions through the medium of the officers. As the officers so the
> army. More true to-day than when it was spoken is Rüchel's
> saying, "The spirit animating the officer-corps is the spirit of
> the army."

The army is the nation/*Volk*/*millet* in arms. The officer corps is the
soul or spirit of this army. They are the receptacle of martial wisdom
and keep the army and hence the nation competitive in the struggle

between nations. The vigor of the masses is not important for the vitality of the "nation in arms," since the decay or vitality of the nation depends on the position of the leading classes. Goltz's insistence on the special duty of the officer corps was translated into a duty of the CUP. As its 1908 program stated, the CUP "is the spirit of the state" (Tunaya 1998, 56 n. 12).

Discipline

Mustafa Kemal used Goltz's representations to conceptualize his own relationship with the Turkish *people* and *nation*. Taha Parla and Andrew Davison argue that the emergence of the Turkish Republic in 1923 saw a discursive conflation of the concepts pertaining to *nation, people, party*, and *leader* (2004, 50).

> Kemal's discourse exhibits three essential, charismatic power dynamics. The first is a false humility wherein he poses as the humble servant of the nation, not as its Great Leader. (160)
>
> [Second,] Kemal described his bond as humble ruler and his followers in emotive terms of love and affection. (163)
>
> The third element of Kemal's rhetorical style in this charismatic relation is the conditionality of his love, expressed in often vituperative diatribes against those who did not love him, who did not recognize his position as humble leader, who did not see that his only ostensible interest was to serve his nation, or who did not accept his logic as such. Those who did not love him, he said, opposed him. (165)

Kemal's position as a charismatic leader was constituted by an exclusive bond between him and his loyal followers—*exclusive* in the sense that it divided the population into those who were *for* him (and thus part of the body politic) and those who were *against* him (who were categorized as external, either as representing foreign powers or belonging to the past order). More to the point, this dual spatial and temporal exclusion reconfigured the relations between Kemal and the Turkish citizens by disciplining the remaining body of citizens and laying down the boundaries for acceptable behavior. This configuration of social relations was stabilized by the emphasis on the concepts of *unity* and *order* in Kemalist discourse of the 1920s and 1930s. The unity of purpose between the *vatandaş* and leadership of the Kemalist Republic was represented as the realization of the *people in arms*. Kemal argued (albeit privately) for the dismemberment of the Ottoman Empire so that the army could rely on a proper nation and did so while the Ottoman dynasty still reigned (similar to the point about "real Turkey" and "colonial Turkey" made by Naci İsmail; see chapter 4). Just as Akçura placed the state (or perhaps rather the Ottoman ruling elite) prior to any kind of "nation" in his musings about the appropriate subjects for the state, Kemal placed the army as primary and the nation as secondary. The nation was created to save the state, rather than the other way around.

The Turkish Republic became a single-party state in 1935, when the Republican People's Party merged with the state structure. Thus, the party not only ruled the state but *was* the state, and every party appointee also held the corresponding post in the state hierarchy. The leader of each municipality was also the leader of the party's municipal branch, the governor of a province was also the leader of the provincial branch of the party, and so forth, up to the president, who was the leader of the party (Ahmad 1977, 6–8). In a parallel move, the Republican People's Party discursively replaced the officer corps as the trustee of the nation. The nation was under the protection of the party rather than the military, although former Ottoman officers educated by Goltz and his colleagues led the party. The Republican People's Party's 1943 program (5) tied the party's trusteeship over the nation to *progress* in *civilization*:

> It is one of the fundamental duties of the party to make the Turkish nation [*millet*] within a short period of time reach an advanced level of civilization and a high degree of standard of living and power and make the Turkish fatherland [*Türk vatanı*] flourish in all ways. The party therefore finds it necessary to profit from all the intercessions and all the endeavors of the individuals in the fatherland and the persons governing and from all the powers of the state at the same time. The statism [*devletçilik*] of our party is born from this necessity.

The relationships between the party, the nation, and the individual were stabilized and legitimized by claiming that the party took upon itself a duty to bring the nation to the level of progressed civilization. The integration of the body politic into an organic whole was a disciplining effort that took place both on the individual level in schools and the military and on the political level through the marginalization of critics as disloyal, foreign, or reactionary.[7] I focus here on the disciplining effort directed at political elites. As Mustafa Kemal represented the matter in 1923,

> The fate of those who do not conform to the nation's will and purpose is disappointment and extinction. (Shouts of "doubtlessly!") Gentlemen, let us bow with all due respect and submission before this enormous will. (Heavy ovations). (Kemal 1945b, 299)

This dichotomizes the political arena into two groups: those who conform to "the nation's will" and those headed for extinction. Unsurprisingly, "the nation's will" was that expressed by the party, and those who were headed for extinction were those who opposed the party. The first and most practical use of this dichotomy as a tool came with the establishment of "Independence Tribunals" (İstiklal Mahkemeleri), which operated in three periods between 1920 and 1927.

> Discernable in these characteristics is a tendency in Kemal's spoken discourse to use terms of an ethno-racialist nationalism alongside terms of a civil or civic nationalism. The effect is that the latter take on hues from the former. For Kemal, the Turkish "nation" is not only defined by social norms of culture and ethos, but also ethnoracial characteristics. . . . If what was meant by "Turkish national" was not only a "common tie regardless of race" but also a member of a "masterful ethnic or racial group," it would have been difficult to be a good civic national Turk if one lacked the right ethnic or racial characteristics. (Parla and Davison 2004, 75)

7. One should of course keep in mind that such processes are never completed, and despite organicist assumptions implicit in scholarly work and in actors' political claims, polities are never organic wholes.

This altered the concept of *citizenship* by drawing on both civic and ethnoracial discourse and linking it to the concept of *Türk* in a meaning closely tied to *Muslim* without displacing it. In short, although civic and ethnoracialist conceptualizations of who was a *Türk* clearly existed, the first prerequisite for consideration as a potential part of the organic whole was to be Muslim. Christians were excluded; non-Turkish-speaking Muslims were (and to some extent still are) forcefully assimilated and disciplined into being *Türk*.

Mustafa Kemal equated his own identity not only with that of the republic but also with the nation and indeed with *justice*. He, the party, and the state were the expression of *general* interests, while other parties and people represented only *particular* interests. Moreover, his opponents were represented as "without fatherland and nationality" (Parla and Davison 2004, 166).

> Kemal's love was always conditional on the mass's showing its love for him by joining him in opposing those who opposed him, those who had other ideas, those who he said could hardly have any ideas at all. His was the only relevant mind. He castigates the others by declaring their brains to be "weak." His is the active mind, their's [sic] the organs of "seducers." He is the brain for the headless mass that is the heart. They need to recognize him as the brain that knows what the body should do. (167)

Furthermore,

> the tendency to dismiss and eliminate principled discussion over fundamental political issues, classifying such issues in ways that purge them of any possible relevance to the nation's goals, is one of Atatürk's most entrenched legacies in Turkish political culture, though it is, of course, neither limited to the Turkish context nor specific to Kemal himself. (172)

Other people's ideas were dismissed as "artificial" and "private," with no relevance for the republic as a whole, as representing the views of private individuals rather than taking into consideration the good of the whole of the Turkish nation/people/republic (173).

The distinction in Kemalist discourse between those who had the general interest of the Turkish people in mind and those who sought mere personal advantage is linked with a narrative of the Ottoman historical experience in the First World War. More specifically, it alludes to Mustafa Kemal's rival, Enver Paşa, who had been minister of war during the First World War and was a leading figure among the Young Turks. Kemalist intellectual Falih Rıfkı's memoir of his war experience on the Palestine front, *Zeytindağı* (Olive Mountain) (Atay 2008 [1932], 99), is rich in representations that distinguish between Mustafa Kemal's nationalist leadership and what is represented as the vainglorious leadership of the Young Turk Triumvirate. Falih Rıfkı claims that each of leaders in the triumvirate had *personal* reasons for pressing for an alliance with the various Great Powers, with little consideration for what was good for the collective. Personal interests and subjectivity were bad and belonged to the past and eastern Ottoman Empire, while general interest and objective methods were traits of Mustafa Kemal Atatürk and the modern Turkish Republic.

Conclusion

The reconfiguration and stabilization of social relations that made up Turkish nation-state formation were part of the struggle to discursively legitimate the state elite's control both over a particular territory and over the population that came to inhabit it. The claims of having reached the "standard of civilization" cannot be detached from the necessity of being a "nation" of citizens. As chapter 6 shows, the individuals within this collective had their place, depending on whether they were to be considered *vatandaş* or merely *halk*, a conceptual pair that bore a certain resemblance to the earlier concepts of *askerī* and *reʿāyā*. This conceptual continuity can be neatly summed up in an expression, "The *halk* descended upon the beach, and so the *vatandaş* could not even get in the sea," that is often attributed to a 1950s mayor of Istanbul. The *vatandaş* somehow considers himself above the *halk*, distinguished from the masses through attachment to *civilization* and having a civilizing mission toward the *halk*. The expression has been extensively used to delegitimize the elite by laying claim to the concepts of *people* (*millet* and *halk*) in the power struggles of the late 1990s and early 2000s. It also sums up some of the previous century's reconfigurations of the Ottoman Muslim subjects into a Turkish nation-state and the tensions inherent in that project, whereby a particular elite used concepts of *the people* to legitimize its own position vis-à-vis other elites. This was similar to developments elsewhere in Europe, and as we shall see in the next chapter, not the last time it happened in Turkish politics.

SIX

Democracy

In this chapter I trace how concepts of *democracy* were translated into Turkish and used as tools to restructure relations between the Turkish state and its citizens to gain international recognition and American economic aid and military protection. The Turkish translation equivalent of *democracy* is *demokrasi.* Despite the two words' apparent similarity, omnipresence in political debates, and frequent equation in translation, *demokrasi* and *democracy* have slightly different histories of use and different connotations and emphases (an argument that has been made in the Senegalese context by Schaffer 1998).[1] Moreover, the configuration of social and political relations that the Turkish concept has been used to stabilize has often been called "undemocratic" in English and other European languages. This creates a lot of potential for misunderstanding in English-Turkish interlingual relations and facilitates claims that mean something slightly different when translated from one language to the other. While competent leaders can use this divergence creatively, it can be a stumbling block for those who are not aware of these semantic differences or not skilled enough to use them to their advantage.

Demokrasi became omnipresent in Turkish political debates beginning in 1945; before that time, the Turkish state elite rarely used the concept to legitimize their rule, and when they did, *demokrasi* often carried meanings that would appear somewhat awkward and selective

---

1. This should, however, not be construed as an argument for or against Turkey's capacity for democratic governance.

when translated into English. Where divine grace had once been the served as the main legitimization for Ottoman rule, translations of key concepts used in French- or English-formulated international law were increasingly used in the struggle to legitimize rule over Anatolia in the aftermath of First World War—a struggle that involved both discursive and military aspects. *Millet* (variously *nation* or *people*) was used in ways that referred to Woodrow Wilson's Fourteen Points, where *nations* were the legitimate basis for sovereignty. In the name of the Turkish *millet*, the Grand National Assembly (Büyük Millet Meclisi) declared a republic (*cumhuriyet*) in 1923. With the exception of aborted attempts at allowing a controlled opposition party to form in 1924 and 1930, the Turkish Republic was organized as a single-party state until 1945. After Atatürk died in 1938, he was succeeded by his close confidant, former officer, prime minister, and CHP representative, İsmet İnönü, who ruled Turkey as *millî şef* (national chief) until 1945, and remained in power as president until 1950. A key turning point was when İnönü sent a delegation to the 1945 San Francisco Conference and officials became concerned about what to tell Americans when they asked the delegates "When will you establish a multiparty democracy?" (Akandere 2003, 17). According to one delegate, İnönü told them to answer that democracy had always been the goal of Atatürk's reforms (Erkin 1974). While Atatürk's writings contain no such statement (nor am I aware of sources confirming the delegate's memory), state discourse used this approach to legitimate multiparty elections in 1946.

Where ruling *on behalf of* the *millet* was enough to legitimize the Turkish state elite's position externally prior to 1945, laying claim to being a *democracy* and anchoring the claim in the practice of multiparty elections became an increasingly important way to seek external legitimacy after this historical juncture. As *democracy* became a key concept for legitimizing Turkey's position within "the Free World," it was and remains a concept that no political actor in Turkey can ignore, however undemocratic others may deem Turkish political practices.

Civilization and Democracy

Just as concepts of *civilization* were used to legitimize continued sovereign control over territory and access to international diplomatic congresses in the late nineteenth and early twentieth centuries, so did concepts of *democracy* become an institutionalized part of the vocabulary of statesmen who engaged in international society language games as the Second World War came to an end. *Civilization* was used to mean the restraint of individual passions, fostering reason and thus avoiding unnecessary war. In *Perpetual Peace*, often cited as the origins of "democratic peace theory," Immanuel Kant argues that republics do not make war. However, Kant rejected *democracy* as such but wrote that the *progress of civilization* (and *Enlightenment*) tempers human emotions, in turn minimizing the propensity for war (2003 [1795], 24).

Around the time of the Second World War, English-language authors started yoking together *civilization* and *democracy*, ultimately coming to use *democracy* where they had previously used *civilization*. Both concepts were used in ways that imbued *democracy* with a teleology similar to that of *civilization* (Bowden 2009, 82–88). There are nevertheless important differences between the uses of the two concepts, and these differences have practical consequences for legitimating political action. One such difference is that the Turkish concept of *medeniyet* came with a horizon of expectation in which its users typically envisioned a *European* future. Even though its *Europeanness* was usually denied, the historical goal of *medeniyet* was associated with practices, institutions, and achievements found in Europe. The horizon of expectation that has been drawn up by those who have relied on *demokrasi* has been more closely associated with social and political organization in the United States.

As in the case of *medeniyet* in the late nineteenth and early twentieth centuries, *demokrasi* became a historical goal—telos—of the grand narrative of Turkish history. But the concept of *medeniyet* did not disappear. Patrick Thaddeus Jackson has shown how concepts of *civilization* were used when German, British, and American leaders legitimized the rearmament and integration of "West Germany" into an American-dominated security complex following the Second World War (2006, 161–72, 201–38). Although I do not take issue with Jackson's point, I would argue that two things happened in international society language games after the Second World War. First, the discursive emphasis shifted from *civilization* to *democracy*. Second, a conceptual fragmentation took place. Where *civilization* had been put to a broad range of usages prior to 1945, a number of different concepts were used to express different aspects of these meanings. *Democracy* took the place of *civilization as condition* and as historical telos. Other usages of *civilization* were replaced by other concepts. *Civilization as entity* (aka Western civilization) was partly superseded by "the Free World," which was largely synonymous in use. *Civilization as process* became replaced to some extent by *modernization* and to some extent by *democratization* and *development*. This increased complexity and diversification of the semantic field of international society increased the possible strategies for reinterpreting Turkey's identity in that language game.

With this international (mostly English) shift in emphasis from *civilization* to *democracy*, it became less useful to argue that one was *civilized* if one could not simultaneously claim to be *democratic*. İnönü's concerns are indicative of just this importance. What the Turkish elite had invested in a cadre-led *progress* toward *civilization* was no longer enough to legitimize their position externally. Furthermore, in English and most importantly American usage, *democracy* is anchored in the practice of multiparty elections.[2] An American ally can do many things, but the practice of multiparty elections is the sine qua non if one wants to argue to an American audience that a country is *a democracy*. In the 1930s, Turkish intellectuals and jurists argued in Turkish that Turkey *was already a demokrasi* but largely either ignored or rejected the issue of multiparty elections and political competition. Whatever İnönü's personal inclinations, he appears to have been well aware of this close connection between *democracy* and elections in English discourse.

Since being *progressive* (*ilerici*) was treated as a mark of social distinction among the Turkish elite, the majority of the population was, almost by definition, linked to various categories of *reactionary, conservative*, or *traditional*, with *irticai* (reactionary) the most important and most damning. They represented the "wrong" side of the progress dialectic, and involving them in politics would mean taking the country away from the telos of *medeniyet*. Since the most widely agreed-upon intersubjective interpretation of *democracy* has long been *selecting governments through majority elections*, progress simply could not be

---

2. For anchoring practices, see Swidler 2001.

synonymous with *democratization* without redefining the purpose of the Turkish republican project. Because of the importance placed on this interpretation in international language games, it became increasingly difficult to maintain a Turkish concept of *demokrasi* that was incompatible with the concept of *democracy*. It appeared impossible to be *ilerici* while also arguing in favor of *demokrasi* at the same time, since the latter would mean involving people linked to the concept *reactionary* in the selection of the government and even the actual running of the state.

Democracy and *Republic* in Late Ottoman Discourse

States legitimizing their rule by reference to concepts other than divine grace was nothing new to the Turkish elite when the Grand National Assembly declared a Turkey a *republic* (*cumhuriyet*) in 1923. In fact, the Ottoman state had been suzerain over republics (known as *cumhûr* in Ottoman), such as Ragusa, and had relations with the Venetian Republic since the fourteenth century. However, in earlier Ottoman writing, a *cumhûr* was a rabble or a mob (Tezcan 2010, 233). As Marinos Sariyannis (2016) shows, when Ottoman statesmen had to interact with polities described as *cumhûr*, Ottoman writers tended to write of their leaders in monarchical terms. Thus, the *stadtholders* of the Commonwealth of the Netherlands (Felemenk Cumhûru [the Flemish *cumhûr*]) were described as *Felemenk kıralları* (the Flemish kings, in this specific context meaning William III of Orange) (45–46). The term *cumhûr*, as Sariyannis puts it,

> deserves a special study: we saw Kâtib Çelebi using it with the meaning "commonwealth, society"; by the early eighteenth century (as seen also in Na'ima's reference) it also denoted a state governed in a more or less democratic form (one will remember Defterdar's description of the Netherlands and Venice), while afterwards, as we are going to see, it was used for the French republic (and, also, its puppet states). (47)

By the late nineteenth century, *cumhûr* had become a conventional and less negatively charged way of speaking and writing about states such as the United States of America (sometimes called the United

Republics of America [Āmerikā Cemāhīr-i Müctemiʿasɪ]; see Şemseddīn Sāmī 1317, 482). However, when discussing its merits as a system of governance rather than merely using the name of a state, it was systematically argued to be inapplicable to the Ottoman polity and its meaning of *mob rule* was foregrounded (see Kul 2014, 159–64).

While *cumhûr* and the neologism *cumhuriyet* (that which is based on the *cumhûr*, previously written as *cumhurluk*) were becoming established in the second half of the nineteenth century, *demokrasi* was barely used until the 1920s. As in so many texts introducing a little-known European concept to an Ottoman audience, Ali Suavi's 1870 article, "Demōḳrāsī: Hükūmet-i Ḥalḳ: Müsāvāt" (Democracy: Government of the People: Equality), has neither a clear definition nor a consistent application of the word *demokrasi*. On the one hand, he linked it to *müsavat* (equality), while on the other to *cumhuriyet* (republic). Answering his own question, "Where do we currently find democracy?" Ali Suavi enumerates *republics,* concluding that "the biggest republic in Europe is Switzerland, which is a place as big as our Danube province" (1096). Even so, Ali Suavi broadened his discussion to nonrepublics such as France and Great Britain (he wrote the text during the Second French Empire),[3] calling the actions of their governments the actions of "republicans."[4]

For the most part, Ali Suavi used *demokrasi* almost synonymously with *müsavat* (*equality*). He referred not only to equality between the subjects but also to equality between ruler and ruled. Moreover, according to Ali Suavi, legitimate rule depends on recognition by those who are ruled (though the examples of those whose recognition needs to be sought by the ruler are only taken from the ruler's immediate entourage). Ali Suavi (1870, 1096, 1084–85) argues that *demokrasi* existed during the early caliphate (that of the first four rightful caliphs), because "all" (meaning Muhammed's companions) shared equally in the spoils of war.

In a discursive move that was typical of the Young Ottomans and that they shared with other Muslim reformist intellectuals of the time, Ali Suavi used Quranic tradition and Hadith to exemplify and

---

3. The text was published on 17 May 1870, four months before the Prussians captured Napoleon III at the Battle of Sedan and the Second French Empire foundered.

4. Ali Suavi generally argued in favor of constitutional monarchy, but this hardly features in his article on democracy.

explain European concepts in translation. This form of entanglement can be exemplified by Ali Suavi's (1870, 1091) claim that "there isn't a person who does not know that democracy is the highest form of egalitarian government and the most in accord with *şeriat* [Sharia]."[5] He transcribed a French concept into Ottoman and claimed that it was the one "most in accord with the holy law." By doing so and substantiating this claim with a story about one of the first four rightful caliphs, he in a sense equated an ancient (and perfect) past with a potential future. Ali Suavi also used a Halidî sheikh, Gümüşhaneli Ahmed Ziyaeddin (1813–1893), as an example of the prototypical person who would be a suitable basis for *demokrasi*, lamenting that not all the people of Istanbul were like him, or they would have *demokrasi* "by now." If men had proper *morality, müsavat* (*equality*) and *demokrasi* would follow.

Chapter 4's discussion of *civilization* stresses that among late-nineteenth-century Ottomans, moderation and honing one's comportment and disciplining one's emotions were ways to both enhance and show one's civilizational level. The concept of *ahlak* (*morality*) was also crucial to how Ali Suavi gives meaning to *demokrasi*. Immediately after discussing how *müsavat* had been a central virtue to the early Muslims and how they practiced *democracy*, he writes,

> Now that it is understood what democracy, rule of the people and equality means, we say that this form of government was practiced by this group and tribe who shared a unity of purpose and were loyal, observant, and pious community. They had no fear other than the fear of God, they had no work other than serving God, they had no institutions [tanẓīmāt] other than good morals; in sum, they were men of God. ([Ali Suavi] 1870, 1087–88)

Rousseau was referred to as making the same argument: "If there exist men of God, they are governed in the manner of democracy" (1093). So, good morals are a prerequisite for *democracy*, with a central virtue being *piousness*. However, Ali Suavi claimed that *democracy* was not working in France, because France as a nation "lacks a moral-

---

5. Ali Suavi uses an adjectival form related to *şeriat: eñ şer'î.*

ity limiting the liberties within the community" (1088–89). "Limiting *liberties* within the community" was a prerequisite for a successful *democracy*. Moreover, *morality*, not *law*, should delimit the individuals' *liberties*.

Ali Suavi furthermore argued that although *democracy* constituted the ideal form of government, it was ill suited to Ottoman conditions. First, the Ottomans were not moral enough and could not control their passions. Second, the Ottoman Empire was too large and heterogeneous to practice democracy. Finally, Ali Suavi made what may somewhat anachronistically be called a geopolitical argument: "The issue that we have to understand is that a state, such as the Ottoman state, has to be [governed] in accordance with its [geographic] location, circumstances and population [and consequently] be a sultanate" (Çelik 1993, 244) In short, *democracy* is an ideal that cannot apply equally everywhere.

The Science of Duty

In the running of the Turkish Republic, the Prussian-educated professional part of the Ottoman officer corps that had led the 1908 revolution was accompanied by European-educated Ottoman jurists, many of whom used the French Third Republic (1871–1940) as an important reference point (Hanioğlu 2011, 134–35). Most of these jurists were educated in France, Switzerland, or Germany, and all drew extensively on French and German legal philosophy when interpreting political concepts (Erozan 2005, 69–95). Although some of them were already becoming central during the Second Constitutional Period (1908–18), these jurists gained increased prestige after the establishment of the Turkish Republic in 1923 and were tasked with legal reform of the state. They took on the specialist functions of the state and lectured at the Darülfünun, which later became Istanbul University. They drew heavily on the legal positivist theories of Hans Kelsen (1881–1973), Georg Jellinek (1851–1911), Léon Duguit (1859–1928), and Maurice Hauriou (1856–1929), developing theories of statecraft and using such concepts as *state* and *society* in ways that became very important for the constitution of the Turkish state. In conjunction with the Turkish adoption of European codified legal practices, European extraterritorial jurisdiction in Turkey (one aspect of the so-called capitulations) was abolished (Turan Kayaoğlu 2010). Non-European states had difficulty claiming to be sufficiently civilized to revoke European extraterritoriality without anchoring this claim in a practice akin to legal positivism.

While using concepts as *hürriyet* (liberty), *terakki* (progress), and later *istiklal* (independence) as something positive, late Ottoman and early Republican Turkish statesmen and intellectuals used *demokrasi* as something by and large negative until the Second World War. As with *cumhûr* in the previous century, the most important use to which *demokrasi* was put was in the meaning of anarchic mob rule (Erozan 2005, 111). Central Ottoman jurists used the concept in the sense "majoritarian oppression" and mostly considered the political participation of commoners as harmful (Erozan 2005, 111–12). This linked the elite-oriented interpretation of the concept of *state* espoused by nineteenth-century French philosophers such as Gustave Le Bon and Auguste Comte with the Goltzian doctrine that the officer corps had a special duty to guide the state (see chapter 5).

A certain similarity also existed between the Goltzian principle that the whole *Volk/millet* should be armed to ensure the survival of the state and the way that Ottoman jurists of the Second Constitutional Period conceptualized subjects' relationship with the state (Erozan 2005, 115). According to Ottoman law professor Ahmed Şuayıb, the key purpose of law was to specify each subject's duties toward the state, and not to specify the duty of the state toward the citizen or guaranteeing freedom from oppression by the state. At this time, subjects' key duty was military service, which, with the possible exception of interaction with tax collectors, was perhaps also the primary relationship that most subjects had with the Ottoman state.

A late Ottoman introductory textbook to constitutional law, which was in fact a translation of French jurist Félix Moreau's *Précis Élémentaire de Droit Constitutionnel* (Mōrō 1327 AH / 1326 HS [1910], 18–19), states that "the state can rightfully subject individuals to indispensable sacrifices for the proper protection of society." Furthermore, "the benefit of the individual should always be sacrificed for public benefits and the law of individuals is inferior to the necessities of the state" (Erozan 2005, 116). The state's needs outweighed individual rights. Policymaking should be conducted according to the needs and nature of the state by politicians who, in Şuayıb's conception, were "doctors of politics" (Erozan 2005, 115). Anyone employed by the state must primarily care for the needs of the state and act accordingly. Ottoman jurists appear to have offered little guidance about what might constitute the "needs of the state," but whatever they might be, they took primacy over the needs of individuals, an argument that would not sound unfamiliar in today's Turkey.

National Sovereignty and the National Will

Although the Ottoman armies in the First World War were soundly beaten and the empire they fought to defend crumbled, the officer class survived and in fact thrived. The nationalist resistance movement in Anatolia, which was mobilized in 1919 with Mustafa Kemal and a handful of other officers as a central node, was an alliance between state officials, merchants and businessmen, magnates and landowners in the countryside, and the new professions in the cities. Its leaders were members of the old Ottoman Harbiyeli officer class trained at the Ottoman Academy of War (Ahmad 1977, 7). Furthermore, although Turkish historiography typically uses 1923 as a watershed, the discourse into which the members of the officer class had been socialized during their education and war experience became the mainstay of the Turkish republican project. In addition to the contributions by Colmar von der Goltz, discussed in the previous chapter, the discourse that they used drew heavily on Ziya Gökalp's translation of *Kultur* (*hars*) in combination with Akçura's "political Turkish millet based on race," both of which were formulated in the decades before the final collapse of the Ottoman Empire. Gökalp's and Akçura's reinterpretations and novel usages of concepts of *millet* were then embedded in a Social Darwinist and solidarist discourse that gave the officers and the state elite a particular duty of leadership in the struggle of survival between nations (Aksakal 2004; see also chapter 5). Having been formulated as an elitist project, this was then propagated through the local cultural branches of the Committee of Union and Progress, the Turkish Hearths (Türk Ocakları). The Turkish Hearths were spread across Anatolia and gave this conceptualization of the Turkish nation wide dissemination also among the lower rungs of the intellectual elite (Poulton 1997, 83). In the wake of the First World War, the territory of the Ottoman polity was reduced to Anatolia, and this was where the Turkish nationalists started their counteroffensive; thus, it was particularly important as a baseline for how the relationship between state and society was formulated in the aftermath of the War of Independence (1919–22).

After defeating the French, the Armenians, and the Greeks in turn; outmaneuvering the Italians; and staring down the British occupiers in Istanbul, the nationalists in Ankara gained the reins of power over Ottoman state institutions. The nationalist resistance movement had partly been formulated in what may called a religious language, and the religious institutions of the Ottoman Empire were put to important use in rallying and bringing together the resistance. However, after the military battles had been won, the newly declared Turkish Republic soon sidelined the religious jurists by abolishing the Sharia courts in 1924, instead giving European-educated jurists a leading role in reforming the state. They did so primarily by translating European laws and passing them in the Turkish Grand National Assembly—the Swiss Civil Code (1926), the Italian Criminal Code (1926), and the German Commercial Code (1928). These changes anchored claims to having a *civilized* legal system, which in turn was used as an argument to permanently abolish the capitulations involving European extraterritorial jurisdiction (Turan Kayaoğlu 2010, 136–47). In addition to the obvious entanglements of Turkish and European legal concepts through the translation of formal law codes, the presence of European-educated jurists in leading positions in the Turkish Republic meant that competing interpretations of key political concepts were increasingly drawn from European sources. European political discourse of the 1910s–1930s, in which the leading Turkish jurists had been educated and from which they drew their interpretations and made translations did to some extent fit with that of the late Ottoman Empire and early Republic.

Not surprisingly, concepts of *demokrasi* were marginal in political discourse of the Turkish Republic prior to 1945. Instead, *demokrasi* was discussed within the confines of academic and intellectual publications, with the law profession leading the way. Not only the European education of the jurists but also the social context in which the Turkish Republic emerged was of consequence for the interpretation of political concepts. French jurist Léon Duguit, who educated a number of important Turkish jurists, claimed that the state is a product of social differentiation between "the strong" (*les forts*) and those whom they govern, "the weak" (*les faibles*) (Erozan 2005, 121–22). Ahmed Salahaddin (1920, 154) used this setup when he found the origin of the state in "those who give orders and those who obey orders. . . . Here is the true material origin of the state!" (Erozan 2005, 122). Neither the Goltzian doctrine of officers' extraordinary duty in directing the state nor the Ottoman conceptual of *askerī* and *teba'a* seems far off. There are those who command and those who obey.

If an individual disagreed with the *national will* as expressed by the leader and his cadres, the individual rather than the state was at fault. In the words of Turkish jurist Sıddık Sami Onar (1941, 61),

> General interest is always superior to particular interests. It follows that the interest of the municipality is superior to that of the individual; and the interest of the state is in turn superior to the interest of the municipality. When these interests conflict it is the superior interest that must be given preference.

Having emerged from what became known as the War of Independence (*İstiklâl Harbı*), the nationalist elite of the newly founded republic placed an even greater emphasis on *unity* and *national sovereignty. Unity* was used in such a way that even Montesquieu's separation of powers threatened the integrity of the nation:

> Gentlemen, there is no separation of powers in reality, in nature, in the world. There cannot be a separation of powers in the power that we call the national will [*iradei milliye*]. (Kemal 1945a, 204)

Since the national will was said to be both the indivisible paramount power, it was argued that it could not be subject to the separation of powers. A division of power was anathema to the discourse of national unity, and Mustafa Kemal (1945c, 300) stated that "there is only one power. And that is national sovereignty."

This unity of purpose was to be embodied in the Republican People's Party (Cumhuriyet Halk Partisi, CHP). The political project was about the pursuit of a higher good; the goals of the Turkish reform (*inkılap*). The CHP would represent all interests in society by incorporating all goals and all wills into itself. As Turkish jurist Fuat Başgil (1940, 14) wrote in a book on Turkish public law,

> The Republican People's Party was not going to be like parties in classical parliamentary countries. This party, in a constant process of formation and perfection, would be formed as a conscientious and active cadre of discipline and education that has as its goal to encompass the entire nation [*millet*]. The nation would find in this cadre the ultimate expression of its unity. [The cadre] would realize the coincidence and identity of the party and the nation, and the nation and the party would in the future take the form of a single organization through the fusion of the nation and the party into one another. This is the organizing idea behind the principles of the Republican People's Party.

The party was to be the expression of all wills as well as the cadre that could lead the nation and in which the nation would find an expression of its own unity.

This semantic configuration was hegemonic in state discourse in the 1930s and gave meaning to *demokrasi* as it was translated into Turkish. In legal writings that explicitly dealt with *demokrasi*, this concept simply meant that "sovereignty belongs to the nation" and did not entail practices such as elections. When the concept was used in this way, Turkey was represented as a *demokrasi* but of a different sort from "classical" or "liberal" democracies. As Turkish law professor and minister of justice Mahmut Esat Bozkurt's (1930, 5555) used *demokrasi*, it meant the sovereignty of the *millet* and not much else. The concept was primarily given meaning by contrasting it with counterconcepts such as *padişahlık* (rule by a sultan) and *müstemleke* (colony). Introducing something that he called *Kemalist demokrasi*, which he differentiated from the latter two concepts, Bozkurt (5556–57) reinterpreted it to include *social and economic democracy* as well as *political democracy*. This *Kemalist democracy*, according to Bozkurt, "does not necessarily require parties"; instead, it required "liberty, equality, justice and sovereignty." *Rights* was not on the list. As long as the Turkish *revolution* was ongoing, there was no need for multiple parties; they would wait until the regime was fully consolidated (Erozan 2005, 167).

In a public lecture after not long after Atatürk's death, Bozkurt claimed to quote from an issue of the *The Times*: "It is a mistake to assume that Atatürk's regime is a dictatorship. The regime is democratic. Only, it completes an important deficiency in our democracies, and that is authority" (1940, 128–29). He concluded that "here is the real meaning of Atatürk's legacy." Furthermore, he linked the concept of democracy to that of *şef* (chief or leader). In the international context of the time, the use of *şef* would be an easily recognizable link to other authoritarian and totalitarian rulers such as Mussolini, "Il Duce"; Franco, whose official title was "Caudillo"; Hitler, "Der Führer"; and Rafael Trujillo, "El Jefe"—all of which carry the meaning of "the leader" or "the chief." Bozkurt (1940, 128) even claimed that Hitler had taken Atatürk as his example and sought to reconcile the German concept of *Führerschaft* with the Turkish *demokrasi*:

> Kemalism is an authoritarian democracy that has its roots in the people, in the Turkish nation. It resembles a pyramid—its base is the people, its apex is the head, who again comes from among the people and whom we call *Şef*. The *Şef* derives his authority from the people. And democracy is nothing but precisely this.

While the thrust of this argument is slightly different, this representation is broadly speaking a variation of Duguit's and Ahmed Salahadin's claims about the weak and the strong combined with Onar's arguments that the general will must always trump individual wills. Each element has its *roots* in the people, but that does not change who commands whom. One may of course wonder whether Bozkurt turned a descriptive ideal type of how the state functions into a normative argument about how it ought to be.

Much as the Turkish Hearths were the Committee of Union and Progress's means of making its ways of conceptualizing relations between state and society available to a broad public, the early republic eagerly disseminated its conceptualizations through the school system. This way, these conceptual changes became an institutionalized part of discourse for a broad section of society and consequently more durable over time. The primary text that was used in these classes was *Vatandaş İçin Medenî Bilgiler* (Civic/Civilized Knowledge for the Citizen), which Kemal dictated to his adopted daughter, Ayşe Afet (İnan), and which was published in 1931. Here, the concept of *demokrasi* received a thorough treatment in a manner that drew heavily on the usage of early republican jurists:

> The ideal of democracy, in its full meaning, prescribes that the general assembly of the nation is in the governing position, or if nothing else, that the final will of the state is nothing but the expression and manifestation of the nation. (Âfetinan 1998 [1931], 32)

The *national will*, which was closely linked with *inkılap* and embodied by the Republican People's Party, was used also to give meaning to *demokrasi*. There was no mention of what Americans or Britons or would consider an important anchoring practice of *democracy*—multiparty elections. The history of using *demokrasi* to stabilize a configuration of social relations that *democracy* usually does not cover is one reason why translation between *democracy* and *demokrasi* involves a surprising amount of semantic reconfiguration.

Democracy Is Coming

Having allied with Britain and France in 1940 but not heeding its treaty obligations until the outcome of the war was clear, Turkey declared war on Germany in February 1945. The rationale for doing so, Turkey's foreign minister explicitly told the Grand National Assembly, was that if the country declared war by March 1, it would gain a place in the United Nations (Turkey 1945b, 126). The United Nations was convening an April 1945 conference in San Francisco to "negotiate the future world order [*nizam*]," and Turkey should not be absent (126). Sitting at the negotiating table with the victors was a matter not only of state prestige but also of securing Turkey's independence and territorial integrity.

The entanglement of *demokrasi* and *democracy* cannot be understood without two important events that occurred on 7 June 1945. In

Moscow, the Turkish ambassador was presented with what have become known as "Stalin's demands": Kars and Ardahan provinces would be "returned" to the USSR; the USSR would be permitted to establish bases in Turkey for the "joint defense" of Istanbul and the Çanakkale Straits; and the two countries would conclude an agreement revising the Montreux Convention governing the straits (Coş and Bilgin 2010, 43). Although these demands were not new and had not previously been considered a serious security threat, with the Soviet Union's increased military capacity and occupation of Eastern Europe, Turkish leaders found themselves in a far more vulnerable position. In addition, in Ankara on the same day, four CHP deputies presented party leaders with the Dörtlü Takrir (Statement of the Four), which demanded greater political liberties in the name of *demokrasi*, a concept to which the leadership had recently declared its commitment. Although it was a coincidence that the two events happened at the same time, together they created a situation where the CHP leadership needed to anchor its English claims to *democracy* in practices that Americans and Brits considered *democratic* to secure American and British protection in the face of Stalin's demands. The situation reinforced the salience of the claims made by the authors of the Statement of the Four, since it was impossible for the CHP to externally legitimize its political position to the extent that they could get Western protection without at the same time reconfiguring social relations domestically by using *demokrasi* as a tool. As a consequence, *demokrasi* and *democracy* became more densely entangled.

As with all new hegemonic usages, İnönü did not simply use *demokrasi* in an entirely new way without any precursors. The newspapers *Tan* and *Vatan*, run by Zekeriya Sertel (1890–1980) and Ahmet Emin Yalman (1885–1972), respectively, had used *demokrasi* in this way from the early 1940s. Both of these men had been educated at Columbia University, and Sertel's wife, Sabiha, who was a frequent contributor to *Tan*, had been educated at New York City's Barnard College. Their writings on *demokrasi* drew extensively on English interpretations, and they started using *demokrasi* by tying it to *hürriyet* (in the meaning of individual liberty) and arguing that it should be anchored in multiparty elections. Although Sertel and Yalman were not particularly important in terms of their personal standing in the political debate, as authors they introduced precursors of a discourse that the United States would soon support with military resources in Turkey (support that the Americans were already providing to other countries) (VanderLippe 2005, 105–7).

As İnönü's concerns at the 1945 San Francisco Conference show, Turkish political leaders would soon have to pay heed to interpretations of *democracy* as a matter of *liberty* linked to the English dichotomies of democracy/totalitarianism and liberty/oppression and anchored in the practice of multiparty elections. Although the Turkish government could close *Tan* and *Vatan* (and indeed did so until the end of the war), sticking to the specific Turkish usage of *demokrasi* discussed above became increasingly difficult in the late 1940s, when it became a key concept in interlingual relations between Turkey and the United States. It also became untenable to ignore American interpretations of this concept, uphold the Kemalist single-party state, *and* participate in the international political community dominated by the United States and Britain (VanderLippe 2005, 161–87).

In addition to the discursive work done by Ahmet Emin Yalman and Sabiha and Zekeriya Sertel, the entanglement of Turkish *demokrasi* with American usage of *democracy* had another precondition in the labeling of different actors in the Second World War. *Demokrasi* increasingly became used in discussions of international relations and geopolitical alignment. When the war turned in 1943–44 and what various actors, among them Turkish media, called the "democratic powers" or "democratic countries" started recording battlefield victories. By the time Turkey declared war on Germany, the concept of *demokrasi* had already come into frequent use in Turkish discourse on international relations, though not on domestic affairs. An unsigned February 1945 editorial in the newspaper *Yeni Sabah* that compared the policies of wartime neutrals Sweden, Switzerland, Spain, and Turkey alleged that Turkey had never been a strict neutral and that it "had long since taken her place on the democratic front" (Deringil 1989, 179). Moreover, Nadir Nadi, a Turkish columnist who had gained a reputation for being pro-Axis, wrote, "We always saw the fate of civilization and mankind as hinging on allied victory" (Deringil 1989, 179). The link between *civilization* and *democracy* in that the "fate of civilization and mankind" was in the hands of the *democratic front* is not entirely different from contemporary English discourse. As the Allies won the war, and Turkey started seeking inclusion in the

Western security community, the English yoking together of *democracy* and *civilization* also became current in Turkish, and was used this way even among people who had been known for Axis sympathies.

Between Turkey's last-minute entry into the Second World War on the side of the "democratic powers" and the election of the Demokrat Parti (Democrat Party, DP) government in 1950, the CHP discourse using these concepts was full of contradictions. On the one hand, the party legitimized and in fact celebrated its decision to announce multiparty elections: "Our decision to take our place alongside the democracies has gained us great sympathy [around] the world" (Turkey 1945a, 13). In this text, the gains to be had from announcing multiparty elections lay not in any virtues inherent in democracy or even the domestic benefits it might bring about but in the sympathy gained internationally and in Turkey's ability to "take its place alongside the democracies"—the most powerful and prestigious countries in the world and largely coextensive with "Western civilization." In other words, *demokrasi* was a matter of prestige.

Having instructed the delegation going to San Francisco to tell the Americans that a democracy with multiparty elections had always been Atatürk's goal, İnönü started using the concept in his speeches. Most important, he declared in his 19 May 1945 Youth Day speech,

> Our homeland's political administration, the administration by the people [*halk*], which was established with the republic [*cumhuriyet*] will continue to be developed with progress in all its facets and all its necessities. Democratic principles will take even greater precedence in the political intellectual life of the country, by abolishing the restrictions that have been made necessary by the precautionary measures in the time of war. Our greatest democratic institution is the Grand National Assembly, which has taken rule into its hand from day one, and continuously led the country along the road of democracy. (Akandere 2003, 25)

While strong on the use of *demokrasi*, the speech was fairly weak on specifics, and it was this that prompted the Statement of the Four on the same day as the Soviet Union issued "Stalin's demands." The four CHP parliamentary deputies—Celal Bayar, Fuad Köprülü, Adnan

Menderes, and Refik Koraltan—proposed that the Republican People's Party give citizens their *siyasî hürriyetler* (political liberties) and make the Grand National Assembly into the democratic institution it was meant to be rather than merely following the letter of the Turkish constitution. Like İnönü before them, they also linked the goal of *demokrasi* back to Atatürk's intentions:

> The Turkish Republic, which was born of the holy War of Independence which is tied to the immortal name of Atatürk, created in the first Law of Constitutional Organization [1921] what was perhaps one of the world's most democratic constitutions and gave wide expression to both individual liberties and *millî* (national/popular) accountability. . . . In these days when the winds of liberty and democracy have won a full victory and blow through the entire world and international security has become tied to the principle of respect for democratic liberties, there can be no doubt that also in our country, the whole *millet*, from the president down to its smallest [member], carries the same democratic ideals. (Akandere 2003, 23)

Tying together individual liberties with *demokrasi* and international security and order, the authors suggested that İnönü be more concrete in the *progress toward democracy* that he had stated as a historical goal of Atatürk's reforms. İnönü rejected the proposal, and the signatories came under a deluge of criticism from the CHP. There is no indication that they intended to set up an opposition party, but as the criticism became unbearable, İnönü suggested that they do so (Akandere 2003). The Demokrat Parti thus emerged through joint action between members of the CHP, where the actors, initially, seem to have intended something else.

The intraparty debates that led to the formation of the Demokrat Parti centered on the appropriate use and meaning of *liberty* (*hürriyet*) and its connection to *demokrasi*. At stake was whether a commitment to *demokrasi* would entail more political liberties. In September 1945, with the end of the war and the CHP government under increasing international and domestic pressure to relax the wartime restrictions on civil liberties, Prime Minister Şükrü Saraçoğlu responded to the Statement of the Four with what he called "the government's reply to the charlatans of liberty [*hürriyet*]" (*Cumhuriyet* 1945a). He claimed that "the Turkish state has been part of the family of democratic states for 20 years" and that "the criticism of the government is unwarranted." Here, *democracy* was not about practice but was about *belonging*. The Turkish Republic *belonged* to the family of *democracies*, regardless of its political practices.

This was argued by using a conceptualization of *hürriyet* that drew on exactly the kind of collectivist political discourse that had been in vogue prior to 1945. One example can be found in "Democracy and Liberty among Us" (Bizde Demokrasi ve Hürriyet), an article published in the government paper, *Cumhuriyet* in which the editor, Yavuz Abadan (1945, 1) challenges those who had formed the DP:

> Those who have clamored for *hürriyet* and *demokrasi* until today have to explain their true goals, and they have not acceded to [giving an] objective analysis of what it is they find lacking in Turkey: the purposes/meanings of *hürriyet*; how do they understand *demokrasi*; and finally, what kind of relationship do they think there is between these two concepts? It is a vain effort to search for a serious answer to all of these answers among the pile of columns and columns of writings [they have produced]. The only common point of principle that catches the eye among all of this noise: to make us look good to the foreigners—or even worse—to present [it] as a tribute [to the foreigners], to pursue the goal of making our regime resemble those of others.

Abadan follows up by arguing that Turkish democracy must be appropriate to "our national character [*millî karakterimiz*]." The CHP was claiming that the DP was merely engaging in *parti kavgaları* (party quarrels) and was motivated by *subjective* rather than *objective* interests—that is, DP members sought personal gain, whereas İnönü, like Atatürk, had the entire *millet* in mind—and that they therefore offered little principled opposition.

While much of the defense launched by Abadan and others relied on established meanings of *demokrasi* in Turkish, Sertel's and Yalman's newspapers gained allies in their search for appropriate ways to use and interpret *demokrasi*. For an explanation of the concept, "which is used very frequently and whose description is being sought these days," the pro-CHP newspaper *Cumhuriyet* (1945c) turned to Winston Churchill's speeches and claimed to be able to identify nine qualities of *demokrasi*:

1. freedom of ideas and the freedom of opposition and criticism;
2. the people's [*halk*] right to bring down a government that does not satisfy it;
3. the possibility for the people to show their will via legal routes;
4. courts are free from interference and able to render decisions without any kind of influence or threats;
5. laws that uphold justice;
6. all individuals, rich or poor, treated with equality, and not to keep civil servants aloof from the people;
7. protecting individuals within the framework of the law so that they can perform their duties toward the state;
8. people do not need to fear the law enforcement [*zabıta*] that exists under single-party rule;
9. all judgments are transparent to protect against torture and ill-treatment.

While neither elections nor majority government were part of the nine main aspects of *demokrasi*, the *Cumhuriyet* article argued that holding elections was nevertheless the best way to conduct affairs and minimize differences within a country. Rather than encouraging *parti kavgaları*, elections sought to maintain a unity of purpose. They did, however, merely constitute *one* aspect of *demokrasi*, and not the main one. *Cumhuriyet* concluded that different countries needed different types of *democracy* according to their national character (*millî karakter*). There was no *Archimedean point* for defining a democracy; it had to spring from the particular traits of the collective practicing it. (One may of course wonder exactly *where* in Churchill's writings the author found this point, if that is in fact its source.) Both Abadan's piece and the *Cumhuriyet* article used Ali Suavi's argument that democracy was not appropriate for Turkey but needed to be adjusted to fit the country's *millî karakter*, geographic position, and other needs.

The 1950 Elections

The experience of the "opposition parties" that were formed and largely controlled by the CHP in 1924–25 and 1930 meant that when the Demokrat Parti was formed in January 1946, its founders had difficulty claiming that the DP was in fact an actual opposition party rather than a mere puppet that was there to legitimize the CHP. Moreover, springing out of the CHP as they did, they struggled to formulate a political platform that was sufficiently distinct from that of the governing party. The CHP also kept claiming that there could be no disagreement about the state's goals (which were those of the Turkish *inkılap*) but only about the *means* of attaining those goals. According to one Turkish jurist and CHP member,

> In the end, we must all gather together around the same goal. In the wide and scientific sense, "politics" is the determination of this one common goal and the connection and harmony between various activities to reach the goal. (Abadan 1943, 3)

Even after Turkey introduced multiparty elections, this jurist continued to argue that multiparty competition in the Kemalist republic involved ways to implement Atatürk's reforms rather than disagreement about what the future should look like (Abadan 1946).

The four founders of the Demokrat Parti—Celal Bayar, Adnan Menderes, Refik Koraltan, and Fuad Köprülü—all had their political backgrounds from the CHP, and were very much part of the Turkish republican project. However, it is noteworthy that none had attended the Ottoman Military Academy, and none were officers (as opposed to e.g. İsmet İnönü, Kemal Atatürk or many of the other central figures in the Republican People's Party).[6] Moreover, as the sons of landowners, jurists, and professionals, their social standing was to some extent independent of their position in the CHP.

---

6. Bayar was the son of a religious scholar and began his career in Ottoman banking and in the Regie, the foreign-controlled Ottoman Tobacco Monopoly. Menderes was the heir to one of the largest estates of the Aegean, said to be five thousand hectares, and educated as a lawyer. Köprülü was an intellectual and leading literary figure descended from the illustrious Köprülü dynasty, which had provided several grand viziers in the seventeenth century. Koraltan was a lawyer who had studied at the Istanbul Faculty of Law before becoming a state employee.

A central point of debate at the time of the formation of the DP was the Land Reform Bill, which sought to redistribute large landholdings—including that of the Menderes family—to landless peasants. Since the peasant voters understood little about what practices should be associated with *demokrasi* and were seldom in a position to exercise them, voting in the countryside was to a great extent directed by local power brokers who were themselves frequently landowners (Birand, Dündar, and Çaplı 1991). The DP itself vehemently denied being very different from the CHP, but as the only other party of significant size, the DP became the focus of voters dissatisfied with the CHP, and given the Land Reform Bill this included many among rural elites. The DP challenged the CHP's monopoly on power by using translation equivalents of concepts that İnönü and his delegation had used to legitimate Turkey's place at the conference in San Francisco. By outmaneuvering the CHP on questions such as the public practice of religion, the DP attracted support from a broad range of voter groups.

The DP challenged the semantic links between the *halk, millet,* and the *şef* that Mustafa Kemal Atatürk and the Republican People's Party had created in the 1920–40s as well as the social configuration that these links stabilized. Colmar von der Goltz's *Das Volk in Waffen* had stressed that the military had a particular duty to *lead* the state but that the nation's survival rested on arming the people. Thus, the state *rests* on the people (*Volk* in the German original, translated into Ottoman as *millet* [nation]) but is led by a cadre of particularly suited men. So, in the run-up to the 1950 election, when Turkish prime minister Şemsettin Günaltay declared that "interpreting democracy as unlimited freedom opens the road for anarchy in the national society," the point was the need for *leadership* and limiting freedoms: "Democracy means to found a state for the people, with the will of the people. . . . [I]f the citizens choose good people, things will go well" (*Ulus* 1950a, 6).

Avni Refik Bekman (1950), a professor of chemistry and parliamentary deputy for the CHP in the 1940s and 1950s, "trusted" that because of its good virtues, the Turkish *millet* would select good leaders, but Bekman also lamented that debate took the form of duels, leading to a struggle of all against all. Where Ali Suavi had once argued that the Ottomans lacked morality (*ahlak*) and therefore could not have democracy, Bekman argued that politics needed to be *ilmî* (scientific). He claimed that the CHP's opponents were *terbiyesiz* (unmannered, uncultured, and perhaps also disobedient), particularly as a consequence of their lack of scientific knowledge and reliance on *hissî* (passionate/feeling-based) and *subjektif* (subjective) methods. Conversely, according to Bekman, "the Great Man"—İnönü—had democracy as his highest ideal and used *objektif* (objective) methods. Bekman here made use of the discourse that Atatürk had used to legitimize his position, Baltacıoğlu used to discuss science as the basis of *civilization,* and Europeans had used to formulate their claims that Turkey had to adopt *objective* legal methods as a prerequisite for recognition as *civilized* and hence as *sovereign* (see chapters 3 and 4).

In 1950, the editor of the government newspaper, *Ulus* (The Nation),[7] equated the danger of other parties with that of the foreign invasion of 1919, linking together the various key concepts I have discussed:

> Today the [Republican] People's Party once again finds itself face to face with the duty to save the fatherland [*vatan*]. . . . The National Struggle [Millî Mücadele, the War of Independence] gave us *millî hakimiyet* [national sovereignty] by saving the Turkish Fatherland [*Türk vatanı*] from foreign invasion and sultanic tyranny [*padişah zulmü*]. Those who at the time adopted national sovereignty in all its comprehensiveness and sincerity now have to save our democracy from anarchy and reaction. Because just as on one side reaction has started rearing its ugly head, so on the other do the activities of external enemies who want to destroy the Turkish Nation [*Türk Milleti*] and their agents on the inside catch one's eye. There are also some brainless people, who, without noticing the severity of the struggle that is taking place, have joined this disturbance that takes the name of party politics [*particilik*], and it is clear that they have long incited the great mass of citizens [*vatandaş*] who have guarded themselves from partisanship and not thought of other

7. This is a Turkic-rooted concept for *nation* that was re-introduced to replace *millet* after the language reform. It has different connotations tied to Turkicness and the sun-language theory, but the configuration of social relations that it was used to stabilize was much the same.

things than the felicity and progress of the country [*memleket*]. The People's Party is the child of the National Struggle. The People's Party is the proponent and standard-bearer [*bayraktar*] of democracy, and it was they who made the decision to create national sovereignty. They are the ones to have bravely, patiently, and in a spirit of tolerance actively propounded democratic principles without losing their composure over the past five years of difficulties. The People's Party has established the nation's external dignity and life, and by making friendships and alliances with the world's most powerful states, it has secured an honorable place for Turkey in Europe and in the community of civilization. (Yalçın 1950, 1)

According to this author, since the War of Independence had established the *millî hakimiyet* (national/popular sovereignty), and since national sovereignty was a prerequisite for democracy, *demokrasi* should also be left to the CHP.

Democracy as Telos

By appealing to voters excluded from the state project by the CHP's othering of explicit religiosity and traditional lifestyles, the Demokrat Parti won the 1950 elections in a landslide. In a move that has few parallels in Turkish history, İnönü conceded defeat and went into opposition, an action the pro-DP press lauded as the final step on the historical road toward the West. *Garb medeniyeti* (Western civilization) and *demokrasi* now became largely synonymous and were projected back in time to become the historical telos of all the political changes that the Ottoman Empire and Turkey had undergone over the past 111 years. *Milliyet*, a newspaper established immediately after the 1950 election, heralded the DP's victory:

It is not necessary to mention that the first step toward democracy could [only] be made after turning to Western civilization. Considering this, we may count the 1839 Tanzimat, which was the beginning of all our efforts on the road of Westernization, the first step toward the goal of democracy. But it was a step without spirit and foundation. (Oksal 1950, 2)

The absence of spirit and foundation, according to *Milliyet*, resulted from the fact that the step had been carried out by an elite that forced the reforms on the people. In this particular use of *demokrasi*, the political system hardly matters. *Demokrasi* is *us*, it is *now* as well as *our future*, more than a political system or set of practices.

While the pro-CHP press and the CHP itself had largely represented the 1950 campaign as an effort to *save* the Turkish *inkılap*, *Milliyet* published an article, "Our Revolutions: Five Stages in Our History" (İnkilâplarımız: Tarihimizde Beş Merhale), arguing that the DP victory was itself an *inkılap* and linking it to all the major political changes in the Ottoman Empire and Turkish Republic:

> 1839 [the Tanzimat], 1876 [the Ottoman Constitution], 1908 [the Young Turk Revolution], 1923 [the establishment of the Turkish Republic], and 1950 are the main stages in the steps we have taken toward the West and toward democracy. (Oksal 1950, 2)

DP discourse thus represented *all* of Turkey's political changes as teleologically pointing to this moment in history, when Turkey *finally* achieved democracy.

There is a contrast between an established CHP discourse that *demokrasi* should be limited by the needs of the *inkılap* or even that it should be run exclusively by the CHP and this new discourse centered on the DP. İnönü persistently defended *demokrasi* as the best way to secure the gains of the *inkılap* after 1945. He argued that it was better for the CHP to let go of government power as soon as possible than to cling to it and risk the *inkılap*. Furthermore, the CHP's newspaper *Ulus* (1950b, c) quoted the *New York Times* as declaring that despite the CHP's defeat, the elections constituted İnönü's greatest achievement. These can be seen as attempts at yoking together *demokrasi* and *medeniyet* as largely synonymous historical teloi by way of entanglement with English. Although this approach mitigated some of the most problematic incompatibilities of the two concepts, the contradiction between *democracy* as majoritarianism and *civilization* as a mark of social distinction and cadre-led *progress* nevertheless persists in Turkish discourse to this day: certain political actors still seek to save "the modernization project" from the masses.

International Dichotomies

The conceptual dichotomies that became the main identity markers of international politics after the Second World War (*democracy* and *communism, capitalism* and *socialism*) were also used in Turkish prewar discourse. As early as 1921, Mustafa Kemal (1945a, 190–91) said,

> Our government is neither a democratic government nor a socialist government. And as a matter of fact it is a government that does not resemble any of the types that are found in books with scientific categories of governments. But it is a government that gives the unique expression of the national will and national sovereignty; it is a government of this nature! If it is necessary to name our government from a social-scientific perspective, we say "popular government" [*halk hükümeti*]. . . . Never mind that it does not resemble democracy or socialism, that it does not resemble anything! Gentlemen, we should take pride in not resembling and not imitating! For we resemble [none but] ourselves!

Falih Rıfkı (from 1934, Atay), who wrote books and newspaper articles about his extensive travels in Europe and Russia during the late 1920s and 1930s, also employed conceptual pairs such as *democracy* and *communism*, but he argued that the Turkish system should be a synthesis of the "best from both systems" (1931, 4). Rather than a telos of Turkish history, *demokrasi* was in the 1930s one of several tools to be employed in the attainment of *progress* toward *medeniyet*.

Totalitarianism and tyranny were largely absent from the semantic field giving meaning to *democracy* prior to 1945 (with the exception of *Tan* and *Vakit*, which started writing about *democracy* versus *totalitarianism* as early as 1943 [VanderLippe 2005, 105–7]). With the end of the war approaching, the dichotomy between *democracy* and a more generalized kind of totalitarianism that was also associated with *racism* also came into use by party-associated newspapers such as *Ulus* (Deringil 1989, 174). A striking example of this dichotomous approach to politics appeared in an article that *Cumhuriyet* (1945b) claimed had been translated from the American magazine *Life*:

In the green hillsides of the Alps the Lake of Konstanz, with its eye-catching, deep blue waters, divides the German nation [*millet*] into two. One of the two nations into which it divides them lives in prosperity and the other in destitution. On the one side of the lake are the Germans of the Third Reich. Their youth are either dead or maimed in the war, their cities are in ruins, and they themselves live under foreign rule. Today they are drenched in poverty, and it is unclear what will become of them in the future. On the lake's other side, however, live the northern Swiss, who are also German, and in addition to being part of the same race, they speak the same language, they have many of the same characteristics/qualities. But for centuries they have not seen the face of war, and their standard of living is very high. The most important of it all is that they live under a free horizon and can be called free humans. What has created this difference between them? The Swiss came to a fork in the road six centuries ago. But they chose the road of *demokrasi* and have not turned back.[8]

By attributing the entirety of the Swiss/German discrepancy in 1945 to *demokrasi*, the article made it difficult to argue against the concept.

Likewise, a Turkish translation of an article from *The Economist* appeared in *Cumhuriyet* in September 1945. This piece posited the primary dichotomy as pitting *kapitalizm* (capitalism) against *komünizm* (communism) and asked whether a war between the two was inevitable (Crowther 1945). This was an important part of the introduction and reiteration of this relatively new but soon dominant dichotomy. *Demokrasi* and *kapitalizm* thus became linked in that both were paired opposites of *komünizm*.

The front page of September 1945 edition of *Cumhuriyet* (1945d) featured a story about how the British Labour Party's *Daily Herald* had asked, "Can there be evidence put forward that the system that the Soviets have today is *Demokrasi?* Definitely not!" By 1951, the Turkish concepts of *hür dünya* (the Free World) and *demokrasi* were also yoked together. Osman Şevki Çiçekdağ (1899–1956), a parliamentarian

---

8. I could find no corresponding article in *Life* magazine's online archive, although given the ubiquitousness of Turkish newspapers' practice of translating English-language articles, *Cumhuriyet* may have named the wrong American publication.

from Ankara, declared that "All the world knows that" the Demokrat Parti's assumption of power "is an enormous and magnificent democratic victory for the Turkish nation, that is remembered by all and followed by the Free World with admiration and appreciation" (Turkey 1951, 636). The link between *the Free World* and *democracy* was such that it was difficult to conceive of one without the other. Being *free* [*hür*] increasingly meant being among the *democracies*, which were also linked to *kapitalizm.*

Since the Universal Declaration of Human Rights in 1948, the concept of *human rights* has attained much the same meaning as "standard of civilization."[9] As Jenna Reinbold (2016) argues, as a nonbinding document with no mechanism for enforcement, the Universal Declaration holds almost no legal authority. Although its authority is virtually entirely moral, its authority formalized *human rights* as a set of standards against which the world's polities are measured and thus placed the concept in a position to structure social relations among states. Following the Universal Declaration's 1949 translation into Turkish, *insan hakları* (human rights) was soon used for distinguishing between a *hür dünya* Us and this collective's Other, *marksizm* (Marxism). The difference between Them and Us was argued to be that "they" do not adhere to the principle of human rights:

> The principle of Marxist political doctrine is oppression—that is to say dictatorship. Because one cannot observe oppression and liberty at the same time, there cannot be a relationship between the political foundation of Marxism and real democracy. On the contrary, the insight consists of the observation that Marxist political interpretation is the opposite of real democracy. In real democracies, the foundations of liberty are the human rights and fundamental freedoms! To keep them safe, human dignity and value must also be protected. In the Marxist understanding of politics, there is no importance given to the dignity of mankind and fundamental human rights.

---

9. Unlike the Statute of the International Court of Justice, which was proclaimed three years earlier and explicitly tied its legitimacy to the laws between "civilized nations," the Universal Declaration of Human Rights does not once mention *civilization* or *civilized nations.*

There, what is important is to create a classless society. (Turkey 1950, 1–2)

In other words, *we* have human rights and fundamental freedoms, whereas *they* have dictatorship and oppression. This refrain has been common in international politics during the postwar period and especially in U.S. foreign policy (Campbell 1992).

Legitimizing the Coups

The Turkish military has intervened directly in the political process by staging coups in 1960, 1971, 1980, and 1997. The 1960 coup ousted the Demokrat Parti government led by Menderes and ended with his execution and those of two other leading DP figures. The military and the CHP press legitimized this coup by contending that it had been carried out to protect *demokrasi*. The CHP's *Ulus* attacked the DP for failing to practice democracy:

> We find ourselves having entered a new era, as a *normal* regime has replaced the outgoing regime. . . . The outgoing regime's name was Democracy. But it itself was not democratic. Today's temporary administration begins by undertaking to rectify the foundations of democracy in the shortest possible time. . . . Democracy needs absolute transparency. Democracy means that the nation sees that its own affairs are run in this or that manner. To see [this], it is absolutely necessary to know or at least learn how things are going and how they are run. (Aral 1960, 2)

This argument hinges on an interpretation of *democracy* as practice rather than as the geopolitical entities of *democracies* as opposed to the *communist bloc* where *totalitarianism* reigned. In a sense, this rhetorically separates the political party known as the Demokrat Parti from the concept of *demokrasi* used to create the party and legitimize its rule. In the decade and a half following the Second World War, concepts of *demokrasi* had become so important that even the military used it to oust an elected government on the grounds that its practices were not democratic.

The interim regime picked up on Atatürk's old conceptual usage when it distinguished between the DP's "subjective" and "passion-based" politics and the new leaders' "objective" and "serious" politics, announcing an *ilmî heyet* (scientific commission) "for identifying anti-democratic laws" (*Ulus* 1960, 1). The DP administration was labeled "morally bankrupt" and was accused of having run the country with policies that amounted to a kind of "domestic colonialism" (Karaosmanoğlu 1960, 1). *Morality*, the absence of which Ali Suavi had cited as the main reason for why *demokrasi* was not appropriate in the Ottoman Empire, was also a key concept in explaining why the DP's rule was illegitimate:

> Since democracies do not rely on virtues, since moral principles did not determine our relationships, this decidedly alienates democracies from their roots and decidedly brings catastrophe to the country. The most blatant example of this is what we have personally experienced with the Demokrat Parti. The Demokrat Parti at first propagated great ideals, [but] the dishonest leader and his entourage soon departed from their virtues and moral principles. The former governing party sought to tie them in by building constructions that would benefit themselves and thereby also benefit [the voters]. (Baban 1960, 1)

Demokrasi was used to mean a system where only individuals' wishes were taken into account, not the collective as a whole. *Demokrasi* then, was not directly linked to political competition but was tied to an organic approach to society as a whole that took into account the interests of *all* components when making decisions. Dispensing with self-serving politicians could then be argued to serve rather than harm democracy.

The military's 1971 intervention—almost exactly a century after Suavi had made his point about how *demokrasi* was not suitable to the Ottoman state—also used a variant of this argument. According to

Turkish prime minister Nihat Erim, *demokrasi* required a certain level of *progress*, and more *liberal* constitutions required further advanced societies:

> The Turkish Constitution is more liberal than many of the constitutions of the European countries. Turkey cannot afford such a luxury. By changing the constitution and by taking out the fundamental rights and freedoms, we will create an authority that prevents them from being abused. (*Milliyet* 1971, 1)

Excessive and luxurious liberty had enabled students to create "anarchic events" that were threatening "public security." Moreover, Erim promised that after making the necessary constitutional changes, Turkey would still be no less democratic than West Germany, Italy, France, or Britain:

> The 1961 constitution was very progressive [*ileri*] and includes principles that are too liberal for Turkey. This liberal constitution, which is a luxury in today's geopolitical situation and our condition, is unbearable for us. After the changes, Turkey, as a member of the Council of Europe [that] takes the standards of the European Council into account, will not constitute an exception in terms of freedoms in the human rights commission. (*Milliyet* 1971, 9)

In terms of a historical teleology, the 1961 constitution was claimed to be out of sync with other temporalities. It was *ahead* of society, which had yet to catch up with the progressive outlook of the military rulers who had imparted this constitution to the Turkish nation. It was therefore not only politically unsuitable but potentially harmful to the security of the nation.

Erim delivered this speech in English at a meeting with leaders of Turkey's Western allies, further demonstrating how Turkish statesmen and media entangled *demokrasi* with *democracy*. Translated into Turkish and published in the newspaper *Milliyet*, Erim's speech then became part of the Turkish tradition *in Turkish*, where the rhetorical commonplaces were part of different conversations and different joint actions. Such translations again entangled Turkish rhetorical commonplaces with their use in English discourse in that Erim's legitimation of the coup and the political changes that followed was played out in the English language game and then translated into Turkish.

Erim used concepts of *demokrasiler* (plural of *demokrasi*) in a way that distributed them implicitly along a historical time scale by reference to how "liberal" they were. The benchmarks of progress toward *medeniyet* in the late nineteenth and early twentieth centuries still served as reference points for Turkish statesmen seeking to legitimize policy, although this time the European Human Rights Convention was used as a formalization of a standard of civilization. Where nineteenth-century Ottoman and British statesmen had spoken and written of "civilized countries" and laid out "backward" and "forward" with respect to the concept of "civilization," Turkish politicians did much the same with respect to *demokrasi* in 1971. Democracy was and remains a gold standard for judging legitimacy of rule in international society language games.

Whereas maintaining sovereignty in the nineteenth century required attaining the standard of civilization, in the late twentieth century and especially after the end of the Cold War, avoiding "falling behind" on the democratic scale was vital, since doing so would imply illegitimacy of rule, which other states could use to legitimize government replacement. There are many examples of how practices such as coups did not necessarily result in a problematic relationship with the "Free World" and withdrawal of U.S. protection, as illustrated not only by Turkey but also by Chile, South Africa, and the Philippines. However, the European community took a slightly different approach. While not as active on the regime-changing front, the European Union and its predecessors have used more stringent membership requirements as an important foreign policy tool. Here, a "democratic scale" is put to important use, both for Self/Other relations and for conceptions of historical time.

Conclusion

Unlike *civilization*, which became entangled with an Ottoman word with established connotations, an Ottoman/Turkish concept of *democracy* was formed by simply transliterating the word and making it a neologism. Most Turkish usages of *demokrasi* have in one way or another been translations of European and later American usages. Some of these usages have become inappropriate in various European rhetorical traditions, but their translations have remained in use in Turkish. The most important such example is how various CHP-supporting journalists following the 1945 announcement of multiparty elections and later the military leaders involved in the 1960 coup linked *demokrasi* to organicist conceptualizations of the state that were propounded by republican jurists in the 1920 and 1930s. This is one way in which Turkish usage of *demokrasi* varies from English *democracy* despite their having common roots in translation and very similar dictionary definitions.

Since roughly 1950, *demokrasi* has been as much a telos of Turkish history as a set of practices. And in Turkish discourse, it is often acceptable to invoke some of the hegemonic usages of the 1930s to legitimize practices as *democratic* in ways that would seldom work in European or American language games. Turkish concepts of *demokrasi* are frequently used to mean majoritarianism through elections, and political leaders, including the present government, frequently represent the protection of minority interests as undemocratic in ways that resemble Atatürk's insistence that his opponents were motivated by *subjective* interests. This strategy has repeatedly been used to legitimize the coalescence of a group of power brokers around a leader who governs by distributing state resources to supporters through patron-client networks. Claiming, as Prime Minister Recep Tayyip Erdoğan did in 2013, that the opposition "should shut up" because the governing party embodies the *millî irade* (national will) is a contemporary variant of this phenomenon.

SEVEN

Teleology

In the previous four chapters I have concentrated on the discursive work and contention that went into reinterpreting key concepts in the conduct of Ottoman and Turkish politics, and how these were used to reform and reshape the Ottoman polity. I focus here on how these concepts have been used to envision the future in specific ways and how this envisioning has been used to legitimize foreign policy. More specifically, this chapter deals with how the concepts treated in this book are used to form a hyper-coherent historical narrative, retrospectively organizing sequences of events so as to point to the present and to the future preferred by the actor in question. This narrative seems to be reproduced without much effort, and is used to legitimize a broad range of policies, both foreign and domestic. I center the analysis on the political discourse used to legitimize four Turkish foreign policy decisions vis-à-vis *Europe* and *the West* after the Second World War: Turkish admission into NATO (1952) and the applications for the Common Market (1963), the European Economic Community (1987), and the European Union (1999). Membership in these international organizations may be seen as teloi in and of themselves or as milestones on the path to some other telos (*democracy* or *civilization*). Whatever the case, the narrative into which these events are organized appears to have been quite consistent between 1952 and 1999, and membership in these international organizations occupies the same position in the Turkish identity narrative. To some extent, the legitimations of all four instances appear discursively interchangeable.

The frequency with which international organizations were founded and treaties signed in the post-1945 period leaves little space for discussions of minor events. Despite the importance of many other treaties, I have chosen to focus on the key events in Turkey's relations with international organizations created by European and Western states, when sweeping grand narratives are most frequently used to legitimize concrete policy. A narrative can be defined as a mode of discourse that arranges discrete events into a meaningful temporal order by tying them into a story and endowing the events with meaning as part of an integrated whole (Hinchman and Hinchman 2001, xvi; see also White 1973). Paul Ricoeur has dubbed a narrative a "linguistically mediated temporal synthesis" (1985, 157). The basic narrative used in Turkish leaders' legitimizations for applications for membership in international organizations holds that since the first half of the nineteenth century, first the Ottoman Empire and now Turkey has been undergoing a political transformation. The historical goal of this transformation is whatever agreement is being signed, negotiated, or argued in favor of on that particular occasion, which "opens a new page in the history of the Turkish Republic" (Turkey 1987, 138), and will allow Turkey to "merge with Europe" (*Avrupa ile bütünleşmek*) (Turkey 1987, 139), or "merge with the West" (*Batı'yla bütünleşmek* [Turkey 2002, 34]).

With the Justice and Development Party (Adalet ve Kalkınma Partisi [AKP]) regime becoming ever more powerful, pundits continue to ask the same question that has arisen since the party came to power in 2002: Is Turkey turning East? Nevertheless, the narrative has remained in use, although the occasions have gotten fewer since 2012. There are variations on this discourse, and the telos of entering Europe or the West has been challenged by an Islamist discourse that more clearly disassociate *medeniyet* (civilization) from *Avrupa*, but Turkish politicians regularly employ such narratives to legitimize and give meaning to political initiatives, agreements, and memberships. The hegemonic Turkish identity narrative relies heavily on the concepts analyzed in the previous four chapters—concepts that have been reinterpreted through entanglement with European political meaning. As such, the narratives Turkish politicians have used to legitimize NATO and EU membership applications are particularly well suited for translation back and forth between Turkish and

French, English, and German, and they are apt to legitimize decisions in international society language games as well as in domestic Turkish language games.

Both in English and in Turkish, canonical works on late Ottoman history and Turkish republican history use some concept of *Westernization, Europeanization, secularization,* or *modernization* to structure their narratives (Tunaya 1960; B. Lewis 1961; Berkes 1998). Yet as with categories of "Westernist," "Islamist," and "Turkist," few authors distinguish between these categories' use as political concepts in Ottoman/Turkish language games and the analytical capacity to which these concepts are put when scholars identify and label changes in Ottoman and Turkish practices and institutions. This literature tends to conflate the two rhetorical traditions and use concepts such as *Westernization* as if it were somehow what the actors in question also meant. Narratives of Ottoman and Turkish transformation frequently explain societal changes by reference to a presumed Ottoman wish to imitate Europeans/Westerners or adopt European political and social practices and institutions, a wish that is usually dated to the beginning of the nineteenth century (B. Lewis 1961, 1988; Ayalon 1987). By the mid-twentieth century, this narrative had become hegemonic in both Turkish and English, within academic texts and in more political texts. A typical example of how this looks in a mid-twentieth century Turkish text is İsmail Hakkı Baltacıoğlu's statement that "from the Auspicious Tanzimat onward, we have seen, read, listened to, and learned from those who want to Europeanize and civilize" (1945, 23). One should of course not take Baltacıoğlu's claim at face value, since no such intention to Europeanize and civilize can be found in mid-nineteenth century Ottoman texts. However, it is worth noting how he linked together the concepts *Europeanize* and *civilize,* and used these to formulate a narrative within which to give meaning to current events and argue for political and social change.

During the first decade of AKP rule, even the most trivial matters have sometimes been legitimized by the deployment of this narrative. For example, in 2012 Turkey's director general for press, media, and information launched an initiative to develop local media. His announcement "underlined that the European Union was one of the most important steps of the modernization period from the Tanzimat to the present and that in this period, local media will fulfill a very important function" (*Haberler* 2012). The European Union is here represented as a step in an unfolding history of progress toward a goal. It is ambiguous whether the telos is *democracy, civilization,* or *modernity* or whether the three are so closely bundled together that they are nearly impossible to keep distinct. The EU and NATO were also sometimes represented as goals in themselves rather than as steps along a historical path. Although this narrative was never all-pervasive, it does seem to be a taken-for-granted discursive framework within which most changes that homogenize Turkish practice with European social and political practice can be legitimized, in part because the narrative has *worked* both in Turkish and in translation into European languages. Even though the EU accession process has foundered, the narrative is reproduced in legitimizing meetings and new developments in the Turkey-EU relationship.

Europeans and Infidels

Europe emerged as a rallying concept with both political and social connotations after the Ottoman conquest of Constantinople in 1453. Pope Pius II used the concept in a way that sought to transcend the schism between the Orthodox and Roman Catholic churches and later gained salience with attempts to unite the various Christian denominations that emerged during the Reformations. The explicit goal of uniting these sects was to fight the *Turk*, as they called the Ottomans (den Boer 1995; I. B. Neumann 1999, 44–45). In a sense, the representation of a Muslim or Ottoman "threat" was both temporally and logically prior to the emergence of Europe as an identity concept, and *Europe* was, at least initially, primarily meaningful through a use that juxtaposed it with an Eastern Other (I.B. Neumann 1999).

Europe is certainly not a static concept, and it has been repeatedly reinterpreted, most famously by Tsar Peter I (the Great) of Russia, who, if not outright successful in representing Russia as European, managed to create a certain ambiguity about the eastern geographical boundary of the concept (I. B. Neumann 1999, 74–76). Pim den Boer (1995, 13, 65–74) points to the Napoleonic Wars as an important watershed in the use of *Europe* as a political concept, when it was linked both to the universalizing ideals of the French Revolution and to the international order that subsequently emerged with the congress system. Since *Europe* as a political entity is not meaningful divorced from its social, political, and religious connotations, it has also been linked to what at some point came to be known as "European ideals." These ideals have changed over time, and their bundling together in a rhetorical commonplace is a relatively new development. Since the 1990s, the commonplace has been used to contrast the current peace and prosperity with the totalitarian and war-mongering European regimes of the 1930s and early 1940s. European identity is often linked to concepts of *peace* and *democracy* in opposition to the wars and authoritarian regimes of yesteryear (Wæver 1998).

In terms of key personnel, reproduction of social practices, and international treaties as well as discursively in both European and Turkish discourses, Turkey is a continuation of the Ottoman Empire (despite both the difference in composition and the differentiation between the two as analyzed in chapter 4). As such it is still in some ways used as a counter-concept to *Europe.* However, it is no longer as stable a counter-concept as it was. The more *Europe* is defined in terms of ideals and practices rather than as an essentialized geography and by its relations to Christianity, the more potential it has for inclusion (Rumelili 2007). Moreover, since the Second World War, new Others have taken the place of "the Turk" in the language games of international society and in European identity discourses. Some of these unite Turkey and Europe. Yet because *Turk* has long been a counter-concept that gave meaning to *Europe,* changing the meaning of the conceptual pairs that represent Turkey and Europe as polar opposites requires a great deal of discursive work. Joint rhetorical action that changes established usage and thus the identity relationship of concepts such *Europe* involves a great many actors, and some of the participants have never let go of the usage that dichotomizes Turks and Europeans.

Through a combination of what Louis Althusser (1972) calls interpolation—speaking from a subject position into which an individual is hailed—and stigmatization of Ottoman Muslim subjects qua *Turks,* a Turkish concept of Europe, *Avrupa,* also came to give meaning to *Türk* in Turkish discourse. The opposition between the two concepts had great importance for the emergence of a Turkish nation-state, which could be treated in the context of what Ayşe Zarakol (2011) has called stigma-management techniques. One such technique to which the "nationalist" part of the faltering Ottoman elite turned when their claims to "Ottoman Empire" failed was appropriating the nation/empire dichotomy that Woodrow Wilson set out in his Fourteen Points. In this way, they "spoke back" and legitimized their claims to sovereignty by using the commonplace of the "Turkish nation" when legitimacy claims qua Ottomans were failing. Moreover, since discourse equating the dichotomy European/Turkish with Western/Eastern is embedded in many different languages, it is particularly difficult to change this conceptual relationship, although Turkey to some extent succeeded in doing so through joint action (Rumelili 2007).

Much as *Europe* replaced concepts of *Christendom* in the European languages, so did *Avrupa* replace its onomasiological predecessor *Frengistan* in Ottoman, becoming the commonly accepted translation equivalent for *Europe* in Turkish. Nevertheless it largely became used as an asymmetric counter-concept—used to speak about what We are not—rather than a concept used for the identity of the Self. Where *Europe* became an important concept in the wake of the Ottoman expansion and conquest of Constantinople, *Avrupa* took the place of *Frengistan* as a result of Ottoman/French and Ottoman/English conceptual entanglements. *Frengistan* can literally be translated as "the land of the Franks" and was used with an ambiguity between what are today called *France* and *Western Europe*. According to the *Encyclopaedia of Islam, frenk*

> probably reached the Muslims via the Byzantines, was originally used of the inhabitants of the empire of Charlemagne, and later extended to Europeans in general. In medieval times it was not normally applied to the Spanish Christians . . . , the Slavs . . . or the Vikings . . . but otherwise was used fairly broadly of continental Europe and the British Isles. The land of the Franks was called *ifrandja* (Persian and Turkish *Firangistān*). . . . Between the 16th and the 19th centuries, "Frank" came to be the common term, in most Muslim countries, for Christian Europeans in general. It was however limited, as Sāmī Frasheri [Şemseddin Sami] explains, . . . to Catholics and Protestants; "Russians, Greeks, Bulgarians, Serbs and other orthodox peoples are not called

Frank." It has also, on occasion, been applied to various things believed to have been introduced by the Franks, such as syphilis, cannon, European dress, and modern civilization. (Hopkins and Lewis 2013 [1960])

In Ottoman, *Frenk* was primarily used in the meaning of an *infidel* whose ruler had not submitted to Islamic suzerainty. The Ottomans' increasing use of *Avrupa* instead of *Frengistan* in the nineteenth century can partly be explained by *Frengistan*'s historically close linkages with *kâfir* (infidel). The substitution of *Avrupa* enabled the deployment of a rhetorical commonplace that did not necessarily draw on the tradition where these two were closely linked, thus opening up for other ways to legitimize interaction with Europeans (Naff 1984).

Europe as the Telos of Reform

Although concepts of *modernity, Europe,* and *civilization* are often used together both in English and in Turkish, authors sometimes make fine distinctions between them. In Turkish, these concepts' translation equivalents are frequently brought together in such expressions as *muasır medeniyetinin seviyesine ulaşmak* (to reach the level of modern civilization), a statement that is often attributed to Mustafa Kemal Atatürk and that appears on statues and memorials around Turkey. The concept of *muasır* and its neologism, *çağdaş*, both of which may be translated as *contemporary* or *modern*, offer different ways to talk about certain (Europe-emergent) practices without explicitly mentioning Europe or the West. Particularly in English, concepts of progress have often been used to mean development along a path toward "Western modernity," with all societies traveling along the same path. The extent to which European and American societies have been used to speak and write about examples of *modernity* and *progress* has yoked together the two concepts, so that the geographical aspect of modernity is often implicit in the use of the word (Fabian 1983). A common European or Western representation can be summed up in Edward Shils' words: "the states of Western Europe and of North America (and the English-speaking dominions of the British Commonwealth)—need not aspire to modernity. They are modern. It has become part of their nature to be modern and indeed what they are is definitive of modernity" (1970, 382).[1] Through entanglements and translations, a variant of this representation has also emerged in Turkish rhetorical tradition, although it is more often than not implicit in discourse.

The representation of Europe or the West as always already modern means that all other societies fall short of reaching the apex in the hierarchy of civilization. As Timothy Mitchell (2000, 3) formulates it,

> Modernization continues to be commonly understood as a process begun and finished in Europe, from where it has been exported across ever-expanding regions of the non-West. The destiny of those regions has been to mimic, never quite successfully, the history already performed by the West. To become modern, it is still said, or today to become postmodern, is to act like the West.

Although *progress, modernity,* and their Turkish translation equivalents can be used in explicitly nonessentialist ways, they can nevertheless also easily be given essentialist overtones through their implicit links with a particular geography of origin. Handling the stigma that comes with this ambiguity is central to Turkey's position in the international order (Zarakol 2011).

Such discourse was not translated into Ottoman or Turkish at a single instance or point in time. Instead, a long series of interlingual conversations has brought about the particular Turkish narratives that rely on concepts of *modernization, Europeanization,* or *Westernization.* In relation to the Ottoman Empire, such discourse appears at least partly to originate in English discourse on the "need for reform." For example, Stanley Lane-Poole's 1888 biography of Stratford Canning, in dialogue with Canning's own discourse, formed a narrative of Ottoman *Westernization* or *modernization* in English. According to Lane-Poole, Canning's

---

1. For a discussion, see Bowden 2009, 47–75.

brain conceived the scheme, the heat of his enthusiasm forged and welded the scattered links of Turkish reform, he alone dreamed of a regenerated Turkey where Christian and Musulman alike should resist in firm unity, shoulder to shoulder, the insidious approach of Russia. . . .

He entered upon his dominion at Constantinople with a fixed purpose—to make the continuance of the Ottoman Empire possible by making it European. His policy was open, avowed, straightforward. Private motives he had none. He would save Turkey in spite of herself if she could be saved at all. . . . He had laid out his road before him, and in that road he and the Sultan were to walk. If any man uprose in the way, he must be made to stand aside. . . . [H]e would pursue the path he had marked out for himself and for the empire over which he dominated. . . . [H]e sought to impose upon the Sultan and his ministers his idea of a New Turkey, an empire worthy to take a place in the councils of European States. (1888, 69–71)

"Turkey" of the future is a Turkey made European, led, in spite of itself, along the historical path by altruistic European diplomats. Lane-Poole's English-language discourse of 1888 is based on Canning's letters, notes, and memoirs but it is not Canning's own. The discursive elements here should strike a familiar note with all those acquainted with Turkish EU accession politics of the early 2000s. Further, Lane-Poole explicitly describes Canning as Sultan Abdülmecid I's "tutor" (80), though it is more than doubtful whether Abdülmecid himself would have considered his relationship with the British ambassador to be one of tutelage. Butrus Abu-Manneh (1994) identifies other people as far more important advisers to the sultan, among them central members of the Halidî brotherhood. "New Turkey" made European was presented as the only alternative to dissolution. Whatever Canning's and Abdülmecid I's representations of this relationship, a version of Lane-Poole's narrative became hegemonic in the twentieth century: Turkey marches along a (westward) path toward *civilization*. The main difference between the various European versions and their Turkish translation was that the Turkish version seldom featured well-intentioned European statesmen. Instead these are represented as engaging in great power schemes and undermining the Ottoman and Turkish state. The fact that Canning had been an important supporter of an independent Greek state in the 1820s was never lost on the Ottomans, and even Lane-Poole admits that the "well-intentioned European statesman" (86) was a problematic aspect of this representation.

Westernization

The well-intentioned European statesman leading the Ottoman Empire along the path of reform to a "New Turkey" became one way of talking about this in English, but no single Ottoman word unified the disparate elements of this representation. I have found neither *Westernization, Europeanization,* nor *modernization* in Ottoman texts. Nor have I found any single Ottoman concept that in a word summed up and stood for the transformative societal process that took place during late Ottoman times. Despite their current ubiquity in texts discussing Ottoman and Turkish historical experience, such concepts were not only absent from Ottoman/Turkish discourse until the 1930s, their lineage in English is also shorter than one may assume. According to the *Oxford English Dictionary Online*, the word *Westernized* first appeared in 1819, and searches in Google Books indicate that the term did not catch on in English-language texts until the turn of the twentieth century, when it primarily appeared not in the context of the Ottoman Empire but in writings on Japan. An 1898 article in *The Nation* illustrates a typical usage of the time:

> It is a growing complaint of travellers who come to visit Japan that the country is fast losing its attractiveness, owing to the rapid process of *Westernization.* . . . The chief cities and towns have gradually acquired, in place of their old picturesqueness and grace, many of the disagreeable characteristics of modern Western civilization. (G.D. 1898, 879)

Westernization was thus used to describe a society as losing its authenticity and uniqueness, a usage that is in fact very similar to how Turkish conservatives currently use the translation equivalent *batılılaşma.* While Lane-Poole was an important actor in piecing together a narrative of the well-intentioned statesman leading "Turkey" on a path of reform, he only once used a concept of *Europeanization* in his biography.

Although no concept of *Europeanization* is to be found in the Ottoman language at this time, there existed discursive elements that came to be yoked together when Ottomans established such a translation equivalent. It is unclear whether earlier common expressions such as *tavr-ı efrence girmek* (to don Frenk attire or to enter into the Frenk mode) can be translated as *Europeanization* (Çağman 2010, 9). I would argue that the propensity to do so after the fact has to do with how old statements, texts, and expressions like this were fitted into a teleological narrative of Westernization that emerged later on. The expression may be interpreted widely (as the suggestion to start "behaving like the Frenk") or narrowly (as a discussion of soldiers' uniforms, or more generally of sartorial practice). This particular expression was first used in debates concerning the introduction of European uniforms for Ottoman soldiers, which is a good reason to interpret it as specifically concerning attire and probably military drill rather than as an argument for wholesale societal transformation. The fact that intellectuals used similar expressions a century later to argue that the Turks should "enter Western civilization" does not change its meaning in early nineteenth-century debate. Although adopting European sartorial practices was highly symbolic and controversial, it is unwarranted to equate arguments for or against European uniforms with arguments for the wholesale adoption of social and political practices that is now summed up by the concepts of *Westernization* and *Europeanization.*

To the extent that the Ottoman words for *east* (*şark*) and *west* (*garb*) had meaning beyond the cardinal directions before the late nineteenth century, they meant the "Islamic East" (*maşrek* [the Levant]) and the "Islamic West" (*mağrib* [the western part of North Africa]) (Meninski 2000 [1680], 2803, 3387). When cardinal directions came to be reified through entanglement with European concepts, they were reinterpretations of the sociopolitical meaning attached to the words for cardinal directions of Arabic origin, in Turkish spelling *şark* and *garb.* Ottoman lexicographer Şemseddin Sami defines *garbî* as "pertaining to Europe, which is situated to the west *in relation to us;*

Western civilization; Western literature" (Şemseddīn Sāmī 1317 [1901–2], 963; emphasis added). Şemseddin Sami's representation is precisely the interpretation of *Europe* around which Iver Neumann (1999) builds his argument in *Uses of the Other*—that it is delineated vis-à-vis the Ottomans, but here the delineation happens in the opposite direction. The Ottoman "we" and "Europe" were used in a co-constitutive relationship not only in English, French, and other European languages, but also in Ottoman. They were used to give meaning to one another in a similar way to *east* and *west* and were closely linked to that conceptual pair. Şemseddin Sami defines *şarkî* as "consist[ing] of and related to those countries that find themselves to the east in relation to Europe" (Şemseddīn Sāmī 1317 [1901/1902], 776). By saying that *Western* means "pertaining to Europe" and it is "to our west," Sami places "us" in a reified East.

The concept of *Westernization* is typically used to speak about a transformative process typified in English by the ending *-ization*.[2] The Turkish equivalent of the English *-ize* (*-lAşmAk*) and *-ization* (*-lAşmA*) are relatively new as productive suffixes.[3] They gained prominence with the Turkish Language Reform started in 1931, but earlier usages include Ziya Gökalp's 1918 essay, "Türkleşmek, İslamlaşmak, Muasırlaşmak" (To Turkify, to Islamify, to Contemporize/Modernize) and Nazım Hikmet's 1923 poem, "Makineleşme" (Mechanization).

A year-by-year search of Turkish parliamentary transcripts reveals

---

2. The Ottoman way of coining neologisms for the various transformative European concepts ending in *-ization* was to use the Arabic verbal noun (*masdar*), form 5, which is often used as a way to express reflexive causation (to make oneself become). Following the 1931 Turkish Language Reform, all "foreign" words were supposed to be replaced with "pure Turkish" (*öztürkçe*) words. This meant that a lot of these Arabic form 5 *masdars* had to be replaced by something that would give a similar meaning but following Turkish grammar. This was done by making extensive use of the suffix *-lAşmAk* (in the verb form) and *-lAşmA* (as a verbal noun) to create neologisms with meaning that has to do with transformative processes. Turkish adheres to vowel harmony, which means that *-lAşmA* (and *-lAşmAk*) can have two different realizations, *-laşma* and *-leşme*. The capital *A* is used to indicate the possibility of both an *a* and an *e* realization, which carry no difference in meaning.

3. A search through the *Tarih Vesikaları*, a corpus of transliterated pre-1928 historical documents published in 1941–42, returned not a single transformative concept with the suffixes *-laşma* or *-leşme* (*andlaşma* and *sözleşme* [both "agreement"] and so forth, but nothing that can directly be called a process). Form 5 Arabic *masdars* may have served a similar function in the Ottoman language, but I have not found any concept in this form with a similar meaning.

the extent to which such concepts were used during the first forty years of the Turkish Republic. Of all the different conceivable ways of writing *Westernization and Europeanization*, there are only three instances of *garblılaşma* prior to the 1960 coup, and there is a single mention of *frenkleşme* in 1940.[4] While *frenkleşme* could be translated as "becoming European," there is some ambiguity in its use, as it originated in "becoming Frankish" and has been more frequently used to talk about the moral defects of Europe than about Europe as an origin of modernity. That was more often articulated by the use of *Avrupa*, today the only word used to mean the continent. The 1940 mention is the first instance I found of any Turkish concept that could be translated as either *Westernization* or *Europeanization* in a single word. The user both acknowledges that the term is fairly new and distances himself from *frenkleşme*, saying that he prefers *garblaşmak* (Westernization):

We were once in the Arab and Persian cultural sphere. Because of this, we naturally took over this sphere's ideology, art, laws, and their emotions, which were naturally conveyed by these, and its techniques of art. . . . Later, times changed and we entered into another cultural sphere, the Western [*garb*] cultural sphere. Recently, there has been the expression *frenkleşme*. I am no great supporter of this expression. Instead, I consider the expression *garblaşmak* more suitable. We have started to count ourselves as a nation that has, for reasons that are not even necessary to mention here, become *garblaşmış* [Westernized], and that is actually what we really are. (Turkey 1940, 130)

The ambivalence toward adopting European practices was given meaning by use of a conceptual pair that distinguished between desirable *garblaşma* and undesirable *frenkleşme*, with the latter clearly carrying more connotations of superficial imitation of European fashions, and perhaps also sounding quite archaic. It is also clear that "the West" was here reified and given object-like qualities—a "cultural sphere."

---

4. I searched for *-laşma* and *-leşme*, so barring misspellings in the transcripts, I should not have overlooked any particular concept. *Garblılaşma* or *garblaşma* appeared once in each of the three years 1940, 1950, and 1960.

The current concept for *Westernization* (*batılılaşma*) did not appear in Grand National Assembly debates until 1963, but even during that decade, its use was limited. The concept may have been used in academic or popular scientific contexts in the intervening years, but its political usage was not widespread. If Westernization was a state-driven project and the Grand National Assembly was a key function of the state, one would expect either *some* kind of treatment of the pros and cons of this concept or a legitimation of political action by reference to this concept. None of the sort can be found.

NATO Membership (1952)

Having discussed the link between the abstract teloi of *demokrasi* and *medeniyet* on the one hand and the reification of *Avrupa* (Europe) and *Batı* (the West) as geographic entities on the other, I now discuss how this narrative was adapted and used to legitimize certain international agreements.

In the struggle over territory and power in Anatolia and Istanbul between 1919 and 1923, the Bolsheviks supported the Turkish nationalists with gold, weapons, and ammunition (Hale 2000, 51). The Bolshevik government also became the first to recognize the Turkish nationalists as treaty partners with the 1921 Treaty of Brotherhood (also known as the Treaty of Moscow). The two groups expressed commonality by invoking a struggle against *imperialism*—a concept that was used against European great powers, as well as those in Russia and the Ottoman Empire who were supported by these powers.

Other than their claimed legitimacy as the negation of imperialism, and their common, though not unified, opposition to the European great powers in the 1920s, the Kemalists and the Bolsheviks had relatively few common interests. Some within the Turkish elite took Soviet social reforms to be a good way to reform Turkish society[5] and Turkish artists looked to Soviet movements within the arts, but generally Turkey and the Soviet Union had little interaction outside government-to-government diplomacy. During the Second World War, Turkey was formally allied with Britain and France but did not

---

5. The mass literacy campaign that followed the Turkish Alphabet Reform of 1928 is perhaps the most clearly Bolshevik-inspired social reform, but also the abolishment of old imperial and religious institutions can be considered in this light.

participate in the fighting and maintained extensive trade relations with Germany and extracted military aid from both Germany and Britain for most of the war.

The Soviet Union had demanded the Istanbul Straits (the Bosporus and Dardanelles, connecting the Black Sea and the Mediterranean) several times during the 1930s, without this creating major diplomatic rupture with Turkey. When they renewed this claim and added a claim to the Turkish provinces of Kars and Ardahan in 1945, Turkey responded much more bluntly than it had previously. As Coş and Bilgin (2010) have argued, the Turkish government's reaction to the renewed demands in 1945 became part of constituting the Soviet Union as a common enemy of Turkey and "the West." In order to succeed in this, Turkish statesmen also saw the need to start using *democracy* for legitimizing Turkey's position internationally (see chapter 6). This very explicit rejection of the Soviet demands gave urgency to the anchoring of claims to *democracy* in political practice. As part of this anchoring, the Republican People's Party started disentangling party and state, allowing opposition parties to form, and declaring multiparty elections. These changes in political practices domestically, in combination with Turkish discourse on the Soviet Union as an important Other (as Europe's and Turkey's *East*), were crucial to legitimizing requests for military and development aid from Britain and the United States. The first major recognition of the legitimacy of these claims came in U.S. president Harry Truman's 1947 speech declaring what became known as the Truman Doctrine. The declared the U.S. willingness to assume Britain's role in supporting the Greek and Turkish governments against communist guerrillas and Soviet military pressure, respectively. Truman's address was as much about supporting the Greek and Turkish *peoples* or *nations* in their *struggle for freedom* as about shoring up existing *democracies*: Truman offered recognition to the two countries for *trying* and for working hard, not for *being democracies*.

In 1952, NATO accepted Turkey and Greece as members, and Turkey's geopolitical discourses became even more entangled and aligned with those of Western European states—that is, threats came from the *east* (despite the fact that much of Soviet Russia and the Warsaw Pact actually lay to the north or northwest of Turkey). *The East* was not merely a cardinal direction but a political entity or quality. In an article on "the meaning of the decision" that appeared the day after Turkey's NATO membership became public, the Turkish newspaper *Cumhuriyet* explained,

> The Great Assembly, which is celebrating in the mood of a national [*millî*] victory this event that we have longed for for years, is doubtlessly expressing the sincere feelings of all Turkish citizens [*Türk vatandaşları*]. Truly, to unify with the Western democracies [*Batılı demokrasiler*] in the face of the dangers that have been formed against the world of liberty [*hürriyet dünyası*, perhaps meant to translate "the Free World"] since the Second World War came to an end has been the most correct path that we could take. [Turkey's] place among nations is as a matter of fact on the side of those who promote freedom [*hürriyetçi*]. . . . From today the Turkish Republic will unconditionally be an essential member of the North Atlantic Pact. This means that our land, which stretches from our eastern border to Thrace, will be considered an inalienable and indivisible part of free Europe. We have created a tight union of fate with the nations that believe in Western civilization and human rights and that live for the defense of this civilization and these rights. . . . With our entry into the pact, the great truth has been put out there, and this is a formal confirmation of the fact that our Turkey is a nation linked to the community of Western civilization. There are reasons for this that we have to give particular importance. Europe has always looked with doubt upon us, and upon our Westernization efforts that started with the Tanzimat but that have gone into reverse from time to time. It is because of the republic and Atatürk's reforms [*inkılablar*] that the Westerners started recognizing us for who we are and for who we have resolved to be. (Nadi 1952, 1)

This excerpt contains all the discursive elements of a narrative of Westernization: the telos that vacillates between *civilization* and *democracy*, sometimes equating the two; the transformation of the Turkish self, starting with the Tanzimat Reforms; the search for Western recognition of Turkey as equal, with guaranteed sovereignty, as expressed in such phrases as "unconditionally be an essential member of the

North Atlantic Pact"; and the "unification with Europe" aspect, which is the most problematic. The article's insistence that "this means that our land, which stretches from our eastern border to Thrace, will be considered an inalienable and indivisible part of free Europe," is reproduced in many writings that celebrate the new cooperation as Turkey's *final* and *much-desired* unification with Europe. However, Western states recognized Turkey as a country in transformation, and one that needed help in its struggle for liberty, not necessarily as a *natural and obvious* part of their collective.

The most important point of contention at NATO's meeting in Lisbon in 1952 did not concern the inclusion of Turkey or Greece in the alliance but instead involved the rearmament of West Germany and its inclusion in a mutual defense system. In his speech on the occasion, the Turkish foreign minister Fuad Köprülü made much use of the concept of *Western civilization* (Turkey 1952, 315). The Atlantic Pact was in Turkish discourse largely synonymous with or at least representative of *Western civilization*, a state of affairs that dovetails neatly with Patrick Thaddeus Jackson's (2006, 151–56, 173) claim that the rearmament of "West Germany" and its inclusion in NATO were argued by reference to *shoring up* its position *in the West* or in *Western civilization*. Conversely, Turkey's NATO membership was legitimized (at least in Turkish) by arguments that NATO would *make* Turkey *Western*. In English, it was also argued that Turkey and Greece were important for *securing the West*, which also meant securing Turkey *in the West*. There is a fine nuance here: Germany was argued to have *always been a natural part of "the West"* at the same time that Turkey was in different ways claimed to be a newcomer, aspirant, and struggling member. This is an example of how Turkey's position in relation to the West has to be argued anew at every historical juncture rather than taken for granted. According to *Cumhuriyet* (1952, 1),

> Just as West Germany has now been accepted as a member of the Atlantic Pact, with equal rights and obligations from now on, the German forces have attained participation in the organization that has been named the European army. In order for the European army, which will be made up of French, Italian, German, Belgian, Dutch, and Luxembourgeois detachments, to defend the democratic world against communist transgres-

sions, it will include forces provided by Turkey and Greece alongside American, English, and Canadian units. . . . This goal is to involve Germany, which is a martial nation [*millet*], in the defense of Europe against communist transgressions.

The representation of the order of international politics in Turkish discourse at this point bears marks of frequent translations from American and British discourse (see chapter 6). Western Europe and the "Free World" (*hür dünya*) were to be defended against "communist imperialism" (*komünist emperyalizmi*) (Turkey 1952, 319–20). Around this time, *hür dünya* was used in much the same places and in the same ways in Turkish discourse as did *Western civilization*, and the two terms therefore took on much of the same meaning. However, *hür dünya* was used in such a way that Turkey was unambiguously included in the concept, whereas its relationship with *Western civilization* was much more ambiguous. This was done by decoupling the concept of *emperyalizm* (imperialism) from the European powers and instead linking it to *komünism* (communism). The old enmity with Frengistan was transcended by reference to a common enemy and transposing one of the main Othering concepts on that common enemy. This was done in a manner that shows entanglements with hegemonic American discourse, which has been covered by Campbell (1992).

Association with the European Economic Community (1963)

In 1959 Turkey applied for association with the European Economic Community, generally known in both English and Turkish as the Common Market (and its direct Turkish translation *Ortak Pazar*). Turkey was accepted as an associate member in 1963, prompting the Turkish newspaper *Akşam* (1963, 1) to declare on its front page, "We entered the Common Market. 'Turkey became a part of Europe through Atatürk's Reforms [*inkılap*].'" *Milliyet* (1963, 1) quoted the head of the Common Market Commission as saying that the treaty was a "confirmation that Turkey had become a part of Europe." According to the main center-right newspaper, *Hürriyet* (1963, 1),

Turkey yesterday reached a goal which it has sought for years and which it has struggled along diplomatic paths to obtain. This goal was for our country to enter the Common Market.

Yesterday, at a great ceremony held in Ankara, Turkey signed an agreement with the Common Market countries. This event is the final step and the most profitable result of the effort Turkey has expended on the road of Westernization and to gain equal rights with the Western world over the past one hundred and fifty years. The Common Market is an organization that will unify Europe first economically and then politically. It is known that great progress has been made along this path. . . . Not only was the road to a bright future opened for Turkey at yesterday's signing ceremony, but the true value of the Westernization efforts over the past 150 years was recognized.

There are some contextual differences between the NATO membership in 1952 and this treaty. The treaty that made Turkey a NATO member concerned military or security matters, whereas membership in the Common Market primarily concerned matters of trade. Nevertheless, the 1963 treaty was legitimized by use of many of the same rhetorical commonplaces as the Lisbon Treaty: both were claimed to be recognitions of Turkey's long-standing Westernization efforts and final steps in the process of unification with Europe. Since Turkey was not self-evident as a *founding* member of these organizations, it has perennially sought later membership—not entirely different from what Jusdanis (1991) calls *belatedness*. This means not only that Turkish diplomats and politicians must use words that "taste of a different context of use" to legitimize their inclusion but also that Turks have no choice but to comply with demands made by the original members of a particular European-emergent or Western-emergent organization if it is to be included in *Europe* or *the West*. Having to adhere to such demands rather than being among the group that defines them create occasions when Turkey's *Westernization* needs to be highlighted. The Westernization narrative reinforced the telos of the Turkish identity narrative as well as Turkey's belatedness in relation to Europe in both domestic Turkish discourse and international English and French discourse.

European Economic Community Application (1987)

By 1987, when Turkish prime minister Turgut Özal sent a letter of application for membership to the European Economic Community (EEC), much of Turkey's political integration into Europe was already under way. Whereas in 1963 columnists and politicians alike depicted the agreement as *the final stage* of Westernization, recognizing Turkey as equal with, or part of, the West, *Milliyet* (1987, 14) labeled Turkey's EEC application "the first step in Europeanization." Echoing the words of newspapers in 1952 and 1963, *Sabah* (1987b, 5) announced that "an entirely new page in our history is about to be turned." In another article, *Sabah* (1987a, 5) said, "Today we are knocking on the door of the EEC." In other words, despite years of diplomatic effort and a succession of claims to having earned acceptance as an equal, Turkey was discursively still at square one in relation to *Europe*.

Turkey's foreign minister presented the application to parliament using much the same narrative:

> Today, a new page in the history of the Turkish Republic has been opened. I again want to express in your presence our deep gratitude to the valuable members of the Great Assembly, which has been a support in the efforts we have exerted for years with perseverance and determination to arrive at this point, and to the representatives of the Turkish press, who have shown us the way with their constructive criticism. I believe that all our institutions are fully attentive to the duties that fall upon them, so that we may arrive at the successful completion of the new road that we have entered today in the shortest possible time. The Turkish Nation [*Türk Milleti*] possesses the virtues [necessary] for reaching a modern [*muasır*] level of civilization, as put up as a goal by Atatürk. I sincerely believe that the European community supports the Turkish Nation in the efforts [it expends] in this direction and shows respect for its will to merge with Europe. With these thoughts I greet your exalted assembly and wish that this important passage in the history of the republic brings our great nation welfare and happiness. (Turkey 1987, 138–39)

While concepts of *civilization* and *modern* were part of this, and the teleological narrative is clearly a structuring device, the transformative concepts such as *Westernization* and *Europeanization* were not frequently or prominently used. The leader of the opposition party

Doğru Yol Partisi (Right Path Party) followed up on the foreign minister's statement by saying,

> Esteemed friends, in the Treaty of Rome, the requirements for becoming part of the European Community are expressed more or less in the following manner: To be European is to have a democratic [form of] rule and have an economic situation on par with the European Community. If we look at the requirements this way, we see that the necessity of being European is given the same meaning with which it was recorded in the Common [Market] Agreement that we signed in 1963. (Turkey 1987, 139)

Because the occasion is different—this was a matter of sending an application, not receiving a letter of acceptance—the tone is less confident than on the two previous occasions analyzed above. The statements accompanying Özal's application merely expressed hope that Europe would recognize Turkey as equal to the other European states, yet it drew upon the same discursive elements and the application is placed in the same teleological narrative as that used to legitimize the 1952 and 1963 agreements.

Whereas the discourse that legitimized NATO membership made much of external communists as a common enemy, Turkish politicians seeking to legitimize the EEC application identified domestic threats as "anti-democratic Islamists" and coup makers as the common enemy of *democracy*. In the muted debate that followed the foreign minister's speech, Erdal İnönü (İsmet İnönü's son and the leader of the opposition Social Democrat Populist Party), argued that

> Turkey, with its history, its geography, the direction of its cultural development, and its attachment to democratic ideals, is a European country. It will naturally take its place in the European Community. Because of this, we positively welcome the government's application. After this application, we want without delay to make the corrections necessary for taking our place in the European Community as soon as possible. Dear Speaker, dear representatives, the European community is not only a community of developed economies; it is a community

of nations that come together in their respect for human rights and their settled understanding of democracy. . . . What the government needs to do, now that it has formally applied to take part in this family, is to set to work correcting the deficiencies and imperfections of our democracy, which we have been pointing out for four years. (Turkey 1987, 141)

Bahar Rumelili (2007) theorizes that European identity contains two aspects: an essentialized (exclusive) identity aspect and a practice-based (inclusive) identity aspect. The former is tied to representations of common descent, common religion, and common historical experiences, and outsiders cannot simply acquire this aspect of a European identity by acting in a certain prescribed manner. The latter has to do with whether a state practices "European ideals" and was in 1999 formalized by the European Union in the Copenhagen Criteria. İnönü claimed that Turkey *was already European* (similar to the discursive work that paved the way for including Germany in "the West" following the Second World War), bolstering his point by mentioning both inclusive and exclusive aspects of European identity. According to Rumelili, for Turkey to claim that it is European by arguing the exclusive aspect is the most tenuous part of Turkey's European identity. Because this aspect is linked to essentialized, ascribed qualities, Turkish politicians can do little except engage systematically in rhetorical commonplaces in European languages and thereby reinterpret *European* identity through joint action. In the practical aspect, however, Turkey *can* change its position by reconfiguring domestic social relations. However, relations between Turkey and Europe is frequently represented in terms of Turkish "delays," "deficiencies," and "shortcomings," not only because these domestic reconfigurations for different reasons fail to anchor legitimacy claims but also because concepts of *Turkey* are linked with these concepts in both European and Turkish rhetorical traditions. As İnönü continued in the debate in the Turkish Grand National Assembly:

The membership negotiations will take years. During this period, it will be necessary to carry out many improvements, even fundamental changes, to all the subsectors of our economy, be they agricultural or industrial. These improvements will also take a great deal of time. No one will object to these, and all of them will be realized in their due course. As for delays in the correction of the deficiencies and imperfections in [our] democracy, . . . they only lubricate the work of those who do not want to accept us into the European Community and open the way for the rejection of our application. (Turkey 1987, 141)

According to İnönü, Turkey needed to avoid giving Europeans reasons for exclusion because some Europeans would seize on any excuse to do so. Delays in "the correction of deficiencies and imperfections in [our] democracy" work to the advantage of those who want to reject Turkey. In addition to being much less celebratory and more careful than the 1952 and 1963 discourses, the discourse on the EEC application introduces a new element into the debate: "Turkey will be an enrichment to Europe's political and cultural life" because "we will enter the European Community while defending our national and cultural traditions" (Turkey 1987, 87). Turkey's *difference*, rather than its conformity, is played up as an argument *for* EEC membership, drawing heavily on an essentialist conception of "our national character" (*millî karakterimiz*) (see chapters 3 and 4), as well as seemingly engaging with or translating European discourses on the benefits of diversity.

European Union Candidacy (1999)

The remarkable consistency in how Turkish politicians from different parties argued the case for membership in NATO, the Common Market, and the European Economic Community continued through the country's 1999 attempt to join the European Union. Even more remarkable, however, is that the historical path appears more like an escalator traveling downward than a stairway to heaven. As the Turks exert themselves, they seem to be standing still, at least discursively, in relation to their ultimate goal at the peak of civilization. They are invited in on others' terms only if they can appropriate and adjust to specific social practices—in the analytic setup of this book, if they can credibly legitimize their position in a language game that has the flavor of European contexts and historical experiences. Often, this involves reconfiguring domestic social relations by the use of translated concepts as tools, which in turn allows Turkish politicians to anchor their arguments for legitimate inclusion in international organizations.

At the first meeting in the Grand National Assembly after Turkey received EU candidate status, Prime Minister Bülent Ecevit argued the case for Turkish membership:

> The [recent] Istanbul meeting of the Organization for Security and Cooperation in Europe was also a great symbolic and psychological influence. Those who participated in this meeting came from different countries, and they got to feel in their hearts that not only does it span the two shores of the Bosporus and has a secular, democratic, and modern lifestyle and multi-dimensional culture, Turkey is a country that joins Europe and Asia, West and East into a healthy synthesis. Some conservative and racist circles in Europe have not yet digested the fact that the Turks have been European for six hundred years while at the same time being Asian, Caucasian, and Middle Eastern. Turkey is a country that has all at once been influenced by the eastern Mediterranean, the Black Sea, and the Balkans. Now Turkey is on the path to becoming an energy terminal country that will bring the oil and gas riches of the Caspian and Caucasus region to world markets. Turkey is a link not only between Europe and Asia but also between Christianity, Judaism, and Islam. Turkey is [also] a promoter of democracy, modernity, and secularism among countries with Muslim-majority populations. Unification with Europe will become easier relative to the extent to which Turkey attains Ataturk['s goals]. . . . The most important requirement for the possibility of EU membership is to harmonize [our] democracy, human rights, rule of law, and economy with the Copenhagen Criteria. . . . Turkey has increased its respectability in the world, especially with the steps that have been made along this path over the past six and a half months. The Grand National Assembly may rectify our deficiencies in a few months by quick and coherent work. In fact, the Copenhagen Criteria are not something the foreigners are forcing upon us; they are something that guarantees

the way of life of which we regard ourselves worthy. (Turkey 1999, 217)

It is noteworthy that Ecevit here makes claims that implicitly challenge the essentialist aspect of the Turkey/Europe identity dichotomy by claiming that "Turkey is a country that joins Europe and Asia, West and East into a healthy synthesis." Using Bahar Rumelili's analytical setup, one might say that Ecevit emphasizes Turkey's Europeanness in the essentialized aspect of identity, while claiming that it needs to rectify its unbecoming and un-European practices. At this point, however, a narrative of *Westernization* or *Europeanization* and the institutionalized political practice of seeking admission, respect, and parity with "the West" and "Europe" seems to have become an established feature of Turkey's identity in relation to Europe and hence also constitutive of a hierarchy in international relations that is a legacy of the nineteenth century. It is difficult to uphold the claim that "Turkey is European" if the speaker at the same time continuously reifies "Europeans" as an entity external to Turkey whose recognition should be sought. Rather than transforming Turkey's relationship with *Europe*, the insistence on *Westernization* stabilizes and institutionalizes this relationship as one of belatedness and insufficiency.

Essentialist Counter-Discourse

The Turkish identity narrative that systematically uses *Westernization* is by no means homogenously reproduced in all contexts across the political spectrum. At the center of political power, it has been challenged by essentialist interpretations of the Turkish nation as Muslim. This discourse typically has a much stronger emphasis on "our culture" (*kültürümüz*) and "our national character" (*millî karakterimiz*) than the discourse analyzed in the three preceding sections. According to a fairly typical speech given by a member of parliament from the socially conservative but economically liberal Motherland Party,

Our culture, which is made up of these values, is what has made us into who we are and set aside an exceptional place on the stage of history for the Turkish Nation [*millet*]. If we had given this the necessary attention and sought to maintain ownership of our own culture, we would have grown to a much greater degree, and we would have developed and progressed much more in science and technology. We regressed when we became estranged from our culture and strove in vain to imitate foreign cultures. From two hundred years ago until today, we have put our own culture in second place, and the venture of Europeanization [*Avrupalılaşma*] and Westernization [*Batılılaşma*] has unfortunately met its disappointing end. (Turkey 1989, 683)

Like other discourses, this speech puts its store in *progress*; however, the speaker argues that since *Westernization* is inorganic and inauthentic, it has failed to provide progress. Such criticisms reject the telos of the narratives of *Westernization* and *Europeanization* but do not exactly make clear what the alternative telos should be.

Although *Frengistan* and *Frenk* have largely gone out of contemporary Turkish use, a search of Turkish parliamentary transcripts shows how the concepts were used in straightforwardly if rarely until the 1980s and 1990s. Even then, *Frenk* seems to have been an ambiguous concept that could mean French, European, or Western (see, e.g., Turkey 1984, 136).

Cultural imperialism is more lethal than economic, military and political imperialism, because sociocultural exploitation is bent on wiping out our national [*millî*] identity. . . . Adoration of foreigners will come to dominate our generations, and command of their brains will be in the hands of the oppressors/ exploiters [*sömürücü*]. . . . Imitators who are under the influence of foreign cultures, . . . are enough to make a nation [*millet*] collapse. . . .

In our age, developed countries have quit conquering land but have [instead] started conquering brains. The least costly form of conquest is brain conquest. Actually, conquest of land is very expensive. Moreover, looking after the land that has been taken into possession has also become a difficult task. Dear representatives, the modern enslavement method of the 19th and 20th centuries [involves the] movement of culture. . . .

For this reason, the capitalist countries wish to form a new type of human who is tied to themselves by using brainwashing technologies. This type will be a creature removed from the idea of nation [*ulus*] . . . ; an "alatype" who has torn up and thrown away his values, his belief system, and national feeling [*millî duygu*]; that is to say, what is called "alaturka."

What does alaturka mean? Is it something like the à la carte menu, where one eats not what one wishes but what is given to you? They say alaturka and unfortunately mean by that those who think like Muslim Turks, believe like Muslim Turks, and live like Muslim Turks. We see that those who act and think like Frenks, like foreigners [*ecnebi*], are called alafranga. . . .

Our outlook is to think like a Turk and to live and behave like a Muslim Turk. I am entreating God not to let us stoop to the characterlessness of resembling foreigners. (Turkey 1996, 228)

This quotation comes from a speech by a representative from the socially conservative and economically liberal Turkish right. It exemplifies the conceptual use of *Turk* as *Muslim* (see chapter 5), with the essentialized Muslimness of Turkish identity privileged in contrast to the counterconcept of *Frenk*. The speaker uses his concepts in a set of dichotomies, some of which I have analyzed in the preceding chapters: the national/imperial dichotomy; imitation versus authenticity (where the latter was expressed by *national* [*millî*]); and the *Frenk/Türk* dichotomy. All of these were bundled together in a semantic field that the speaker uses in a way that are very similar to how they were used a century earlier. To the extent that *Frenk* was used during the last decades of the twentieth century, it primarily appeared in discourse that emphasized the essential and superior qualities of Turks and did so with explicit appeals to the religious aspects of Turkish identity. The single mention of *Frenk* does not indicate that it was a key concept in this text, but it was embedded in a part of the Turkish rhetorical tradition where other concepts had come to give meaning in ways that *Frenk* was previously used: "the foreigners," "the developed capitalist countries," "the imperialists" were now trying to conquer our youths' brains in the same way that they had previously tried to take our lands. These ways of making meaning would probably not work well in translations, and this discourse also appears to be largely confined to Turkish, whereas the narrative of Westernization is apt to be translated and can be used to legitimize decisions to multiple audiences. Versions of a discourse of Western powers as scheming imperialists threatening Turkey and its national character are not only counterdiscourses used against government policy. They can also be used by governments, especially in times of crisis, something that the AKP government has been increasingly doing to domestic audiences since the summer of 2013.

Belatedness

The representation of Turkish *belatedness* in relation to Europe that emerged in the nineteenth century is still used in interlingual joint action between Turkish and EU politicians. Just as Turkish politicians appear to repeat themselves when seeking to legitimize their decisions to join NATO, the Common Market, the EEC, and the EU, there appears to be a continuity between the discourse of nineteenth-century British diplomats and the representatives of the European Union. Members of the European Parliament, members of the Accession Commission, and other European officials frequently phrase Turkey's deficiencies in terms of historical belatedness. Central to the argument is *reform*, of which legal reform is still an important aspect. As it is commonly expressed in European discourses, though less frequently in Turkish, the goal is for Turkey to become like a European state. In relation to the EU, the goal is to *become European*, which after the creation of the European Union is difficult to separate from an attempt to become a member. Although the political context has changed beyond recognition since the middle of the nineteenth century, the discourse is surprisingly similar. In an 1858 report on the Ottoman legal system, the judge of the British Supreme Court at Istanbul, Edmund G. Hornby, stated that

> it is useless to disguise the fact that the Turkish government will resist to the last anything like practical reform. They will continue to promise everything. Commissions will be formed; codes will be undertaken, but nothing, however slight in the

way of practical change in details, will be voluntarily submitted to. (Turan Kayaoğlu 2010, 124–25 n. 50)

Similarly, according to a press statement from the European Parliament after the debate about the *2013 Progress Report on Turkey*,

> Constitutional reform must remain the top priority for [Turkey's] modernization and democratization. [Members of the European Parliament] also said [Turkey's] negotiations with the EU must continue to provide a clear framework for Turkey's reforms. . . . "Turkey has embarked on reform for the benefit of its own citizens. Recent developments in the area of fundamental freedoms, independence of the judiciary, freedom of expression and others are however a cause of grave concern for us. We now need a serious, constructive dialogue with Turkey on these subjects and Turkey needs to show true commitment to its European aspirations and to the values upon which the EU is founded," said rapporteur on Turkey Ria Oomen-Ruijten. (European Parliament 2014)

Despite all the legal, social, and political changes in Turkey; despite its *progress, Europeanization,* and *Westernization*; and despite its representations of having entered Europe and being accepted as an equal in 1952 and 1963, officials in Europe still speak of Turkey as a laggard in need of *reform.* Essentialist counter-discourses also exist in European debates, representing Turkey as inherently unsuited for European practices or vice versa, but official spokespersons, presidents, or foreign ministers seldom use these counter-discourses, and especially not when addressing international audiences. Turkey is not always said to be moving in the right direction along a path of Europeanization, Westernization, and modernization, but from these positions, cultural, political, and legal differences between Turkey and European states have systematically been spoken of in temporal terms. In typical EU discourse, Turkish reform is conducted for the benefit of Turkish citizens under the tutelage of well-intentioned Europeans, but Turkey remains behind. EU reports on Turkey's potential membership are replete with these representations (see, e.g., European Commission 2011, 72).

Civilization has been used in a great number of ways in relations between European states and the Ottoman Empire and Turkey. While the concept is now less used, many of the ways of speaking and writing about such relationships use EU membership in much the same way that *civilization* was used as a historical goal. To put this in Koselleckian terms, they are placed in the same semantic field. In a perspective more in line with Shotter, the *EU as historical goal* is now used as a tool, put to much the same use as *civilization* previously was. Where *civilization* was used in the meaning of historical process, *modernization* and *democratization* have taken its place. Tools that can bring Turkey into alignment with Europe are, however, still yoked to concepts of *reform.* Implementation of the Copenhagen Criteria has taken the place of *civilization* as a particular set of refined practices. Progress reports on Turkey can be read as formalized evaluations of the extent to which Turkey has reached "the standard of civilization," although that phrase has been replaced by "the values upon which the EU is founded." In all such statements, Turkey has been represented as belated, with more *progress* and *reform* needed.

Conclusion

The Turkish decisions to join NATO and the Common Market and to apply for membership in the EEC and EU have been legitimized by use of a narrative of Turkey's transformation from an Eastern and backward polity to a Western, progressive, and civilized nation-state. The concepts of *medeniyet* (civilization), *demokrasi* (democracy) and to some extent *çağdaş* or *muasır* (modern) have been used to envision specific futures for Turkey. All of these futures have been yoked to concepts of *Avrupa* (Europe) and *Batı* (the West). The distinctions are typified by fine nuances like specifying that Turkey should "reach the level of modern civilization," while saying that the Western states have already reached that level. Even the counter-discourses use concepts of *progress* and claim that the reason for "our lack of *progress*" is that "we" have embarked on an unfruitful path of Westernization, thus losing "our" national characteristics. While I do not analyze the counter-discourses here in their full extent, they often also use the concept of *progress* to mean progress toward *civilization.* While conservative parties and actors may argue for a very different future for

Turkey, they nevertheless use a common conceptual vocabulary that has in other contexts been linked to a European or Western future. Moreover, this narrative of Westernization seems to be a structural feature of Turkish politics in that it can also be used by politicians who previously used essentialist conceptions of Turkishness. As the conservative AKP came to power, it also appropriated this particular type of discourse, arguing for Turkish membership in the European Union by employing the kind of historical narrative analyzed in this chapter. Despite the increasing use of essentialist counter-discourses on the domestic arena and in relation to voters, when speaking on the issue of European Union membership on more formal occasions, the AKP has largely reproduced the same type of discourse as that used to legitimize earlier efforts to join international organizations.

EIGHT

Conclusion

In this work I develop a toolkit for studying how political elites govern and "reform" their polity using translation and interaction with interlocutors who use different languages. The proof of the tools lies in their analytical purchase when explaining the set of events that transformed the Ottoman Empire into the Turkish nation-state, as well as how this transformation was part of a reconfiguring of relations with Europeans and Westerners. To make sense of this transformation, I have traced how the actors used certain key concepts in important events and interactions with Europeans and Westerners while allowing actors, levels of analysis, and strategies to emerge. My way to approach this has been to analyze text and follow how Ottoman and Turkish meaning-making and legitimation practices have changed as the actors have established translation equivalents of European and Western political concepts. Moreover, I have followed not only how meaning has changed but also how these changed meaning-making practices have been used to reconfigure and stabilize social relations and how these new configurations then become an important context for the use of concepts. These social relations then become part of social reality in which the emergent rhetorical tradition is imbricated.

This book constitutes not only a social-scientific account of changing Ottoman and Turkish legitimation practices and domestic social relations but also an exhortation to study international relations interlingually. While I do not mean to imply that all international studies scholars should follow my approach, international studies scholars would greatly benefit from an increased awareness that not only is politics conducted in language, often international politics is conducted "between languages," in networks that span linguistic boundaries. By limiting study to English language games, or taking English-language meaning to be universal, international studies runs the risk of parochialism. Interlinguality is a matter of degree. No two individuals are the same, and one human cannot perfectly "transmit" a message to another, even when they speak "the same" language. Some form of creative disturbance (Lotman 1990, 13) or joint action (Shotter 1993, 46–47) will inevitably be part of a conversation between two or more individuals. A conversation is more than its parts. It is not about the transformation of highly individualized cognitive processes into speech but about what comes out of the interaction, and that outcome cannot be reduced to a sum of different intentions. People who engage in a conversation can end up somewhere unknown, not just learning and appropriating from one another through the transfer of meaning but making something more in the process. Diplomats and politicians acting in the name of states do so all the time, yet observers—in the Middle East and elsewhere—have a tendency to look at a particular course of events as the realization of some hidden master plan. Doing so often ignores the fact that when conversations take place across linguistic boundaries, it is often impossible to claim to know beforehand what will come out of an engagement. The joint action potential in an interlingual relationship is less likely to conform to expectations than those that happen in intralingual relations.

An Interlingual International Relations

This book has dealt with long-term changes in a particular tradition and a polity's position in international order through conceptual entanglements. Further work might use the analytical setup presented here to look at entanglement as a consequence of denser webs of interlingual relations that are part of globalization, and then to consider whether this setup has analytical purchase for other polities and historical traditions. Does it make sense to talk of conceptual entanglement for Japanese, Russian, and Mandarin? Moreover, what would be the case for changing political languages in those polities that have been directly colonized and ruled more directly by foreigners? Regardless of whether researchers find *conceptual entanglement* useful as a tool, an interlingual approach would be fruitful for the study of these polities. Even though this is a study of Turkey's relationship with Europe, there clearly is more at stake, namely whether it is possible to approach relationships between states that conduct their politics in different languages without taking translation into account.

An interlingual research program would realize more of its potential if philological research could be complemented with research using ethnographic methods. While change in a rhetorical tradition must be studied historically over longer periods of time, the social dynamics of interlingual practice should also be explored through participatory observation (where the only notable work is Schaffer 1998). This goes for both "high politics" and everyday life, and many of the arenas and sites along the spectrum in-between. Politicians, diplomats, and others use knowledge and ways of interacting developed in everyday life to interact in their professional life. Moreover, "high politics" is embedded in a wider network of interlingual relations from which it cannot be kept separate. Further, a number of social arenas occupy an ambiguous position along this continuum, with translation part of everyday office practice—for example, foreign ministries and the secretariats of international organizations.[1] Since we do not know in advance when joint action involving concept formation or reinterpretation will happen—probably often in informal conversations—it is almost impossible to have ethnographers present to document these processes as they unfold. While my approach here emphasizes some watershed moments of concept formation, where new configurations of meaning come about, I believe that more ethnographic research in multilingual sites across the spectrum from high politics to everyday life would greatly benefit our understanding of the interlingual aspects of international relations.

Interlingual meaning-making practices are often conventionalized and institutionalized within particular professional fields and

---

1. Translation studies offers some insights into the role of translators and interpreters in conflicts, wars, and war crimes tribunals, but little of this has been taken into studies more explicitly concerned with political relations between polities. See Baker 2006; Inghilleri and Harding 2010.

organizations, so much so that translation appears to work seamlessly and effortlessly. This is in itself interesting, and it is worthwhile to look at how translation becomes almost invisible when it is successful and uncontested. It would also be useful to look at sites where conversation breaks down as a result of the absence of shared practices of meaning making to find out how and why such breakdowns occur. Just as John Shotter (1993) claims that academic discourse is realized through scholarly use of meaning made in everyday affairs, I believe that politics is conducted by use of concepts similarly embedded in everyday meaning-making practices. They are part of a wider rhetorical tradition not limited to politics. This means that at the microlevel end of a program for interlingual relations study, research could look at a wide variety of contexts, among them exchange students and playground interactions between children who are used to oral communication in other contexts but have no common language. My own observations indicate that play breaks down not because of a lack of common oral language per se but through misunderstandings or disagreements about the game that emerge from the lack of an ability to establish common rules of conduct. Children as young as two or three expect games to have rules and are extremely creative in making them, but they inevitably have problems communicating such complex rules to other children who do not speak their tongue. Play thus emerges more slowly, and children (at least mine) tend to take longer in warming mutual relations. When rules pertaining to a game are already known and the social situation can easily be interpreted to the effect that those rules apply—as with musical chairs—there is no reason that play should break down while the game is ongoing. It is extremely difficult, however, for children who do not speak the same tongue to agree on their own to play musical chairs and how to play it.

States are not children, and it is important to take care when using observations made on a playground when talking about states and their elites or leaders. Historically, however, there appears to be a parallel: those states that lack common language take longer to establish mutual rules of conduct; they interact, but amicable relations are more likely to break down in the absence of a common language in the sense of conventionalized practices of mutual meaning making, and states (or rather members of their elites) are wont to resort to bullying when they do not understand one another, taking the re-fusal to play along with the rules as a snub to a state's integrity as a rule-making peer.

Interlingual Joint Action

Emerging as Turkey does from an imperial tradition in which the polity was not merely one of several rule makers but expected that others would at least symbolically defer to its rules, Ottoman and Turkish elites have persistently struggled to gain acceptance for their state as a rule-making peer in international society circles. The story that international society rules were made in Europe and then ex-ported whole has been shown not to hold up to empirical scrutiny (Keene 2002; Turan Kayaoğlu 2010). Yet the issue of acceptance as a rule-making peer still makes Turks anxious (Zarakol 2011). As chap-ter 7 shows, Turkey's attempts to gain recognition and inclusion in Western-emergent international organizations have repeatedly re-sulted in celebrations of "having finally arrived" or of "having set out on this path of progress." Contrary to much IR literature on Turkey-EU relations, Turkish narratives of *Westernization* and *Europe-anization* are used as a structural feature of relations between the European Union and Turkey, rather than as a way to change Tur-key's position (Rumelili 2007). These relationships are *stabilized* by the use of this narrative, which may explain why the actors involved have been so reluctant to give up this narrative even after Turkey's commitment to EU accession has come into question.

Debates about Turkish membership in international organiza-tions cannot easily be confined to a particular language. Regardless of which language actors use, their statements quickly become part of interlingual joint action in ways that are difficult to compartmental-ize into neat categories of this or that language. Despite this increas-ingly quick translation from one language to another, there is a dif-ference between Turkish-language discourse on potential membership in these organizations and the discourses on Turkey in European languages. It may seem paradoxical, then, that even those Turkish discourses that emphasize the superiority of essentialized qualities of Turkish culture and that would be likely to evoke puzzle-ment if they were translated into English use concepts entangled with

English-language meaning. The particular semantic configurations of such discourses are specific to Turkish, but since concepts are entangled, discourse can be translated. Although an English-reading audience is likely to disagree with a particular statement in translation, it is understandable in ways that translations of Ottoman discourse seldom were two centuries ago. In short, even those statements with which English-speakers are likely to disagree require less semantic reconfiguration in translation from Turkish to English.

The rhetorical tradition within which Ottoman and Turkish concepts of Europe are put to use often gives them connotations such as *infidel, Christianity,* and *Great Power,* and concepts such *Avrupa* (Europe) are still used to mean foreignness and something of which Turkey is not part. Moreover, the concept is open for use that implies ambivalence about foreigners' intentions. The dynamic between Turkey and EU representatives has to some extent become its own language game, where changes in the established discourse of "it's a matter of time before Turkey becomes a member, all it needs to do is mend its ways" can have unforeseen consequences. The fact that this language game has a dynamic that is only partly entangled with "domestic" language games in Turkey and the various EU member countries means that both EU and Turkish leaders will engage in multivocal signaling—that is, *double communication.* As networks of translation and bilingual interaction densify, actors are increasingly caught "speaking with two tongues," which undermines trust between the states involved. In the case of Turkey and the EU, the fact that actors must legitimize their actions in incompatible language games clearly adds to the complexity of the interaction.

Turkey and the West

Turkey's membership in NATO and partial inclusion in "the West" was legitimized by the use of concepts such as *demokrasi/democracy* and *hür dünya/the Free World.* This was slightly different from what Patrick Thaddeus Jackson (2006) claims in relation to West Germany's "rehabilitation" in international society around the same time: he argues that the German case relied heavily on the concept of a common *Western civilization, where Germany was already a natural part.* Claiming that Turkey was part of *Western civilization* was clearly more difficult. Because of its relatively new use as a key concept in international society, however, *democracy* was more "open" and was linked not primarily to essentialized qualities but to political practices, which the Turkish leadership changed to anchor claims to *democracy* in practice.[2] Reinterpreting Turkish identity by linking it to the "Free World" was easier than claiming that it was part of "Western civilization" despite the fact that these two concepts were often used synonymously. During the Cold War, the defining Other of the "Free World" was the Soviet Union, while the binary opposite of *democracy* was *communism*. These two conceptual pairs have many similarities with discourses that rely on *civilization* in the singular as the unifying practice and telos of all human societies. The Soviet Union's disappearance as a unifying common enemy and defining Other created problems for the coherence of NATO and in particular for the "Westernness" of Turkey. In the absence of a *communism* that Turkey could demarcate itself vis-à-vis, arguing that Turkey was *democratic* became increasingly difficult. Instead, the representation of Turkey's belatedness in progress toward a common human goal was reinforced.

In the 1990s and early 2000s, particularly after the 9/11 attacks, *civilization* was again increasingly used in connection with *democracy* and *freedom*. Sometimes the three were used synonymously; sometimes *democracy* and *freedom* came to be used in a manner similar to civilization in the singular, while *civilization* came to be used in the plural in ways that drew very explicitly on Samuel Huntington's *The Clash of Civilizations* (1996). Whereas Turkey had been represented in English as *democratic* when *democracy* was primarily distinguished by juxtaposition with *communism*, it was less easy to claim that Turkey was *democratic* when *democracy*'s main counterconcepts were linked to *Islamism*, which in English was sometimes conflated with *Islam*. Such claims became even more difficult after the religiously conservative AKP came to power in Turkey in 2002 and refused to support the U.S.-led invasion of Iraq in 2003.

---

2. It is of course possible to claim that a determining factor for discursively being part of the "Free World" was inclusion in binding security arrangements with the United States rather than actual democratic practice. This is a complex issue, with the different concepts in continuous mutual adjustment, and a specific set of practices could be "democratic" in one place but "socialist" in another. However, in Turkey's case, laying claim to *democracy* necessitated multiparty elections, and Turkish *democracy* was a prerequisite for American aid and Turkish NATO membership.

Both Bahar Rumelili and Ayşe Zarakol have argued that Turkey's identity in relation to "Europe" is *liminal*—neither fully European nor totally outside, occupying an ambiguous position at the boundary of European identity (Rumelili 2007, 64–94; Zarakol 2011). I see Turkey's liminality as stemming at least partly from its incompatible positions in different taxonomies and languages—for example, how Turkey and Germany were included in the NATO by slightly different use of concepts. Although the categories within these taxonomies are often treated as synonymous (e.g., the Free World = the democracies = international society = civilization = Western civilization), they nevertheless come with slightly different connotations and practical implications. States such as Britain, France, and the Netherlands are usually represented coherently in such schemata without having to do any discursive work arguing their own inclusion in the wider collective. Turkey is not. Turkey's liminal position in relation to Europe means that Turkish leaders must do discursive work every time the vocabulary of international society changes or new "Western" or "European" organizations are set up. Unlike nonliminal European states, Turkey will not automatically be extended an invitation to join in the initial making of a new organization and get a chance to shape the attendant rules and practices that makes up its language game. Unless Turks either adapt to rules made by others or gerrymander the boundaries for appropriate concept usage, Turkey is left out. Like children using a foreign language on the playground, Turkey's acceptance as a rule-making peer is tenuous. It may be allowed to join the game but often has to play by others' rules.

References

Note for the Reader: Coherently alphabetizing references from the period treated presents a number of problems. As a rule, Ottomans did not have surnames, and Turkey only introduced them in its surname reform of 1934. Sources written prior to 1934 should typically be alphabetized according to the first of an author's names. There are specific exceptions to this convention, where the name the author is best known by can be used (such as Ibn Khaldun). Moreover, Turks who published works before 1934, but then received a surname, often have their works republished (or reprinted) under a name that includes their new surname. I here list references by the names as they appear in the sources I have used, with all the confusion that arises from having works by the same person appearing in different places in the list of references. Another matter that creates confusion is that the names of the places of publication has frequently been an issue of much political contention. Again, I have noted the place of publication as indicated in the source itself and not imposed present-day place names.

Transcripts, Primary Documents, and Newspaper Articles

Abadan, Yavuz. 1945. "Bizde Demokrasi ve Hürriyet." *Cumhuriyet,* 7 September, 1.

Abadan, Yavuz. 1946. "Türk Demokrasisi ve Yeni Parti." *Ülkü* 9 (104): 2.

Akşam. 1963. "Ortak Pazara Girdik." 13 September, 1.

[Ali Suavi]. 1870. "Demōḳrāsī: Hükūmet-i Ḥalḳ: Müsāvāt." *ʿUlūm Ġazetesi,* 17 May, 1083–1107.

Aral, Namık Zeki. 1960. "Meselelerimiz: Demokrasi ve Aleniyet." *Ulus,* 4 June, 2.

Baban, Cihad. 1960. "Fazilet ve Ahlak." *Ulus,* 2 June, 1.

Başbakanlık Osmanlı Arşivleri (Prime Ministry Ottoman Archives), Istanbul. 1218 [1803]. Hatt-ı Hümayūn Tasnifi, 31, 1483, 29 Muharrem [21 May].

Başbakanlık Osmanlı Arşivleri (Prime Ministry Ottoman Archives), Istanbul. 1220 [1805]. Hatt-ı Hümayūn Tasnifi 31 1448F, 18 Muharrem [18 April].

Baysun, Mehmet Cavit. 1941. "Mustafa Reşit Paşanın Siyasî Yazıları I: Atabei Bülent Mertebei Veliyyünniamilerine Maruzi Çakeri Kemineleridir ki." *Türk Tarih Vesikaları* 1 (1): 30–44.

Bekman, Avni Refik. 1950. "Demokrasi ve Partiler: Anarşiye Gidilemez." *Ulus*, 15 April, 2.

Crowther, Geoffrey. 1945. "Dünyayı Meşgul Eden Meselelerden: Kapitalizm ile Komünizm Mutlaka Çarpışacak mı?" *Cumhuriyet*, 8 September, 2.

Cumhuriyet. 1945a. "Başbakanın Dünkü Mühim Beyanatı: Dün Ankara Gazetecileri Kabul Eden Şükrü Saraçoğlu iç ve dış Siyasetimiz etrafında Toplu İzahatta Bulundu: 'Hürriyet Şarlatanlarına Hükûmetin Cevabı.'" 6 September, 1.

Cumhuriyet. 1945b. "İktibas: Demokrasi Bahsinde Dünyaya Ders Veren İsviçre." 4 October, 2.

Cumhuriyet. 1945c. "İktibaslar. Demokrasi nedir?" 29 September, 2.

Cumhuriyet. 1945d. "İngiliz işçi gazetesi Rusyaya hücum ediyor." 15 September, 1.

Cumhuriyet. 1952. "Batının silâhlanma plânı dün açıklandı." 25 February, 1.

Erkin, Feridun Cemal. 1974. "İnönü, Demokrasi ve Dış İlişkileri." *Milliyet*, 14 January, 2.

European Commission. 2011. *Communication from the Commission to the European Parliament and the Council: Enlargement Strategy and Main Challenges, 2011–2012.* Brussels: European Commission.

European Parliament. 2014. "Turkey: Credible Commitment and Strong Democratic Foundations Needed, MEPs say." In *Plenary Session Press Release—External Relations.* Brussels: European Parliament. http://www.europarl .europa.eu/news/en/press-room/20140307IPR38301/turkey-credible-commitment-and-strong-democratic-foundations-needed-meps-say

G.D. 1898. "Economic Transition in Japan." *The Nation*, 9 May, 379–80.

Haberler. 2012. "'Türk Yerel Medyası AB Yolunda' Projesi." 30 January. http:// www.haberler.com/turk-yerel-medyasi-ab-yolunda-projesi-3315415-haberi/

Hürriyet. 1963. "Türkiye Ortak Pazarda." 13 September, 1.

Jouannin, M. 1833 [1526]. "Lettre de Sultan Suleyman El Kanouni (Le Législateur) à François Ier pendant sa Captivité à Madrid, (Février 1526). Traduite par M. Jouannin, Premier Secrétaire-Interprète du Roi. Paris: Unpublished manuscript found in Gallica: Bibliothèque Numérique." Folder: Recueil de lettres et de pièces originales, et de copies de pièces indiquées comme telles dans le dépouillement qui suit. Author: Süleyman I (sultan; 1494–1566). Identifiant: ark:/12148/btv1b9059854s. Source: Bibliothèque Nationale de France, Département des Manuscrits, Français 2982 (Imprimerie de Firmin Didot Frères).

Karaosmanoğlu, Y[akup]. K[adri]. 1960. "İç Sömürgeciler." *Ulus*, 2 June, 1.

[Mahmut Esat]. 1932. "Maarif Vekili Esat Beyefendinin Açma Nutku." 1932. In *Birinci Türk Tarih Kongresi: Maarif Vekâleti ve Türk Tarihi tetkik Cemiyeti tarafından tertip edilmiştir: koferanslar müzakere zabıtları*, 5–15. Istanbul: T. C. Maarif Vekâleti.

Mahmut Esat. 1930. "Muasır Demokrasilerin Istırapları." *Ayın Tarihi: Aylık Siyasî Mecmua*. 21 (71): 5555–68.

Mālūmat. 1313 [1897]. "Devlet-i ʿAlīye-i ʿOsmānīye ve Jāponyā İmparāṭörluğu." 12. Ağustos [24 August].

Milliyet. 1963. "'Ortak Pazar' Anlaşması İmzalandı." 13 September, 7.

Milliyet. 1971. "Erim: Bugünkü Anayasa Türkiye İçin Lükstür." 2 May, 1, 9.

Milliyet. 1987. "AET'ye tam üyelik başvurusunu bugün yapıyoruz: Avrupalılaşmada ilk adım." 14 April, 14.

Mustafa Kemal 1945a. "Bakanlar Kurulu Görev ve Yetkisini Belirten Kanun Teklifi Münasebetiyle, 1 Aralık 1921 (1337)." In *Atatürk'ün Söylev ve Demeçleri I. T. B. M Meclisinde ve C. H. P. Kurultaylarında (1919–1938)*, 182–214. Istanbul: Maarif Matbaası.

Mustafa Kemal. 1945b. "Dördüncü Toplanma Yılını Açarken, 1 Mart 1923 (1339)." In *Atatürk'ün Söylev ve Demeçleri: T. B. M Meclisinde ve C. H. P. Kurultaylarında (1919–1938)*, 273–99. Istanbul: Maarif Matbaası.

Mustafa Kemal. 1945c. "Seçimin Yenilmesi Hakkında Karar Münasebetiyle, 1 nisan 1923 (1339)." In *Atatürk'ün Söylev ve Demeçleri: T. B. M Meclisinde ve C. H. P. Kurultaylarında (1919–1938)*, 299–300. İstanbul: Maarif Matbaası.

Mustafa Kemal. 1952. "Akhisar'da Bir Konuşma. 10. X. 1925." In *Atatürk'ün Söylev ve Demeçleri II. (1906–1938)*, 226–27. Ankara: Türk Tarıh Kurumu Basımevi.

Nadi, Nadir. 1952. "Kararın Manası." *Cumhuriyet*, 19 February, 1.

Oksal, Sedat. 1950. "İnkilâplarımız: Tarihimizde Beş Merhale." *Milliyet*, 21 May, 2.

[Republican People's Party]. 1943. *C. H. P. Programı: Partinin VI. Büyük Kurultayının 14. VI. 1943 Tarihindeki Toplantısında Kabul Edilmiştir*. Ankara: Zerbamat Basımevi.

Sabah. 1987a. "AET'nin Kapısını Bugün Çalıyoruz!" 14 April, 5.

Sabah. 1987b. "Tarihimizde Yepyeni bir Sayfa Açılıyor." 15 April, 5.

Truman, Harry S. 1947. "Special Message to Congress on Greece and Turkey: The Truman Doctrine." March 12. https://www.trumanlibrary.org/audio/mp3s/play.php?aud=sr64-47.mp3

Turkey, Republic of. 1336 [1920]a. *T.B.M.M Zabıt Ceridesi*. Devre: I., Cilt: 2, İçtima Senesi: 1, Ondokuzuncu İçtima 22.5.1336.

Turkey, Republic of. 1336 [1920]b. *T.B.M.M Zabıt Ceridesi*. Devre: I, Cilt: 6, İçtima Senesi: 1, Yüz beşinci içtima, 29.11.1336.

Turkey, Republic of. 1338 [1922]. *T.B.M.M. Zabıt Ceridesi*. Devre: I, Cilt: 24, İçtima Senesi: 3, Yüzotuzuncu İçtima 1 November 1338.

Turkey, Republic of. 1934a. "İskân Kanunu, Kanun No: 2510, Kabul tarihi: 14/6/1934." *T. C. Resmî Gazete* (2733): 21 June 1934.

Turkey, Republic of. 1934b. *T.B.M.M. Zabıt Ceridesi*. Devre: IV, Cilt: 23, İçtima: 3, Altmış Sekizinci İnikat. 14 June 1934.

Turkey, Republic of. 1940. *T.B.M.M. Zabıt Ceridesi*. Devre: VI, Cild 11, İçtima: 1, Elli birinci inikad, 15 May 1940.

Turkey, Republic of. 1945a. *T.B.M.M. Tutanak Dergisi*. Dönem: VII, Cilt: 20, Toplantı: 3, On üçüncü birleşim, 18 December 1940.

Turkey, Republic of. 1945b. *T.B.M.M. Zabıt Ceridesi*. Dönem: VII, Cilt: 20, Olağanüstü İnikat, 23 February 1945.

Turkey, Republic of. 1950. "Gerekçe." In *T.C. Başbakanlık Muamelât Genel Müdürlüğü, Tetkik Müdürlüğü*. No. 71-1710, 6/4166, 1 December 1950.

Turkey, Republic of. 1951. *T.B.M.M. Tutanak Dergisi*. Dönem: IX, Cilt: 9, Toplantı: 1 Yüz onuncu Birleşim, 7 August 1951.

Turkey, Republic of. 1952. *T.B.M.M. Tutanak Dergisi*. Dönem: IX, Cilt: 13, Toplant: 2, Kırk birinci Birleşim Session: 41, 18 February 1952.

Turkey, Republic of. 1984. *T.B.M.M. Tutanak Dergisi*. Dönem: 17, Cilt: 5, Yasama Yılı: 1, 89uncu Birleşim, 12 July 1984.

Turkey, Republic of. 1987. *T.B.M.M Tutanak Dergisi*. Dönem: 17, Cilt 39, Yasama Yılı: 4, 89uncu Birleşim, 14 April 1987.

Turkey, Republic of. 1989. *T.B.M.M. Tutanak Dergisi*. Dönem: 18 Cilt: 37: Yasama Yılı: 3, 55inci Birleşim, 23 December 1989.

Turkey, Republic of. 1996. *T.B.M.M Tutanak Dergisi*. Dönem: 20, Cilt: 17, Yasama Yılı: 1, 35inci Birleşim, 16 December 1996.

Turkey, Republic of. 1999. *T.B.M.M. Tutanak Dergisi*. Dönem: 21, Cilt: 19, Yasama yılı: 2, 33üncü Birleşim, 14 December 1999.

Turkey, Republic of. 2002. *T.B.M.M. Tutanak Dergisi*. Dönem: 21. Yasama Yılı: 4, 77'inci Birleşim, 21 March 2002.

Ulus. 1950a. "Başbakan Dün Sabah Ankara'ya Döndü: Günaltay'ın Zonguldak Nutku: Demokrasiyi Hudutsuz Hürriyet Telâkki Etmek Millî Cemiyette Anarşiye Yol Açar." 13 April, 6.

Ulus. 1950b. "Seçimler Bütün Dünyada Büyük Akisler Uyandırdı: Bir Amerikan

Gazetesi Diyor ki: Demokrasi Yolunda en İleri Adımı İnönü Attırmıştır." 18 May, 1.

Ulus. 1950c. "Türkiye Seçimlerinde: İsmet İnönü'nün Şeref Payı Çok Büyüktür." 17 May, 1.

Ulus. 1960. "Antidemokratik Kanunlar için İlmî Heyet Kuruldu." 2 June, 1.

United Nations. 1945. *Charter of the United Nations and Statute of the International Court of Justice.* San Francisco: United Nations.

Yalçın, Hüseyin Cahit. 1950. "Hakikat Karşısında." *Ulus*, 17 April, 1.

Books and Secondary Sources

Abadan, Yavuz. 1943. *Hukuk Başlangıcı ve Tarihi.* İstanbul: İstanbul Üniversitesi Hukuk Fakültesi Talebe Cemiyeti.

Abou-El-Haj, Rifa'at Ali. 1991. *Formation of the Modern State: The Ottoman Empire Sixteenth to Eighteenth Centuries.* Albany: State University of New York Press.

Abu-Manneh, Butrus. 1982. "The Naqshbandiyya-Mujaddidiyya in the Ottoman Lands in the Early 19th Century." *Die Welt des Islams*, n.s., 22 (1/4): 1–36.

Abu-Manneh, Butrus. 1990. "The Sultan and the Bureaucracy: The Anti-Tanzimat Concepts of Grand Vizier Mahmud Nedim Pasa." *International Journal of Middle East Studies* 22 (3): 257–74.

Abu-Manneh, Butrus. 1994. "The Islamic Roots of the Gülhane Rescript." *Die Welt des Islams* n.s., 34 (2): 173–203.

Acharya, Amitav. 2004. "How Ideas Spread: Whose Norms Matter? Norm Localization and Institutional Change in Asian Regionalism." *International Organization* 58 (2): 239–75.

Âfetinan, A. 1998 [1969]. *Medenî Bilgiler ve M. Kemal Atatürk'ün El Yazıları, Atatürk Kültür, Dil ve Tarih Yüksek Kurumu: Türk Tarih Kurumu Yayınları XVI. Dizi.* Ankara: Türk Tarih Kurumu Basımevi.

Ağaoğlu Ahmet. 1972 [1927]. *Üç Medeniyet.* Transliterated by Tezer Taşkıran. İstanbul: Başbakanlık Kültür Müsteşarlığı Kültür Yayınları/Millî Eğitim Basımevi.

Ahmad, Feroz. 1977. *The Turkish Experiment in Democracy, 1950–1975.* London: C. Hurst.

Aḥmed Ṣalāḥaddīn. 1920. *Ḥuḳūḳ-ı 'āmme.* N.p.: Mekteb-i Mülkiye Maṭbaʿası.

Ahmet Midhat Efendi. 2000 [1891]. *Müşahedat.* In *Ahmet Midhat Efendi Bütün Eserleri*, Romanlar XIII. Ankara: Türk Dil Kurumu.

Ahmet Mithat Efendi. 2016 [1896]. *Avrupa Adab-ı Muaşereti Yahut Alafranga*. Edited and transliterated by Fazıl Gökçek. İstanbul: Dergâh.

Akandere, Osman. 2003. "Bir Demokrasi Beyannamesi Olarak 'Dörtlü Takrir'in Amacı ve Mahiyeti." *Selçuk Üniversitesi Sosyal Bilimler Enstitüsü Dergisi* 9:5–28.

Akçura, Yusuf [Akçuraoğlu Yusuf]. 2005 [1904]. *Üç Tarz-ı Siyaset*. İstanbul: Lotus yayınları.

Aksakal, Mustafa. 2004. "Not 'By Those Old Books of International Law, but Only by War': Ottoman Intellectuals on the Eve of the Great War." *Diplomacy and Statecraft* 15 (3): 507–44.

Aksan, Virginia H. 2004. "Ottoman Sources of Information on Europe in the Eighteenth Century." In *Ottomans and Europeans: Contacts and Conflicts*, 13–23. İstanbul: İsis Press.

Albachten, Özlem Berk. 2004. *Translation and Westernization in Turkey: From the 1840s to the 1980s*. İstanbul: Ege Yayınları.

Alfonce, Ian. 1559 [1544]. *Les Voyages Avantureux du Capitaine Ian Alfonce sainctongeois: Contenant les Reigles et Enseignemens Necessaires à la bBonne & Seure Navigation*. Poitiers: de Marnesz et Boucherz.

Althusser, Louis. 1972. *Lenin and Philosophy, and Other Essays*. New York: Monthly Review Press.

Anderson, Benedict. 2006. *Imagined Communities: Reflections on the Origin and Spread of Nationalism*. New York: Verso.

Anderson, M. S. 1966. *The Eastern Question, 1774–1923: A Study in International Relations*. New York: St. Martin's Press.

Anscombe, Frederick F. 2014. *State, Faith, and Nation in Ottoman and Post-Ottoman Lands*. New York: Cambridge University Press.

Anscombe, G. E. M. 2000. *Intention*. Cambridge: Harvard University Press.

Apter, Emily. 2006. *The Translation Zone. A New Comparative Literature*. Princeton: Princeton University Press.

Arai, Masami. 1994. *Jön Türk Dönemi Türk Milliyetçiliği*. Translated by Tansel Demirel. İstanbul: İletişim Yayınları.

Argens, Jean-Baptiste de Boyer, marquis d'. 1738. *Lettres juives; ou, Correspondance philosophique, historique, et critique entre un juif voïageur en différens Etats de l'Europe et ses correspondans en divers endroits*. 6 vols. La Haye: Pierre Paupie.

Arı, Kemal. 1995. *Büyük Mübadele: Türkiye'ye Zorunlu Göç (1923–25)*. Istanbul: Tarih Vakfı Yurt Yayınları.

Arıkan, Zeki. 1989. "Balkan Savaşı ve Kamuoyu." In *Bildiriler: Dördüncü Askeri Tarih Semineri*, 168–88. Ankara: Genelkurmay Basımevi.

Atay, Falih Rıfkı. 2008 [1932]. *Zeytindağı*. İstanbul: Pozitif Yayınları.

Austin, John L. 1962. *How to Do Things with Words: The William James Lectures deliv-*

ered at Harvard University in 1955. Edited by James Opie Urmson and Marina Sbisà. Oxford: Clarendon.

Ayalon, Ami. 1987. *Language and Change in the Arab Middle East: The Evolution of Modern Political Discourse*. New York: Oxford University Press.

Aybars, Ergün. 1995. *İstiklâl Mahkemeleri*. 3rd ed. İzmir: İleri Kitabevi.

Al-Azmeh, Aziz. 1990. *Ibn Khaldūn*. London: Routledge.

Babinger, Fr., and C. E. Bosworth. 2013. "Pādishāh." In *Encyclopaedia of Islam*, 3rd ed., edited by P. Bearman, Th. Bianquis, C. E. Bosworth, E. van Donzel, and W. P. Heinrichs. Leiden: Brill Online.

Badem, Candan. 2010. *The Ottoman Crimean War (1853–1856)*. Leiden: Brill.

Badie, Bertrand. 2000. *The Imported State: The Westernization of the Political Order*. Stanford: Stanford University Press.

Baker, Mona. 2006. *Translation and Conflict: A Narrative Account*. London: Routledge.

Bakhtin, Mikhail. 1981. *The Dialogic Imagination: Four Essays*. Translated by Caryl Emerson and Michael Holquist. Austin: University of Texas Press.

Baltacıoğlu, İsmail Hakkı. 1945. *Batıya doğru*. İstanbul: Sebat Basımevi.

Balzac, Jean-Louis Guez de. 1631. *Le prince*. Paris: T. du Bray, P. Roccolet, et C. Sonnius.

Barkey, Karen. 2008. *Empire of Difference: The Ottomans in Comparative Perspective*. Cambridge: Cambridge University Press.

Barthold, Wilhelm [Vasilij V. Bartol'd]. 1962 [1932–35]. *Zwölf Vorlesungen über die Geschichte der Türken Mittelasiens*. Hildesheim: Olm.

Başgil, A. Fuad. 1940. "Esas Teşkilât ve Siyasî Rejim." In *Milletlerin hukuki hayatı serisinden Türkiye*, edited by M. Cemil Bilsel, 1–48. Istanbul: Üniversite Kitabevi.

Bassnett, Susan. 1990. *Translation Studies*. London: Routledge.

Baykara, Tuncer. 2007. *Osmanlılarda Medeniyet Kavramı*. İstanbul: IQ Kültür Sanatı Yayıncılık.

Behnke, Andreas. 1997. "Citizenship, Nationhood, and the Production of Political Space." *Citizenship Studies* 1 (2): 243–65.

Bellah, Robert N., Richard Madsen, William M. Sullivan, Ann Swidler, and Steven M. Tipton. 1985. *Habits of the Heart: Individualism and Commitment in American Life*. Berkeley: University of California Press.

Ben-Dor, Zvi Aziz. 2002. "'Even unto China': Displacement and Chinese Muslim Myths of Origin." *Bulletin of the Royal Institute for Inter-Faith Studies* 4 (2): 93–114.

Berkes, Niyazi. 1998. *The Development of Secularism in Turkey*. New York: Routledge.

Bielsa, Esperanza. 2011. "Some Remarks on the Sociology of Translation: A Reflection on the Global Production and Circulation of Sociological Works." *European Journal of Social Theory* 14 (2): 199–215.

Birand, Mehmet Ali, Can Dündar, and Bülent Mehmet Çaplı. 1991. *Demirkırat: Bir Demokrasinin Doğuşu.* Istanbul: Milliyet Yayınları.

Boer, Pim den. 1995. "Europe to 1914: The Making of an Idea." In *The History of the Idea of Europe*, edited by Jan van der Dussen and Kevin Wilson, 13–82. London: Routledge.

Bowden, Brett. 2009. *The Empire of Civilization.* Chicago: University of Chicago Press.

Bozkurt, Mahmut Esat. 1940. *Atatürk İhtilâli: Türk İnkılâbı Tarihi Enstitüsü Derslerinden.* İstanbul: İstanbul Üniversitesi.

Brubaker, Rogers. 1990. "Immigration, Citizenship, and the Nation-State in France and Germany: A Comparative Historical Analysis." *International Sociology* 5 (4): 379–407.

Brubaker, Rogers. 1996. *Nationalism Reframed: Nationhood and the National Question in the New Europe.* Cambridge: Cambridge University Press.

Brummett, Palmira Johnson. 2000. *Image and Imperialism in the Ottoman Revolutionary Press, 1908–1911.* Albany: State University of New York Press.

Brunner, Otto, Werner Conze, and Reinhart Koselleck eds. 1972–97. *Geschichtliche Grundbegriffe: Historisches Lexikon zur politisch-sozialen Sprache in Deutschland.* Stuttgart: Klett-Cotta.

Buğday, Korkut. 2009. *The Routledge Introduction to Literary Ottoman.* Translated by Jerold C. Frakes. London: Routledge.

Bull, Hedley. 1977. *The Anarchical Society: A Study of Order in World Politics.* London: Macmillan.

Bull, Hedley, and Adam Watson, eds. 1984. *The Expansion of International Society.* Oxford: Clarendon.

Çağaptay, Soner. 2006. *Islam, Secularism, and Nationalism in Modern Turkey: Who Is a Turk?* London: Routledge.

Çağman, Engin. 2010. *III. Selim'e Sunulan Islahat Layihaları.* İstanbul: Kitabevi.

Campbell, David. 1992. *Writing Security: United States Foreign Policy and the Politics of Identity.* Minneapolis: University of Minnesota Press.

Campos, Michelle U. 2010. *Ottoman Brothers: Muslims, Christians, and Jews in Early Twentieth-Century Palestine.* Stanford: Stanford University Press.

Çekiç, Can Eyüp. 2009. "'Savoir Vivre Cosmopolite': Ahmed Midhat's Avrupa Adab-ı Muaşereti yahut Alafranga as a Source for Modernization of the Codes of Social Behavior in the Late Nineteenth Century Ottoman Empire." Master's thesis, Graduate School of Social Sciences, Middle Eastern Technical University, Ankara.

Çelik, Hüseyin. 1993. *Ali Suavî.* Series: Türk Büyükleri. Ankara: T.C. Kültür Bakanlığı Yayınları.

Cevdet Paşa [Ahmed Cevdet Paşa]. 1991. *Tezâkir. 40—Tetimme.* Vol. 4. Ankara: Türk Tarih Kurumu Basımevi.

Chalcondyle, Laonicus. 1577. *L'Histoire de la Décadence de l'Empire Grec et Establissement de Celuy des Turcs, Comprise en dix Livres, par Nicolas Chalcondyle.* Translated by Blaise de Vigenère. Paris: Nicolas Chesneau.

Chatterjee, Partha. 1993. *The Nation and Its Fragments: Colonial and Postcolonial Histories.* Princeton: Princeton University Press.

Checkel, Jeffrey. 2005. "International Institutions and Socialization in Europe: Introduction and Framework." *International Organization* 59 (4): 801–26.

Çiçek, Nazan. 2010. *The Young Ottomans: Turkish Critics of the Eastern Question in the Late Nineteenth Century.* London: I.B. Tauris.

Cohen, Raymond. 1997. *Negotiating across Cultures: International Communication in an Interdependent World.* Rev. ed. Washington, DC: United States Institute of Peace Press.

Cohen, Raymond. 2001. "Language and Conflict Resolution: The Limits of English." *International Studies Review* 2 (1): 25–51.

Collin, Richard Oliver. 2013. "Moving Political Meaning across Linguistic Frontiers." *Political Studies* 61:282–300.

Connolly, William E. 1993. *The Terms of Political Discourse.* 3rd ed. Oxford: Blackwell.

Coş, Kıvanç, and Pınar Bilgin. 2010. "Stalin's Demands: Constructions of the 'Soviet Other' in Turkey's Foreign Policy, 1919–1945." *Foreign Policy Analysis* 6 (1): 43–60.

Çulpan, Cevdet. 1966. "Kanuni Sultan Süleyman Eserlerinden: Moldavya'da Bender Kalesi kitabesi (H. 945–M. 1538)." *Türk Kültürü* 4 (46):881–883.

Daborne, Robert. 1612. *A Christian Turn'd Turke; or, The Tragicall Lives and Deaths of the Two Famous Pyrates, Ward and Dansiker.* London: William Barrenger.

Darling, Linda T. 2013. *A History of Social Justice and Political Power in the Middle East: The Circle of Justice from Mesopotamia to Globalization.* Abingdon: Routledge.

Davison, Roderic H. 1963. *Reform in the Ottoman Empire, 1856–1876.* Princeton: Princeton University Press.

Davison, Roderic H. 1976. "'Russian Skill and Turkish Imbecility': The Treaty of Kuchuk Kainardji Reconsidered." *Slavic Review* 35:463–83.

Deringil, Selim. 1989. *Turkish Foreign Policy during the Second World War: An "Active" Neutrality.* Cambridge: Cambridge University Press.

Deringil, Selim. 1998. *The Well-Protected Domains: Ideology and the Legitimation of Power in the Ottoman Empire, 1876–1909.* London: I.B. Tauris.

Deringil, Selim. 2003. "'They Live in a State of Nomadism and Savagery': The Late Ottoman Empire and the Post-Colonial Debate." *Comparative Studies in Society and History* 45 (2): 311–42.

Deringil, Selim. 2012. *Conversion and Apostasy in the Late Ottoman Empire*. New York: Cambridge University Press.

Derrida, Jacques. 1985. "Des Tours de Babel." In *Difference in Translation*, edited by Joseph F. Graham, 165–207. Ithaca: Cornell University Press.

Derrida, Jacques. 2004. "What Is a 'Relevant' Translation?" In *The Translation Studies Reader*, edited by Lawrence Venuti, 423–46. London: Routledge.

Doğan, Atila. 2006. *Osmanlı Aydınları ve Sosyal Darwinizm*. Istanbul: İstanbul Bilgi Üniversitesi Yayınları.

Drakulic, Slavenka. 1993. *The Balkan Express: Fragments from the Other Side of War*. New York: Norton.

Dubos, l'Abbé Jean-Baptiste. 1742 [1734]. *Histoire Critique de l'établissement de la Monarchie Françoise dans les Gaules*. 4 vols. Paris: Ganeau.

Duguit, Léon. 1922. *Souveraineté et Liberté: Leçons Faites a l'Université Columbia, 1920–1921*. Paris: Librairie Félix Alcan.

Dündar, Fuat. 2008. *Modern Türkiye'nin Şifresi: İttihat ve Terakki'nin Etnisite Mühendisliği, 1913–1918*. İstanbul: İletişim.

Eco, Umberto. 2003. *Mouse or Rat? Translation as Negotiation*. London: Weidenfeld and Nicolson.

Ecsedy, Hilda. 1972. "Tribe and Tribal Society in the 6th Century Türk Empire." *Acta Orientalia Hungarica* 25:245–62.

Ejdus, Filip, ed. 2017. *Memories of Empire and Entry into International Society: Views from the European Periphery*. Abingdon: Routledge.

Eldem, Edhem. 1999. *Banknotes of the Imperial Ottoman Bank, 1863–1914: Based on the Ottoman Bank Archives and the Tahsin İşbiroğlu Collection*. Istanbul: Osmanlı Bankası Arşiv ve Araştırma Merkezi.

Elias, Norbert. 2000. *The Civilizing Process*. Oxford: Blackwell.

Epstein, Charlotte. 2008. *The Power of Words in International Relations: Birth of an Anti-Whaling Discourse*. Cambridge: MIT Press.

Erozan, Hüseyn Boğaç. 2005. "Producing Obedience: Law Professors and the Turkish State." PhD diss., University of Minnesota.

Everett, Daniel. 2008. *Don't Sleep, There Are Snakes*. London: Profile Books.

Fabian, Johannes. 1983. *Time and the Other*. New York: Columbia University Press.

Fahmy, Khaled. 1997. *All the Pasha's Men: Mehmed Ali, His Army, and the Making of Modern Egypt*. Cambridge: Cambridge University Press. Rpt., American University in Cairo Press, 2002.

Falih Rıfkı [Atay]. 1931. *Yeni Rusya.* Ankara: Hakimiyet-i Milliye Matbaası.

Ferguson, Adam. 1995 [1767]. *An Essay on the History of Civil Society.* Cambridge: Cambridge University Press.

Findley, Carter V. 1980. *Bureaucratic Reform in the Ottoman Empire: The Sublime Porte, 1789–1922.* Princeton: Princeton University Press.

Findley, Carter V. 2005. *The Turks in World History.* New York: Oxford University Press.

Findley, Carter V. 2010. *Turkey, Islam, Nationalism, and Modernity: A History.* New Haven: Yale University Press.

Finnemore, Martha, and Kathryn Sikkink. 1998. "International Norm Dynamics and Political Change." *International Organization* 52 (4): 887–917.

Fisher, Alan W. 1987. "Emigration of Muslims from the Russian Empire in the Years after the Crimean War." *Jahrbücher für Geschichte Osteuropas, Neue Folge* 35 (3): 356–71.

Fleischer, Cornell H. 1983. "Royal Authority, Dynastic Cyclism, and 'Ibn Khaldunism' in Sixteenth-Century Ottoman Letters." *Journal of Asian and African Studies* 18 (3–4): 198–220.

Foucault, Michel. 1970. *The Order of Things: An Archaeology of the Human Sciences.* New York: Pantheon.

Foucault, Michel. 2003. *Society Must Be Defended.* London: Penguin.

Gadamer, Hans-Georg. 2004. *Truth and Method.* Translated by Joel C. Weinsheimer and Donald G. Marshall. London: Continuum.

Garner, Bryan. 2009. *Garner's Modern American Usage.* 3rd ed. Oxford: Oxford University Press.

Garsten, Bryan. 2006. *Saving Persuasion: A Defense of Rhetoric and Judgment.* Cambridge: Harvard University Press.

Geertz, Clifford. 1973. *The Interpretation of Cultures: Selected Essays.* New York: Basic Books.

Gibb, H. A. R., and Harold Bowen. 1950. *Islamic Society and the West: A Study of the Impact of Western Civilization on Moslem Culture in the Near East.* London: Oxford University Press.

Ginzburg, Carlo. 1980. *The Cheese and the Worms: The Cosmos of a Sixteenth-Century Miller.* Baltimore: Johns Hopkins University Press.

Göçek, Fatma Müge. 1996. *Rise of the Bourgeoisie, Demise of Empire: Westernization and Social Change.* New York: Oxford University Press.

Gökalp, Ziya. 1968. *Principles of Turkism.* Leiden: Brill.

Golden, Peter B. 1982. "Imperial Ideology and the Sources of Political Unity amongst the Pre-Činggisid Nomads of Western Eurasia." *Archivum Eurasiae Medii Aevi* 2:37–76.

Golden, Peter B. 1992. *An Introduction to the History of the Turkic Peoples: Ethnogenesis and State-Formation in Medieval and Early Modern Eurasia and the Middle East.* Wiesbaden: Otto Harrassowitz.

Goltz, Colmar von der. 1884. *Das Volk in Waffen: Ein Buch über Heerwesen und Kriegsführung unserer Zeit.* 3rd ed. Berlin: Decker.

Goltz, Colmar von der. 1301 [1886]. *Millet-i Musellaḥa: Asrımızın Usūl ve Ahvāl-i Askeriyesi.* Translated by Meḥmed Ṭāhir. Ḳonsṭanṭīnīye: Matba'a-ı Ebüzziya.

Goltz, [Colmar] von der. 1914. *The Nation in Arms.* Translated by Philip A. Ashworth. London: Hodder and Stoughton.

Gong, Gerrit W. G. 1984. *The Standard of "Civilization" in International Society.* Oxford: Oxford University Press.

Gözübüyük, Şeref, and Suna Kili, eds. 1982. *Türk Anayasa Metinleri, 1839–1980.* 2nd ed. Ankara: Ankara Üniversitesi.

Gramsci, Antonio. 1971. *Selections from the Prison Notebooks.* Translated by Quentin Hoare and Geoffrey Nowell Smith. London: Lawrence and Wishart.

Granovetter, Mark S. 1973. "The Strength of Weak Ties." *American Journal of Sociology* 78 (6): 1360–80.

Greene, Molly. 2010. *Catholic Corsairs and Greek Merchants: A Maritime History of the Mediterranean, 1450–1700.* Princeton: Princeton University Press.

Greene, Molly. 2015. *The Edinburgh History of the Greeks, 1453–1768: The Ottoman Empire.* Edinburgh: Edinburgh University Press.

Gummer, S. Chase. 2010. "The Politics of Sympathy: German Turcophilism and the Ottoman Empire in the Age of the Mass Media, 1871–1914." PhD diss., Georgetown University.

Günay, Bekir. 1992. "Mehmed Sadık Rıfat Paşa'nin Hayatı Eserleri ve Görüşleri." Master's thesis, Sosyal Bilimler Enstitüsü, İstanbul Üniversitesi, Istanbul.

Gürçağlar, Şehnaz Tahir. 2008. *The Politics and Poetics of Translation in Turkey, 1923–1960.* Amsterdam: Rodopi.

Gürkan, Emrah Safa. 2015. "Mediating Boundaries: Mediterranean Go-Betweens and Cross-Confessional Diplomacy in Constantinople, 1560–1600." *Journal of Early Modern History* 19:107–28.

Gutas, Dimitri. 1998. *Greek Thought, Arabic Culture: The Graeco-Arabic Translation Movement in Baghdad and Early 'Abbasid Society (2nd–4th/8th–10th Centuries).* London: Routledge.

Guth, Stephan. 2010. "Politeness, Höflichkeit, 'adab: A Comparative Conceptual-Cultural Perspective." In *Verbal Festivity in Arabic and Other Semitic Languages: Proceedings of the Workshop at the Universitätsclub Bonn on 16 January, 2009*, edited by Lutz Edzard and Stephan Guth, 9–30. Wiesbaden: Harrassowitz Verlag.

Haarman, U. 2014. "Waṭan." In *Encyclopaedia of Islam*, 3rd ed., edited by P. Bearman, Th. Bianquis, C. E. Bosworth, E. van Donzel and W. P. Heinrichs. Leiden: Brill Online.

Hale, William M. 2000. *Turkish Foreign Policy, 1774–2000*. London: Cass.

Hanioğlu, M. Şükrü. 1995. *The Young Turks in Opposition*. New York: Oxford University Press.

Hanioğlu, M. Şükrü. 2011. *Atatürk: An Intellectual Biography*. Oxford: Princeton University Press.

Hansen, Lene. 2006. *Security as Practice: Discourse Analysis and the Bosnian War*. London: Routledge.

Haskins, Charles Homer. 1927. *The Renaissance of the 12th Century*. Cambridge: Harvard University Press.

Hasse, Dag Nikolaus. 2008. "Influence of Arabic and Islamic Philosophy on the Latin West." In *The Stanford Encyclopedia of Philosophy*, edited by Edward N. Zalta. Stanford: Stanford University. https://plato.stanford.edu/

Herzog, Christoph, and Raoul Motika. 2000. "Orientalism 'Alla Turca': Late 19th/Early 20th Century Ottoman Voyages into the Muslim 'Outback.'" *Die Welt des Islams*, n.s. 40 (2): 139–95.

Hinchman, Lewis P., and Sandra Hinchman. 2001. *Memory, Identity, Community: The Idea of Narrative in the Human Sciences*. Albany: State University of New York Press.

Hobson, John M. 2012. *The Eurocentric Conception of World Politics*. Cambridge: Cambridge University Press.

Holbrook, Victoria Rowe. 1994. *The Unreadable Shores of Love: Turkish Modernity and Mystic Romance*. Austin: University of Texas Press.

Holt, P. M. 1984. "Some Observations on the 'Abbāsid Caliphate of Cairo." *Bulletin of the School of Oriental and African Studies* 47:501–7.

Hopkins, J. F. P., and B. Lewis. 2013 [1960]. "Ifrandj." In *Encyclopaedia of Islam*, 2nd ed., edited by P. Bearman, Th. Bianquis, C. E. Bosworth, E. van Donzel and W. P. Heinrichs. Leiden: Brill Online.

Huntington, Samuel P. 1996. *The Clash of Civilizations and the Remaking of World Order*. New York: Simon and Schuster.

Hussain, Nasser. 2003. *The Jurisprudence of Emergency: Colonialism and the Rule of Law*. Ann Arbor: University of Michigan Press.

Ibn Khaldûn. 1967. *The Muqaddimah: An Introduction to History*. Translated by Franz Rosenthal. Princeton: Princeton University Press.

İbn Haldun. 2008. *Mukaddime: Osmanlı Tercümesi: Mütercim Ahmed Cevdet Paşa*. Vol. 3. Edited and transliterated by Yavuz Yıldırım et al. İstanbul: Klasik Yayınları.

Ilicak, Şükrü. 2011. "A Radical Rethinking of Empire: Ottoman State and Society during the Greek War of Independence (1821–1826)." PhD diss., Harvard University.

İnalcık, Halil. 1994. *The Ottoman Empire: The Classical Age, 1300–1600.* London: Phoenix.

İnce, Başak. 2012. *Citizenship and Identity in Turkey: From Atatürk's Republic to the Present Day.* London: I.B. Tauris.

Inghilleri, Moira, and Sue-Ann Harding. 2010. "Translating Violent Conflict." *The Translator* 16 (2): 165–73.

Jackson, Patrick Thaddeus. 2002. "Rethinking Weber: Towards a Non-Individualist Sociology of World Politics." *International Review of Sociology* 12 (3): 439–68.

Jackson, Patrick Thaddeus. 2006. *Civilizing the Enemy: German Reconstruction and the Invention of the West.* Ann Arbor: University of Michigan Press.

Jackson, Patrick Thaddeus. 2011. *The Conduct of Inquiry in International Relations: Philosophy of Science and Its Implications for the Study of World Politics.* London: Routledge.

Jackson, Patrick Thaddeus. 2017. "Causal Claims and Causal Explanation in International Studies." *Journal of International Relations and Development* 20 (4): 689–716.

Jackson, Patrick Thaddeus, and Daniel H. Nexon. 1999. "Relations before States: Substance, Process, and the Study of World Politics." *European Journal of International Relations* 5:291–332.

Jakobson, Roman. 2000. "On Linguistic Aspects of Translation." In *The Translation Studies Reader,* edited by Lawrence Venuti, 113–18. London: Routledge.

Jung, Dietrich. 2011. *Orientalists, Islamists, and the Global Public Sphere: A Genealogy of the Modern Essentialist Image of Islam.* Sheffield: Equinox.

Jusdanis, Gregory. 1991. *Belated Modernity and Aesthetic Culture: Inventing National Literature.* Minneapolis: University of Minnesota Press.

Kafadar, Cemal. 1993. "The Myth of the Golden Age: Ottoman Historical Consciousness in the Post-Süleymânic Era." In *Süleymân the Second and His Time,* edited by Halil İnalcık and Cemal Kafadar, 37–48. İstanbul: The Isis Press.

Kafadar, Cemal. 1995. *Between Two Worlds: The Construction of the Ottoman State.* Berkeley: University of California Press.

Kafadar, Cemal. 2007. "A Rome of One's Own: Reflections on Cultural Geography and Identity in the Lands of Rum." *Muqarnas* 24:7–25.

Kant, Immanuel. 2003 [1795]. *To Perpetual Peace: A Philosophical Sketch.* Translated by Ted Humphrey. Indianapolis: Hackett.

Kara, İsmail, and Nergiz Yılmaz Aydoğdu, eds. 2005. *Namık Kemal: Osmanlı Modernleşmesinin Meseleleri: Bütün Makaleleri 1.* İstanbul: Dergah Yayınları.

Karimullah, Kamran. 2012. "Rival Moral Traditions in the Late Ottoman Empire, 1839–1908." *Journal of Islamic Studies* 24 (1): 37–66.

Kasaba, Reşat. 2009. *A Moveable Empire: Ottoman Nomads, Migrants, and Refugees.* Seattle: University of Washington Press.

Katz, David S. 2016. *The Shaping of Turkey in the British Imagination, 1776–1923.* Basingstoke: Palgrave Macmillan.

Kayalı, Hasan. 1997. *Arabs and Young Turks: Ottomanism, Arabism, and Islamism in the Ottoman Empire, 1908–1918.* Berkeley: University of California Press.

Kayaoğlu, Taceddin. 1998. *Türkiye'de Tercüme Müesseseleri.* İstanbul: Kitabevi Yayınları.

Kayaoğlu, Turan. 2010. *Legal Imperialism: Sovereignty and Extraterritoriality in Japan, the Ottoman Empire, and China.* Cambridge: Cambridge University Press.

Keene, Edward. 2002. *Beyond the Anarchical Society: Grotius, Colonialism, and Order in World Politics.* Cambridge: Cambridge University Press.

Keohane, Robert. 1984. *After Hegemony.* Princeton: Princeton University Press.

Keyder, Çağlar. 1989. *Türkiye'de Devlet ve Sınıflar.* Istanbul: İletişim.

Kirecci, Mehmet Akif. 2007. "Decline Discourse and Self-Orientalization in the Writings of Al-Ṭahṭāwī, Ṭāhā Ḥusayn, and Ziya Gökalp." PhD diss., University of Pennsylvania.

Koç, Haşim. 2004. "Cultural Repertoire as a Network of Translated Texts: The New Literature after the Tanzimat Period (1830–1870)." Master's thesis, Institute for Graduate Studies in Social Sciences, Boğaziçi Üniversitesi, Istanbul.

Kogaciolu, Dicle. 2004. "The Tradition Effect: Framing Honor Crimes in Turkey." *Differences* 15 (2): 119–51.

Köprülüzade M. Fuat. [Fuat Köprülü] 1931. "Bizans Müesseselerinin Osmanlı Müesseselerine Tesiri Hakkında Bazı Mülâhazalar" *Türk Hukuk ve İktisat Tarihi Mecmuası* 1 (1): 165–313.

Koselleck, Reinhart. 2002. *The Practice of Conceptual History: Timing History, Spacing Concepts.* Stanford: Stanford University Press.

Koselleck, Reinhart. 2004. *Futures Past: On the Semantics of Historical Time.* New York: Columbia University Press.

Koselleck, Reinhart. 2011. "Introduction (*Einleitung*) to the *Geschichtliche Grundbegriffe.*" *Contributions to the History of Concepts* 6 (1): 7–25.

Koselleck, Reinhart, and Klaus Schreiner. 1994. *Bürgerschaft: Rezeption und Innovation der Begrifflichkeit vom Hohen Mittelalter bis ins 19. Jahrhundert.* Stuttgart: Klett-Cotta.

Koskenniemi, Martti. 2010. *The Gentle Civilizer of Nations: The Rise and Fall of International Law, 1870–1960*. Cambridge: Cambridge University Press.

Krebs, Ronald R., and Patrick Thaddeus Jackson. 2007. "Twisting Tongues and Twisting Arms: The Power of Political Rhetoric." *European Journal of International Relations* 13 (1): 35–66.

Kreiser, Klaus. 2008. *Atatürk: eine Biographie*. Munich: Verlag C. H. Beck.

Kürkçüoğlu, Ömer. 2004. "The Adoption and Use of Permanent Diplomacy." In *Ottoman Diplomacy: Conventional or Unconventional?*, edited by A. Nuri Yurdusev, 131–50. Basingstoke: Palgrave Macmillan.

La Fontaine, Jean de. 1991 [1679]. *Fables*. Paris: Gallimard.

Landau, Jacob. 1995. *Pan-Turkism: From Irredentism to Cooperation*. London: Hurst.

Lane-Poole, Stanley. 1888. *The Life of the Right Honourable Stratford Canning Viscount Stratford de Redcliffe, K.G. G.C.B D.C.L. LL.D. etc. From His Memoirs and Private and Official Papers*. Vol. 2. London: Longmans, Green.

Le Moyne, Pierre. 1653. *Saint Louys; ou, Le Héros Chrestien, Poëme Heroïque*. Paris: Du Mesnil.

Leonhard, Jörn. 2013. "Introduction: The Longue Durée of Empire: Toward a Comparative Semantics of a Key Concept in Modern European History." *Contributions to the History of Concepts* 8 (1): 1–25.

Lerner, Daniel. 1958. *The Passing of Traditional Society: Modernizing the Middle East*. Glencoe, IL: Free Press.

Lewis, Bernard. 1953. "The Impact of the French Revolution on Turkey: Some Notes on the Transmission of Ideas." *Cahiers d'Histoire Mondiale* 1 (1–4): 105–25.

Lewis, Bernard. 1961. *The Emergence of Modern Turkey*. Oxford: Oxford University Press.

Lewis, Bernard. 1982. *The Muslim Discovery of Europe*. London: Weidenfeld and Nicolson.

Lewis, Bernard. 1988. *The Political Language of Islam*. Chicago: University of Chicago Press.

Lewis, Bernard. 2002. *What Went Wrong? Western Impact and Middle Eastern Response*. Oxford: Oxford University Press.

Lewis, Geoffrey. 1999. *The Turkish Language Reform: A Catastrophic Success*. Oxford: Oxford University Press.

Lindner, Rudi Paul. 2007. *Explorations in Ottoman Prehistory*. Ann Arbor: University of Michigan Press.

Linnaeus, Carolus. 1735. *Systema naturae*. Lugduni Batavorum.

Linnaeus, Carolus. 1753. *Species plantarum, exhibentes plantas rite cognitas, ad genera relatas, cum differentiis specificis, nominibus trivialibus, synonimis selectis, locis naturalibus, secundum systema sexuale digestas.* Holmiae: Impensis Laurentii Salvii.

Liu, Yameng. 1999. "Justifying My Position in Your Terms: Cross-cultural Argumentation in a Globalized World." *Argumentation* 13 (3): 297–315.

Lotman, Yuri M. 1990. *Universe of the Mind: A Semiotic Theory of Culture.* Bloomington: Indiana University Press.

Lowry, Heath W. 2003. *The Nature of the Early Ottoman State.* Albany: State University of New York Press.

Makdisi, Ussama. 2002. "Ottoman Orientalism." *American Historical Review* 107 (3): 768–96.

Manela, Erez. 2007. *The Wilsonian Moment: Self-Determination and the International Origins of Anticolonial Nationalism.* New York: Oxford University Press.

Mardin, Şerif. 2000 [1962]. *The Genesis of Young Ottoman Thought: A Study in the Modernization of Turkish Political Ideas.* Syracuse: Syracuse University Press.

Mardin, Şerif. 2008. "Conceptual Fracture." In *Transnational Concepts, Transfers, and the Challenge of the Peripheries,* edited by Gürcan Koçan, 4–18. Istanbul: Istanbul Technical University Press.

Mareschal, André. 1971 [1637]. *Le Railleur; ou, La Satyre du Temps.* Bologna: Casa Editrice Prof. Riccardo Pàtron.

Marjanen, Jani. 2009. "Undermining Methodological Nationalism: Histoire Croisée of Concepts as Transnational History." In *Transnational Political Spaces: Agents—Structures—Encounters,* edited by Mathias Albert, Gesa Blum, Jan Helmig, Andreas Leutzsch, and Jochen Walter, 239–64. Frankfurt a. M.: Campus.

Marot, Clément. 2005 [1538]. *L'Adolescence clémentine.* Paris: Le Livre de poche.

Marot, Jean. 1977 [1526]. *Le Voyage de Venise.* Geneva: Droz.

Mattern, Janice Bially, and Ayşe Zarakol. 2016. "Hierarchies in World Politics." *International Organization* 70:623–54.

Meisami, Julie Scott. 1987. *Medieval Persian Court Poetry.* Princeton: Princeton University Press.

Meninski, Franciszek (Franciscus à Mesgnien). 2000 [1680]. *Thesaurus Linguarum Orientalum Turcicae-Arabicae-Persicae.* Vol. 2. Istanbul: Simurg.

Meyer, John W., John Boli, George M. Thomas, and Francisco O. Ramirez. 1997. "World Society and the Nation-State." *American Journal of Sociology* 103 (1): 144–81.

Minawi, Mostafa. 2016. *The Ottoman Scramble for Africa: Empire and Diplomacy in the Sahara and the Hijaz.* Stanford: Stanford University Press.

Mitchell, Timothy. 1991. *Colonising Egypt.* Berkeley: University of California Press.

Mitchell, Timothy. 2000. "The Stage of Modernity." In *Questions of Modernity*, edited by Timothy Mitchell, 1–34. Minneapolis: University of Minnesota Press.

Mitchell, Timothy. 2002. *Rule of Experts: Egypt, Techno-Politics, Modernity*. Berkeley: University of California Press.

Mitchell, Timothy. 2006. "Society, Economy, and the State Effect." In *The Anthropology of the State: A Reader*, edited by Aradhana Sharma and Akhil Gupta, 169–86. Malden, MA: Blackwell.

Moran, Berna. 1977. "Alafranga Züppeden Alafranga Haine." *Birikim* 27:6–17.

Mōrō, Felīks. 1327 AH / 1326 HS [1910]. *Medḥal-i Ḥuḵūḵ-ı Esāsīye*. Translated by İbrāhīm Şināsī. Ḳonya: Maṣreḵ-i ʿİrfān Maṭbaʿası—Vilāyet Maṭbaʿası.

Mouradgea d'Ohsson, Ignatius. 1787. *Tableau général de l'Empire othoman, divisé en deux parties*. Vol. 1. Paris: De l'Imprimerie de Monsieur [Firmin Didot].

Naff, Thomas. 1984. "The Ottoman Empire and the European States System." In *The Expansion of International Society*, edited by Hedley Bull and Adam Watson, 143–69. Oxford: Clarendon.

Nāmıḳ Kemāl. 1327 [1909]. "Wa shāwirhum fīl amr." In *Maḵālāt-ı Siyāsiye ve Edebīye*, 165–75. İstanbūl: Selānīk Maṭbaʿası. Originally published in *Hürriyet* [Liberty] (London), 20 July 1869, 1–4.

Namık Kemal. 2014 [1909]. *Namık Kemal: Makalât-ı Siyasiye ve Edebiye*. Transliterated and edited by Erdoğan Kul. Ankara: Birleşik Yayıncılık.

Neumann, Christoph K. 1999. *Araç Tarih Amaç Tanzimat: Tarih-i Cevdet Siyasi Anlamı*. İstanbul: Tarih Vakfı Yurt Yayınları.

Neumann, Iver B. 1996. *Russia and the Idea of Europe: A Study in Identity and International Relations*. London: Routledge.

Neumann, Iver B. 1999. *Uses of the Other: "The East" in European Identity Formation*. Minneapolis: University of Minnesota Press.

Neumann, Iver B. 2011. "Entry into International Society Reconceptualised: The Case of Russia." *Review of International Studies* 37 (2): 463–84.

Neumann, Iver B. 2012. *At Home with the Diplomats: Inside a European Foreign Ministry*. Ithaca: Cornell University Press.

Neumann, Iver B., and Einar Wigen. 2018. *The Steppe Tradition in International Relations: Russians, Turks, and European State Building, 4000 BCE–2018 CE*. Cambridge: Cambridge University Press.

Nexon, Daniel H. 2009. *The Struggle for Power in Early Modern Europe*. Princeton: Princeton University Press.

Nexon, Daniel H., and Thomas Wright. 2007. "What's at Stake in the American Empire Debate." *American Political Science Review* 101 (2): 253–71.

Nida, Eugene. 2000. "Principles of Correspondence." In *The Translation Studies Reader*, edited by Lawrence Venuti, 126–40. London: Routledge.

Oğuz, Ahmet. 1994. "Ceride-i Havadis Gazetesi'nde Çıkan Haber-Yazılar ve Değerlendirmesi (1840–1844)." Master's thesis, Gazi University.

Onar, Sıddık Sâmi. 1941. "Hukuk Bakımından Şehir ve Hemşehri." In *Üniversite Haftası: Erzurum, 13-7-1940–19-7-1940*, 56–67. İstanbul: Ahmed İhsan Matbaası.

Ortaylı, İlber. 1983. *İmparatorluğun en Uzun Yüzyılı.* İstanbul: Hil Yayın.

Ó Tuathail, Gearóid, and John Agnew. 1992. "Geopolitics and Discourse: Practical Geopolitical Reasoning in American Foreign Policy." *Political Geography* 11 (2): 190–204.

Özsu, Umut. 2015. *Formalizing Displacement: International Law and Population Transfers.* Oxford: Oxford University Press.

Padgett, John F., and Christopher K. Ansell. 1993. "Robust Action and the Rise of the Medici, 1400–1434." *American Journal of Sociology* 98 (6): 1259–1319.

Palabıyık, Mustafa Serdar. 2010. "Travel, Civilization, and the East: Ottoman Travellers' Perception of 'The East' in the Late Ottoman Empire." PhD diss., Middle East Technical University.

Parla, Ayse. 2001. "The 'Honor' of the State: Virginity Examinations in Turkey." *Feminist Studies* 27 (1): 65–88.

Parla, Taha, and Andrew Davison. 2004. *Corporatist Ideology in Kemalist Turkey.* Syracuse: Syracuse University Press.

Parsons, Talcott. 1949. *The Structure of Social Action: A Study in Social Theory with Special Reference to a Group of Recent European Writers.* 2nd ed. New York: Free Press.

Pernau, Margrit. 2012. "Whither Conceptual History? From National to Entangled Histories." *Contributions to the History of Concepts* 7:1–11.

Pernau, Margrit, Helge Jordheim, Orit Bashkin, Christian Bailey, Oleg Benesch, Jan Ifversen, Mana Kia, Rochona Majumdar, Angelika C. Messner, Myoung-kyu Park, Emmanuelle Saada, Mohinder Singh, and Einar Wigen. 2015. *Civilizing Emotions: Concepts in Nineteenth Century Asia and Europe.* Oxford: Oxford University Press.

Pocock, J. G. A. 1972. "Virtue and Commerce in the Eighteenth Century." *Journal of Interdisciplinary History* 3 (1): 119–34.

Poulton, Hugh. 1997. *Top Hat, Grey Wolf, and Crescent: Turkish Nationalism and the Turkish Republic.* London: Hurst.

Raby, Julian. 1982. "A Sultan of Paradox: Mehmed the Conqueror as a Patron of the Arts." *Oxford Art Journal* 5 (1): 3–8.

Racine, Mr. 1672. *Bajazet. Tragédie.* Paris: Pierre Le Monnier.

Redhouse, James W. 1890. *A Turkish and English Lexicon, Shewing in English the Significations of the Turkish Terms.* Constantinople: A.H. Boyajian.

Reinbold, Jenna. 2016. *Seeing the Myth in Human Rights.* Philadelphia: University of Pennsylvania Press.

Reinkowski, Maurus. 2005. "The State's Security and the Subjects' Prosperity: Notions of Order in Ottoman Bureaucratic Correspondence (19th Century)." In *Legitimizing the Order: Ottoman Rhetoric of State Power*, edited by Hakan T. Karateke and Maurus Reinkowski, 195–212. Leiden: Brill.

Ricoeur, Paul. 1985. *Time and Narrative*. Vol. 2. Chicago: University of Chicago Press.

Risse, Thomas. 2010. *A Community of Europeans? Transnational Identities and Public Spheres*. Ithaca: Cornell University Press.

Robert, Paul, and Alain Rey. 2001. *Le Grand Robert de la langue française, 2. éd. du Dictionnaire alphabétique et analogique de la langue française*. Paris: Le Robert.

Rodinson, Maxime. 1988. *Europe and the Mystique of Islam*. Translated by Roger Veinus. London: Tauris.

Rogers. J. M. 2005. "Mehmed the Conqueror: Between East and West". In *Bellini and the East*, edited by Caroline Campbell and Alan Chong, 80–97. New Haven: Yale University Press.

Roshchin, Evgeny. 2013. "(Un)Natural and Contractual International Society." *European Journal of International Relations* 19:257–79.

Rumelili, Bahar. 2007. *Constructing Regional Community and Order in Europe and Southeast Asia*. Basingstoke: Palgrave Macmillan.

Said, Edward W. 1978. *Orientalism*. New York: Vintage Books.

Sariyannis, Marinos. 2013. "Ruler and State, State and Society in Ottoman Political Thought." *Turkish Historical Review* 4:92–126.

Sariyannis, Marinos. 2016. "Ottoman Ideas on Monarchy before the Tanzimat Reforms: Toward a Conceptual History of Ottoman Political Notions." *Turcica* 47:33–72.

Saussure, Ferdinand de. 1983. *Course in General Linguistics*. Translated by Roy Harris. London: Open Court.

Schaffer, Frederic C. 1998. *Democracy in Translation: Understanding Politics in an Unfamiliar Culture*. Ithaca: Cornell University Press.

Şemseddīn Sāmī. 1317 [1901–2]. *Ḳāmūs-i Türkī*. Dersaʿādet: Aḳdām Maṭbaʿası.

Sessions, Jennifer E. 2011. *By Sword and By Plow: France and the Conquest of Algeria*. Ithaca: Cornell University Press.

Shils, Edward. 1970. "Political Development in the New States—The Will to Be Modern." In *Readings in Social Evolution and Development*, 379–82, edited by S. N. Eisenstadt. Oxford: Pergamon.

Shotter, John. 1993. *Cultural Politics of Everyday Life: Social Constructionism, Rhetoric, and Knowing of the Third Kind*. Buckingham: Open University Press.

Skinner, Quentin. 1978. *The Foundations of Modern Political Thought*. Cambridge: Cambridge University Press.

Skinner, Quentin. 2002. *Visions of Politics*. Vol. 1, *Regarding Method*. Cambridge: Cambridge University Press.

Skinner, Quentin. 2009. "A Genealogy of the Modern State." *Proceedings of the British Academy* 162:325–70.

Spruyt, Hendrik. 1994. *The Sovereign State and Its Competitors: An Analysis of Systems Change*. Princeton: Princeton University Press.

Steiner, George. 1998. *After Babel: Aspects of Language and Translation*. 3rd ed. Oxford: Oxford University Press.

Strauss, Johann. 1989. "Türkische Übersetzungen zweier europäischer Geschichtswerke aus Muḥammad ʿAlī's Ägypten: Botta's 'Storia d'Italia' und Castéra's 'Histoire de Catherine.'" In *XXIII. deutscher Orientalistentag: Vom 16. bis 20. September 1985 in Würzburg: Ausgewählte Vorträge*, edited by Einar von Schuler, 244–58. Wiesbaden: Franz Steiner Verlag.

Strauss, Johann. 1995. "Diglossie dans le domaine ottoman: Évolution et péripéties d'une situation linguistique." *Revue du Monde Musulman et de la Méditerranée* 75–76:221–55.

Strauss, Johann. 2003. "Who Read What in the Ottoman Empire (19th–20th Centuries)?" *Middle Eastern Literatures* 6 (1): 39–76.

Stritzel, Holger. 2014. *Security in Translation: Securitization Theory and the Localization of Threat*. Basingstoke: Palgrave Macmillan.

Swidler, Ann. 2001. "What Anchors Cultural Practices?" In *The Practice Turn in Contemporary Theory*, edited by Theodore R. Schatzki, Karin Knorr Cetina, and Eike von Savigny, 74–92. London: Routledge.

Swidler, Ann. 2003. *Talk of Love: How Culture Matters*. Chicago: University of Chicago Press.

Tezcan, Baki. 2010. *The Second Ottoman Empire: Political and Social Transformation in the Early Modern World*. New York: Cambridge University Press.

Tilly, Charles. 1992. *Coercion, Capital, and the European States, AD 990–1992*. Cambridge: Blackwell.

Thackston, Wheeler M. 2001. "Resmülhatt-ı Osmani: An Introduction to the Orthography of Ottoman Turkish." In *Intermediate Ottoman Manual*, edited by Selim S. Kuru and Wheeler M. Thackston. Cunda/Ayvalık: Harvard-Koç University.

Topal, Alp Eren. 2017a. "Against Influence: Ziya Gökalp in Context and Tradition." *Journal of Islamic Studies* 28:283–310.

Topal, Alp Eren. 2017b. "From Decline to Progress: Ottoman Concepts of Reform, 1600–1876." PhD diss., Ihsan Dogramaci Bilkent University.

Tristan L'Hermite, François. 1975 [1655]. *Le théatre complet de Tristan L'Hermite: Èdition critique*. Tuscaloosa: University of Alabama Press.

Tunaya, Tarik Zafer. 1960. *Türkiyenin Siyasî Hayatında Batılılaşma Hareketleri.* İstanbul: Yedigün Matbaası.

Tunaya, Tarık Zafer. 1998. *Türkiye'de Siyasal Partiler, Cilt 1, İkinci Meşrutiyet Dönemi, 1908–1918.* İstanbul: Hürriyet Vakfı.

Ursinus, M. O. 2014. "Millet." In *Encyclopaedia of Islam,* 3rd ed., edited by P. Bearman, Th. Bianquis, C. E. Bosworth, E. van Donzel, and W. P. Heinrichs. Leiden: Brill Online.

Üstel, Füsun. 2004. *"Makbul Vatandaş" ın Peşinde: II. Meşrutiyet'ten Bugüne Vatandaşlık Eğitimi.* İstanbul: İletişim Yayınları.

VanderLippe, John M. 2005. *The Politics of Turkish Democracy: İsmet İnönü and the Formation of the Multi-Party System, 1938–1950.* Albany: State University of New York Press.

Venuti, Lawrence. 1998. "Strategies of Translation." In *Encyclopedia of Translation Studies,* edited by M. Baker, 240–44. London: Routledge.

Venuti, Laurence. 2008 [1994]. *The Translator's Invisibility: A History of Translation.* 2nd ed. London: Routledge.

Vucetic, Srdjan. 2011. *The Anglosphere: A Genealogy of a Racialized Identity in International Relations.* Stanford: Stanford University Press.

Wæver, Ole. 1998. "Insecurity, Security, and Asecurity in the West European Non-War Community." In *Security Communities,* edited by Emanuel Adler and Michael Barnett, 69–118. Cambridge: Cambridge University Press.

Weber, Max. 1968. *Economy and Society: An Outline of Interpretive Sociology.* Vol 1, ed. Guenther A. Roth and Claus Wittich. New York: Bedminster Press.

Wehr, Hans. 1976. "Ḥarṣ." In *A Dictionary of Modern Written Arabic,* edited by J. Milton Cowan, 166. Ithaca, NY: Spoken Language Services.

Wescott, Roger W. 1990. "Reflections on the Etymology of Some Words for 'Peace.'" *International Journal of World Peace* 7 (3): 94–97.

Wheaton, Henry. 1916 [1863]. *Wheaton's Elements of International Law.* 5th ed. London: Stevens and Sons.

White, Hayden. 1973. *Metahistory: The Historical Imagination in Nineteenth-Century Europe.* Baltimore: Johns Hopkins University Press.

Windler, Christian. 2001. "Diplomatic History as a Field for Cultural Analysis: Muslim-Christian Relations in Tunis, 1700–1840." *Historical Journal* 44 (1): 79–106.

Wittgenstein, Ludwig. 1975. *On Certainty.* Translated by Gertrude E. M. Anscombe, Georg Henrik von Wright, and Denis Paul. Oxford: Blackwell.

Wittgenstein, Ludwig. 1982. *Last Writings on the Philosophy of Psychology.* Vol. 1, *Preliminary Studies for Part II of the Philosophical Investigations.* Oxford: Blackwell.

Wittgenstein, Ludwig. 2009. *Philosophical Investigations*. Rev. 4th ed. Chichester: Wiley-Blackwell.

Worringer, Renée. 2001. "Comparing Perceptions: Japan as Archetype for Ottoman Modernity, 1876–1918." PhD diss., University of Chicago.

Yaycioglu, Ali. 2016. *Partners of the Empire: Crisis of the Ottoman Order in the Age of Revolutions*. Stanford: Stanford University Press.

Yeğen, Mesut. 1996. "The Turkish State Discourse and the Exclusion of Kurdish Identity." *Middle Eastern Studies* 32 (2): 216–29.

Yeğen, Mesut. 1999. "The Kurdish Question in Turkish State Discourse." *Journal of Contemporary History* 34 (4): 555–68.

Yurdusev, A. Nuri, ed. 2004. *Ottoman Diplomacy: Conventional or Unconventional?* Basingstoke and New York: Palgrave Macmillan.

Zarakol, Ayşe Nur. 2010. *After Defeat: How the East Learned to Live with the West*. Cambridge: Cambridge University Press.

Zarakol, Ayşe Nur, ed. 2017. *Hierarchies in World Politics*. Cambridge and New York: Cambridge University Press.

Ze'evi, Dror. 2004. "Back to Napoleon? Thoughts on the Beginning of the Modern Era in the Middle East." *Mediterranean Historical Review* 19 (1): 73–94.

Index